The Secrets of Success Cookbook

The Secrets of Success Cookbook

Signature Recipes and Insider Tips from San Francisco's Best Restaurants

MICHAEL BAUER

CHRONICLE BOOKS

SAN FRANCISCO

Library of Congress
Cataloging-in-Publication Data:
Bauer, Michael.
    The secrets of success cookbook: signature recipes
and insider tips from San Francisco's best restaurants /
by Michael Bauer.
        p.   cm.
    Includes index
    ISBN 0-8118-2502-7 (pb)
    1. Cookery—California—San Francisco   2. Cookery,
American—California style.   I. Title.

    TX715.B3493 2000
    641.59794'616dc21

99-053772

Printed in the United States of America.

Designed by Aufuldish & Warinner.
Interior photographs by Bob Aufuldish.
Bob Aufuldish wishes to thank Girard Hirigoyen at
Fringale; Jack Kreitzman and Michael Blackburn at Cucina
Jackson Fillmore; Heidi Krahling at Insalata's; Bradley
Ogden and Rudy Rahbar at the Lark Creek Inn; Roland
Passot, Phyllis Evans, and Sarah Neylon at Left Bank;
Luis Delgado, and Henrik Kam.
Cover photograph by Frankie Frankeny.
Frankie Frankeny gives special thanks to James
Ormsby of Red Herring and Gail Defferari of XYZ.
Food styling by Wesley Martino.

Front and back cover: Tamarind Crab, page 199.

Distributed in Canada by Raincoast Books
8680 Cambie Street
Vancouver, British Columbia V6P 6M9

10 9 8 7 6 5 4 3 2 1

Chronicle Books
85 Second Street
San Francisco, California 94105

www.chroniclebooks.com

||||

DEDICATION

To the chefs who have made the San Francisco Bay Area the best place in the United States to eat and cook.

ACKNOWLEDGMENTS

Translating 200 recipes from the professional to the home kitchen was a constant challenge, and this book wouldn't have seen print without the help of a lot of people.

❊

First I'd like to thank the chefs who provided the recipes I requested. Only a couple forgot to give me the secret.

❊

Catherine Alioto tested and perfected the bulk of the recipes. She's a former pastry chef who can think like a chef and write like a home cook. It's a rare combination that saved dozens of recipes.

❊

Many friends served as a sounding board and offered advice and encouragement: Marion Cunningham, Flo Braker, Marlene Sorosky, and Michael Murphy.

❊

The Food Department interns from the California Culinary Academy also helped with recipe testing: Mary Margaret Pack, Tilde Herrera, Jennifer Straus, Tara Duggan, and Steven Baker.

❊

Some friends turned my book work into a party and gathered to try some of the recipes in their homes, including: Dave and Sonja Hyams, Debbie Zachareas, Mike Drumm, and Dorian Serris.

❊

Lesli Neilson not only tested recipes, but kept me sane by organizing the book and making sure it came out of the computer in unbroken English.

❊

Sonja Hyams spent tireless hours testing recipes and double-checking them.

❊

Robin Davis, both a colleague and a friend, edited the recipes and asked all the right questions.

❊

Bill LeBlond, the cookbook editor at Chronicle Books, was an enthusiastic supporter of the project.

❊

And finally I'd like to salute the staff members of the Food Department, who are a continual source of inspiration: Gerald Boyd, Robin Davis, Janet Fletcher, Fran Irwin, Miriam Morgan, Holly Ocasio Rizzo, Karola Saekel, and Kim Severson.

TABLE OF CONTENTS

Restaurant kitchens are a storehouse of tricks and techniques that can help the home cook. At first glance some of these secrets may not seem so special, but they make a big difference in the finished dish.

I first realized that little things really do mean a lot when I ate the fennel salad at Zinzino, a cute Italian restaurant in the Marina. With only half a dozen ingredients—mint, lemon, olive oil, Parmesan cheese, salt, and pepper—I wondered why the flavor was so much better than others I'd tasted.

The reason came down to one difference: slicing the fennel paper thin, which allowed all the elements to blend, creating a distinct and unified taste. When I eat a dish this good I remember it forever, which is saying a lot. As the food editor and restaurant critic for the *San Francisco Chronicle* I taste recipes and sample new products all day and dine out every night. Conservatively speaking, I fork into more than 2,000 restaurant specialties a year.

It is at least 10,000 dishes ago that I savored the rich, silken pot de crème at 42 Degrees, and I still remember that first bite. I also retain a vivid memory of the caramel chicken at Slanted Door, the juicy hamburger at Zuni, and the puffy twice-baked goat cheese soufflé at Zax's.

As I amassed the recipes for this book I uncovered hundreds of techniques, and a few "general truths" that give the restaurant chef an advantage over the home cook.

Here are a few of those secrets:

❊

Marinating meat and vegetables is the main reason that many restaurant dishes have so much flavor. Rarely will you see a piece of meat that's not first coated with a dry rub or soaked in an aromatic liquid. That's the secret for the chicken at Chez Panisse, which is brined for twenty-four hours in a salt and sugar solution, adding flavor and keeping it plump and moist during cooking. And if you're in love with the coq au vin at Bistro Jeanty in Yountville, you'll understand why once you see the recipe. Philippe Jeanty soaks it in a red wine–based marinade before he sautés the pieces to assemble his incredible stew.

❊

Using more than one method of cooking is another way restaurants top the home cook. For example, the chef will often sear a slab of meat or a fish fillet on top of the stove to get a concentrated caramel crust and to seal in the juices. Then the pan containing the meat is transferred to a hot oven to finish cooking. In some cases, like the tropical-inspired ribs at Ginger Island in Berkeley, the meat is cooked three times. First the ribs are steamed, then baked with aromatic ingredients, and right before serving they're grilled to add deep smoky nuances.

❊

Swirling in a little butter is like waving a magic wand over the pan. A last minute addition to a tomato pasta sauce or pan juices smooths the flavors and add a richness to the dish.

❊

Reduce. Reduce. Reduce. This isn't a diet mantra, but a cooking mantra. Boiling away the liquid several times is a way to coax complex layers of flavor out of food. On recipes like Scala's lamb pasta sauce with artichokes and kalamata olives, the stock is reduced by three-quarters. It's then reduced to a thick glaze once the cubes of meat are added, again intensifying the flavor.

❊

Finishing pasta in the sauce gives the dish a deeper, more unified flavor. If you look at Delfina's orecchiette with broccoli rabe, you'll discover that the chef adds the almost-done pasta to the sauce along with a little of the pasta water. By the time the melange is reduced to a glaze, the pasta is still al dente and has absorbed some of the wonderful flavors. It's a technique that makes even the simplest pasta taste so much better.

❋

Cranking up the heat on the stove or oven seems to be a natural for the restaurant cook. As you look through these recipes you'll see that a 400-degree oven is common for cooking meat, fish, and even vegetables.

❋

Weighing ingredients is more precise in ensuring success of baked goods. We tried to change the recipes to measures, but in some cases we left them in ounces because the finished product came out better.

❋

Balancing flavors is the most consistent and challenging element of a chef's job. If you study these recipes, you'll begin to understand how that works. Here's the best example I can give. Try dressing a salad the traditional American way: combine all the ingredients and toss with the dressing. Then use the same amount of ingredients and vinaigrette, but try the French method of dressing all the elements individually. Logically it seems there would be little difference, but taking time to season each ingredient produces a more vibrant salad.

❋

Collecting and ferreting out the difference in these benchmark recipes became my obsession. That led to a weekly column in the *San Francisco Chronicle*, a cooking segment on *Bay Cafe* on Bay TV, and more importantly to this book.

> Each recipe contains a
> **SECRETS OF SUCCESS**
> box that spotlights what makes the recipe special. Translating a restaurant recipe wasn't always an easy task. At times we gave up, realizing that some great dishes should stay in the professional kitchen.

All the recipes in this book have been adapted and tested for the home cook. In most cases we were able to substitute canned or store-bought stock with little or no compromise in quality. Even with the testing, however, results may vary depending on the ingredients—your tomatoes may be more acidic than mine, for example— the equipment, and even the heat source. So follow the recipe, but taste as you go.

Complex recipes are kept to a minimum in this book. When a preparation requires special effort I'll try to alert you to that fact. The truth is that simple is usually best whether it's in the home or the restaurant kitchen.

You don't need a lot of fancy equipment, either. If you own the usual amount of pots, pans, baking sheets, and knives, you have most of what you need. Beyond the basics, I'd recommend a scale for weighing baking ingredients, a blender, food processor, strainer, food mill, and a mandoline for slicing vegetables (see Equipment for the Home on page 365 for specifics). I'd also invest in a large stockpot, a commercial-sized frying pan, and a grill pan in case you don't want to light up the outdoor grill.

To try to further demystify the cooking process, I've included a glossary of techniques and tips that will help you perform like a chef in the kitchen.

And if you don't want to cook, you can use this book as a guide to the best dishes at the best restaurants in the Bay Area. Service information including address, phone numbers, and days of operation are listed alphabetically in the Restaurant Resource Guide on page 366. So if you crave the Zuni hamburger but don't feel like cooking it at home, you can do the next best thing and make reservations.

PORTOBELLO MUSHROOM FRITTERS WITH AIOLI

Few appetizers are as enticing as Wendy Brucker's Portobello Mushroom Fritters, but then few chefs are as talented as she is either. ❊ The fritters are a brilliant combination of sliced mushrooms that are crunchy outside and juicy-soft inside. But that's not all; they're also served with an arugula and Parmesan salad, enhanced with a sherry vinaigrette, and drizzled with a creamy aioli. It's an unbeatable combination. ❊ That's just one of the great dishes she prepares at Rivoli in Albany, which she owns with her husband, Roscoe Skipper. The room has an open casual feel, thanks to large windows that overlook a manicured garden in back.

Aioli
2 medium garlic cloves, finely chopped
2 egg yolks
3 teaspoons fresh lemon juice
½ teaspoon salt
¾ cup pure olive oil
¼ cup extra-virgin olive oil

Vinaigrette
3 tablespoons sherry vinegar
1 tablespoon minced shallot
1 teaspoon salt
1½ teaspoons freshly ground black pepper
5 tablespoons extra-virgin olive oil
¼ cup pure olive oil

Fritters
4 cups all-purpose flour
Pinch of salt plus 1 tablespoon
4 eggs
¼ cup water
4 cups panko crumbs (see Note)
1 tablespoon chopped fresh thyme
1 pound stemmed portobello mushrooms, cut into ½-inch-thick strips
6 cups peanut oil for frying

4 cups loosely packed arugula
½ cup thinly shaved Parmesan cheese
1 tablespoon rinsed and coarsely chopped capers

—*To make the aioli:* Whisk the garlic, egg yolks, lemon juice, and salt in a medium bowl. Gradually whisk in both oils until the mixture resembles mayonnaise. Cover and refrigerate until ready to use.

—*To make the vinaigrette:* Whisk the vinegar, shallot, salt, and pepper in a small bowl to blend. Gradually whisk in both oils until well blended.

—*To make the fritters:* Combine the flour and a pinch of salt in a large bowl. In another bowl, whisk the eggs and water until frothy. In a third bowl, combine the crumbs, thyme, and 1 tablespoon salt.
—Dip the mushroom strips one at a time into the flour, then in the egg mixture, then finally in the crumbs. Transfer to a cookie sheet until ready to fry. This may be done 3 to 4 hours ahead.
—Heat the peanut oil in a large saucepan to 350 degrees. Fry the mushrooms 6 at a time until golden brown. Using a slotted spoon, transfer the mushrooms to paper towels to drain.
—Toss the arugula with 9 tablespoons of the vinaigrette in a large bowl. Divide among 6 salad plates. Top with the hot mushrooms. Scatter shaved Parmesan over the salads. Mix the capers with the remaining vinaigrette and drizzle over. Serve the aioli in small individual cups for dipping.

Serves 6

Note: *Panko (Japanese bread crumbs) are available in Japanese markets and some other supermarkets.*

> ### SECRETS OF SUCCESS:
>
> *Hot and cold.* The hot mushrooms with the cold arugula and lemon aioli is an incredible combination.
>
> *Two kinds of oil.* Using both regular and extra-virgin olive oil lends a bolder flavor to the vinaigrette.

Roman Eggplant

Eggplant simmered with tomato sauce is a classic combination, and at Bella Trattoria in the Richmond District, it's given a Roman treatment by chef owner Fabrizio Laudati. ✻ This is a straightforward dish where the sautéed rounds of eggplant are gently placed on the tomato sauce, topped with fresh mozzarella and Parmesan, and then allowed to simmer a few minutes to melt the cheese. ✻ It's served by gently transferring the tender eggplant slices, along with the sauce, to a serving plate. The combination of the sweet, acidic sauce, creamy cheese, and earthy vegetables forms a triumphant triad. ✻ The eggplant is always on the menu at this 48-seat trattoria, which features a large mural of boats and water along one wall and French doors that open onto Third Avenue along the other. Although small, the interior has an open and airy feel.

2 medium eggplants, sliced into ½-inch-thick circles
Salt
4 tablespoons plus 1 teaspoon extra-virgin olive oil
4 garlic cloves, pressed
1½ tablespoons dry white wine
One 28-ounce can peeled pear tomatoes with juices
6 to 10 leaves of fresh basil, coarsely chopped
Ground white pepper
1 cup diced fresh mozzarella
2 tablespoons grated Parmesan cheese

—Sprinkle the eggplant with salt. Set aside in a colander for 30 minutes.

—Meanwhile, in a large sauté pan over medium-high heat, heat the 4 tablespoons of oil. Add the garlic and sauté until golden brown, about 5 minutes. Add the wine and cook until most of the liquid evaporates, about 20 seconds. Add the tomatoes and their juices, breaking the tomatoes apart with the back of a wooden spoon. Reduce the heat to medium-low; add the basil. Simmer about 30 to 40 minutes to thicken slightly and blend flavors. Season to taste with salt and white pepper.

—Pat the eggplant dry with paper towels. Heat the remaining 1 teaspoon of oil in a large nonstick skillet over medium heat. Working in batches, cook the eggplant until tender, about 10 minutes per batch.

—Transfer the eggplant to the tomato sauce. Sprinkle the eggplant with the cheeses. Cover the pan. Simmer until the cheeses melt, about 2 minutes.

—To serve, divide the sauce onto each of four plates and place 2 slices of eggplant on top.

Serves 4

SECRETS OF SUCCESS:

Salting the eggplant. Adding salt to the slices pulls out the bitter juices.

Simmering the vegetable. Adding the eggplant to the sauce after sautéing it during the final minutes of cooking helps to meld the flavors.

BATTER-FRIED GREEN BEANS WITH MEYER LEMON AIOLI

When I had to do a television piece putting together my favorite three-course meal, I chose to begin with the batter-fried green beans at Bizou. They're really that good—hot and crunchy with a delicate beer batter. ✽ At this charming restaurant that feels like an intimate French brasserie, Loretta Keller serves the beans with several different sauces including the Meyer Lemon Aioli, my favorite, or a fig puree, which brings a note of sweetness to the table. ✽ It's hard to choose a dish to order at Bizou because everything is so good. Keller, who was the chef/manager at Stars Cafe before venturing out on her own several years ago, is a master at rustic dishes. ✽ It's the type of food that's perfect for the cool evenings in San Francisco. With the first sign of fog, my thoughts always turn to Bizou.

Green Beans
One 12-ounce bottle of ale
1 egg
1 cup plus 3 tablespoons all-purpose flour
½ cup cornstarch
1 teaspoon salt
¼ teaspoon balsamic vinegar
Pinch of cayenne pepper
6 cups peanut or canola oil for frying
1½ pounds green beans, trimmed
2 cups Meyer Lemon Aioli (recipe follows)

Meyer Lemon Aioli
2 egg yolks
Pinch of salt
Pinch of ground white pepper
1 teaspoon Dijon mustard (optional)
½ garlic clove, smashed to a paste
1 to 1½ cups olive, safflower, or vegetable oil
1 tablespoon fresh Meyer lemon (or other lemon) juice
1 tablespoon Meyer lemon (or other lemon) zest (about 1 lemon), finely minced

—*To make the green beans:* Beat the ale and egg together in a mixing bowl. Sift in the flour and cornstarch. Add the salt, vinegar, and cayenne. Whisk until smooth. The mixture should be the consistency of pancake batter.

—Heat the oil in a large pot to 375 degrees. Working with a handful at a time, dip the green beans into the batter and carefully drop them in the hot oil. Cook each batch until golden brown, stirring gently to separate any beans that may have joined, about 3 minutes. Using a slotted spoon, transfer the beans to paper towels and drain. Serve immediately with Meyer Lemon Aioli.

Serves 6

—*To make the aioli:* In a mixing bowl, season the egg yolks with salt and white pepper. Add the mustard, if using, and garlic paste and whisk until smooth. Slowly whisk the oil into the egg yolk mixture, about 1 tablespoon at a time. Once the mixture begins to thicken, begin to add the oil in a steady thin stream, whisking constantly. When the mixture becomes very thick, add a few drops of warm water and the lemon juice. Continue to whisk in enough of the oil until the mixture looks like thick mayonnaise. Whisk in the lemon zest. Adjust the seasoning as needed.

Makes 2 cups

SECRETS OF SUCCESS:

The beans. Keller won't make this dish unless she knows the beans are tender and sweet. Blue Lake beans work particularly well.

The batter. The ale and the cornstarch give the beans that lacy, crunchy coating when fried.

POTATO ROQUEFORT CAKES WITH RIPE PEARS

Fabrice Marcon was born and raised in France and started cooking when he was fourteen, coming to the United States after serving as a sous chef under Paul Bocuse. The guy knows how to cook, and at his charming Hyde Street Bistro, which he bought in 1997, he brings his talents to the table to create simple, straightforward French-California food. ✳ His Potato Roquefort Cakes are a great example of that philosophy. The creamy mashed potatoes are mixed with crumbly Roquefort cheese, formed into patties, and sautéed to crispen the outside. He then puts them on a bed of greens studded with juicy ripe pears, setting up a sweet-tangy contrast. To bring it all together, he drizzles a little hazelnut oil over the salad, adding a nutty nuance and creating a clever twist to the classic nuts, cheese, and fruit combination.

Potato Roquefort Cakes
4 large russet potatoes, scrubbed
8 ounces firm Roquefort cheese, crumbled
2 tablespoons olive oil
Salt and pepper
1½ ripe Anjou pears, diced
½ pound mixed salad greens
1 teaspoon chopped fresh tarragon
Vinaigrette (recipe follows)
Hazelnut oil

Vinaigrette
1 tablespoon red wine vinegar
1 teaspoon Dijon mustard
1 shallot, minced
3 tablespoons olive oil
Salt and pepper

—*To make the cakes:* Preheat the oven to 375 degrees. Bake the potatoes until tender, about 1 hour. When cool enough to handle, peel the potatoes. Transfer the insides of the potatoes to a medium bowl. Mash with a fork. Add the Roquefort and 1 tablespoon olive oil. Stir to form a soft mixture. Season to taste with salt and pepper. Form the mixture into four equal patties, about ¼- to ½-inch thick. Cover and refrigerate until chilled, about 2 hours.

—Preheat the oven to 350 degrees. Heat the remaining 1 tablespoon of oil in a skillet over medium heat. Add the cakes and brown on both sides, about 5 to 7 minutes. Transfer the cakes to a baking sheet. Bake until heated through, about 5 minutes.

—Toss the pears with the salad greens and chopped tarragon. Toss with vinaigrette and divide among 4 small plates. Top each with a Roquefort cake and drizzle with a little hazelnut oil.

Serves 4

—*To make the vinaigrette:* Whisk the vinegar, mustard, and minced shallot in a small bowl to blend. Slowly whisk in the oil. Season to taste with salt and pepper.

Makes ⅓ cup

SECRETS OF SUCCESS:

Firm blue cheese. If the cheese is too soft, the potato cake will fall apart when frying. You want the cheese to be firm and crumbly.

Ripe pears. The soft texture and sweetness sets up a pleasing contrast to the pungent, hot cheese in the cakes.

Hazelnut oil. Drizzling the oil over the top completes a classic triad of flavors: fruit, cheese, and nuts.

POTATO SKINS WITH SMOKED SALMON AND HORSERADISH CRÈME FRAÎCHE

Bradley Ogden is known for his brunch and breakfast dishes served at the Lark Creek Inn in Larkspur. Housed in a charming Victorian, the restaurant overlooks the proverbial babbling brook, and the outdoor patio is ideal for weekend brunches. ❊ Of course, you can get all the traditional brunch dishes, but one of the best is the Potato Skins with Smoked Salmon and Horseradish Crème Fraîche. While a similar dish with caviar has been popular in years past as an elegant appetizer, it was Ogden who thought of adapting it to breakfast. ❊ And why not? Many people love lox and bagels as an early morning repast. Of course, crisp fried potatoes are a natural morning option, so putting them together makes perfect sense. For this dish, the combination of roasted potatoes, salmon, and lemony cream is unbeatable. It truly is a great brunch dish, but it's also just as good as a snack, appetizer, or a passed hors d'oeuvre. ❊ The red onion relish, made with lemon, chives, and chervil, is designed to be sprinkled around the plate, but you can sprinkle it on top of the smoked salmon in place of the optional caviar, if you like.

Potato Skins

20 (about 1 pound) 1-inch diameter yellow
    potatoes or Yukon Golds, scrubbed
Kosher salt
3 tablespoons minced red onion
2 tablespoons chopped fresh chives
2 tablespoons fresh lemon juice
1½ tablespoons olive oil
1 tablespoon chopped fresh chervil
2 teaspoons finely grated lemon zest
Fresh ground black pepper
1 quart grapeseed oil for frying

6 to 8 ounces smoked salmon, sliced paper thin
    (approximately 1½ to 2 ounces per serving)
    and cut into thin strips
2 tablespoons smoked salmon caviar (optional)
1 tablespoon Osetra caviar (optional)
Horseradish Crème Fraîche (recipe follows)
14 small sprigs fresh chervil for garnishing

Horseradish Crème Fraîche

⅓ cup sour cream
½ cup crème fraîche
2 tablespoons grated tart red apple
1 tablespoon peeled and finely grated fresh
    horseradish
¼ teaspoon finely grated lemon zest
Kosher salt
Freshly ground black pepper

—*To make the potato skins:* Place the potatoes in a large saucepan with enough cold salted water to cover. Bring to a boil over high heat, then reduce the heat to a gentle simmer. Cook until the potatoes are just tender but still firm, about 8 to 10 minutes. Drain. Cool.

—While the potatoes are cooking, combine the red onion, chives, lemon juice, olive oil, chopped chervil, and lemon zest in a small bowl. Stir to mix. Season the relish to taste with salt and pepper.

—Cut the potatoes in half. Using a melon ball scoop, dig out the center of the potatoes and discard (or reserve for another dish).

—Heat the grapeseed oil in a large saucepan to 350 degrees. Working in batches, fry the potato skins until golden brown, about 3 to 4 minutes. Using a slotted spoon, transfer the potato skins to paper towels and drain. Season with salt and pepper.

—Arrange the potatoes on four 12-inch dinner plates, using 5 halves per plate and forming them into a star pattern in the center of the plate. Fill the center of each potato with 1 teaspoon of Horseradish Crème Fraîche. Arrange a few strips of smoked salmon over the potatoes. Top each with a dot of Horseradish Crème Fraîche and a little of each of the caviars, if desired.

—Sprinkle the red onion relish around the plates. Garnish plates with the chervil sprigs.

Serves 8

—*To make the Horseradish Crème Fraîche:* Whisk the sour cream in a small bowl until smooth. Using a rubber spatula, fold in and remaining ingredients, seasoning to taste with salt and pepper. Set aside and refrigerate until needed.

Makes 1 cup

SECRETS OF SUCCESS:

The potato skins. The potatoes are boiled then the skins are fried in oil until golden brown, making a crisp contrast to the silken salmon.

The Horseradish Crème Fraîche. Spooned into the potato and on the salmon, this adds a pleasant surprise to the blend.

PARMESAN BUDINI WITH WARM ASPARAGUS AND PEA SHOOTS

You'll find many versions of savory cheese custards, called budini, all over Italy, but in the Bay Area they're rare. At Acquerello, chef Suzette Gresham introduced many Northern Californians to this creamy delight, served with asparagus and intensely flavored pea shoots. ❊ Although the Parmesan Budini has rustic origins, it's given a refined twist, achieved by baking in a slow oven. ❊ If pea shoots aren't available, simply omit them or substitute a scattering of fresh peas. The budino's wonderfully nutty flavor pairs well with just about any spring vegetable. It's also good accompanied by an arugula or watercress salad. It works equally well with Parmesan or Grana Padano. ❊ Gresham first got this recipe from Todd English, the well-known chef of Olives in Boston, but she's made it her own by adding a few twists along the way. ❊ This is only one of the great dishes that Gresham and her partner, Giancarlo Paterlini, have served at the restaurant over the last decade. They've created the most refined Italian restaurant in San Francisco. The formal professional service and the excellent Italian wine list are part of the reason the *Wine Spectator* named Acquerello the second-best Italian restaurant in the nation behind Valentino in Santa Monica and ahead of Felidia in New York.

Nonstick vegetable oil spray
3 tablespoons unsalted butter
2 tablespoons all-purpose flour
¾ cup half-and-half
¾ cup heavy cream
¼ cup milk
1 egg
2 egg yolks
¾ cup grated Parmesan cheese or Grana Padano, plus additional for garnishing
¼ teaspoon kosher salt, plus additional to taste
⅛ teaspoon ground white pepper, plus additional to taste
Pinch of ground nutmeg
18 stalks of asparagus, cut into 1½-inch lengths
½ cup chicken stock
1 to 2 tablespoons finely chopped parsley
2 to 3 ounces pea shoots
Splash of extra-virgin olive oil
Splash of fresh lemon juice

—Preheat the oven to 350 degrees. Spray six 4-ounce ramekins with
nonstick spray.

—In a small heavy saucepan over medium-low heat, melt 1 tablespoon of the butter. Add the flour, mixing well. Remove from the
heat. Slowly whisk in the half-and-half, cream, and milk. Add the
egg and yolks, one at a time, whisking well after each addition. Stir
in the ¾ cup cheese, salt, pepper, and nutmeg. Mix until fully
incorporated.

—Divide the mixture equally among the prepared ramekins. Place
the ramekins in a large pan. Fill the pan with enough water to
come halfway up the sides of the ramekins. Transfer the pan to
the oven and bake until the budini are set or until the tops are
lightly browned and a skewer inserted into the center comes out
clean, about 20 to 25 minutes.

—Meanwhile, blanch the asparagus in a large pot of boiling water
for 30 seconds. Drain; transfer asparagus immediately to a bowl of
ice water to cool. Drain. Set aside.

—In a medium sauté pan, bring the chicken stock to a boil. Reduce
the heat to low. Add the remaining 2 tablespoons of butter and
whisk until melted. Add the asparagus. Toss to coat; season to
taste with salt and white pepper. Sprinkle with the parsley. Keep
warm.

—In a small bowl, gently toss the pea shoots with the olive oil and
lemon juice. Season to taste with salt and pepper. Set aside.

—Remove the budini from the oven. Using a small sharp knife,
loosen the sides. Turn each budino out onto a warm plate. Spoon
the asparagus and sauce around the budinis. Top the budini with
the pea shoots and the additional grated cheese. Serve immediately.

Serves 6

> **SECRETS OF SUCCESS:**
>
> *The water bath.* Placing the ramekins in water while baking evenly distributes the heat and creates a silky texture.
>
> *The cooking temperature.* Baking in a moderate oven prevents the custard from curdling or breaking.

MUSHROOM CUSTARD IN EGG CUPS

Sometimes it's not only the taste but also the presentation that makes the dish. Take the Mushroom Custard prepared by Ron Siegel at Charles Nob Hill, for example. ❖ The custard is absolutely delicious, creamy smooth with the unmistakable earthy flavors of mushrooms. But baking and presenting the custard in eggshells always brings a smile. ❖ This impressive dish is a complimentary appetizer, given to diners after they sit down in the elegant dining room, located atop one of San Francisco's most famous hills. ❖ Siegel knows a few things about custards. In 1998, he became the first American to win a unanimous decision from the four "Iron Chef" judges in Japan. This program has developed a cult following in the Bay Area, based on the idea that competing chefs have the same ingredients and an hour to cook a meal that will wow the judges. Siegel apparently had the competition clinched when he presented a lobster custard similar to this version with mushrooms. ❖ The restaurant, formerly Le Club, is owned by the same team that produce Aqua. Siegel has worked with Michael Mina on the French-Italian inspired menu. In an industry that's increasingly turning to boisterous casual restaurants, Charles Nob Hill harks back to the days of smooth service, hushed conversations, and grand surroundings.

1 tablespoon butter
½ cup chopped mushrooms
12 eggs at room temperature
1 cup milk
1 cup heavy cream
Salt and ground white pepper
Sprigs of fresh watercress, parsley, or dill for
    garnishing

—Preheat the oven to 275 degrees. Melt the butter in a medium skillet over medium heat. Add the mushrooms and sauté until tender, about 7 to 10 minutes. Cool.

—Working over a bowl to catch any spills, remove the top quarter of each eggshell, either with small, sharp shears or by decapitating the eggs with a whack of a chef's knife. Place the contents of 3 eggs into a medium bowl. Save the shells and the egg carton. Whisk the eggs; set aside. Reserve the contents of the remaining eggshells for an omelet or other use.

—Trim the tops of the shells as neatly as possible. Rinse the shells with hot tap water and carefully remove any membrane. Place the shells upside down to dry.

—Combine the milk and cream in a small saucepan and bring to a boil. Add the mushrooms and return to a boil. Pour the mixture into a blender and puree on high speed until liquefied. Rinse the saucepan. Pour the mixture back into the rinsed saucepan and bring to a boil once more.

—Whisk the hot mixture slowly into the 3 beaten eggs. Strain through a fine sieve. Season with salt and white pepper.

—Set the cleaned eggshells into the bottom half of the egg carton; divide the custard mixture among the shells. Place the carton in a large baking pan; add enough hot water to the pan to come ½ inch up the sides of the egg carton.

—Cover the pan loosely with foil and bake until just set, about 40 to 45 minutes. Cool to room temperature.

—Serve in individual egg cups. Garnish with sprigs of watercress, parsley, or dill. If you don't have egg cups you can make the shells stand upright on the plate by using a teaspoon to crack the bottom of the shell.

Note: *If cooking in the eggshells seems too time consuming, line 12 small muffin tins with paper liners, divide the custard mixture among them, place in a shallow pan with 1 inch of hot water and bake as above. Cool and unmold onto small plates; garnish as desired.*

Serves 12

SECRETS OF SUCCESS:

Warming the ingredients. Make sure the eggs are at room temperature; whites expand to their maximum volume at about 75 degrees.

Using a blender. Processing the cream and mushroom mixture in the blender gives the finished custard an airy, smooth texture.

The presentation. While the custard is delicious and can be baked in individual muffin cups, the shells give it a celebratory feel.

MARINATED TOMATOES WITH GARLIC TOASTS

Bruschetta is all the rage these days and just about every combination of ingredients is finding its way onto toasted bread: cauliflower and anchovy, peas and artichokes, cheese and salad greens. ❋ The most popular, however, is the simple mixture of tomato, basil, and garlic. This combination is one of the draws at Chow, an inexpensive Italian restaurant in the Castro. ❋ It's easy for the home cook, too. Roma tomatoes are marinated and allowed to soak up the flavors for several hours, so even winter tomatoes taste great. ❋ Chef/owner Tony Gulisano has worked in many fancy restaurants, including Spago and Chinois on Main in Southern California and Monsoon and Il Fornaio in the Bay Area, but his heart is in the simple food he's now cooking at Chow, which opened in 1997. The restaurant looks like it's been around for decades with wainscoting, wood floors, and Depression-era pendant lights hanging from the ceiling.

8 ripe Roma tomatoes, peeled (see page 363)
1 cup (or more) extra-virgin olive oil
2 garlic cloves, minced
8 fresh basil leaves, torn into pieces
1 teaspoon sea salt
½ teaspoon cracked black pepper
12 half-inch thick slices of chewy bread
4 whole garlic cloves

—Cut the peeled tomatoes in half lengthwise and cut each half into eighths. Add ½ cup of the olive oil, the minced garlic, basil, salt, and pepper. Adjust seasonings as needed. Gently squeeze the tomato mixture with your hands to distribute the flavor and release the juices. Cover and set aside in a cool place for at least 1 hour and up to 4 hours before serving.

—Prepare a grill (medium heat) or heat a stovetop grill pan over medium heat. Dip your fingers into the remaining ½ cup oil and rub each slice of bread with an even film. Grill the bread evenly on both sides to a deep golden color. Remove and quickly rub the hot surface with a garlic clove. The clove will dissolve and leave its perfume on the toast.

—Arrange the toasts on a platter. Spoon the tomato mixture onto the grilled bread. Drizzle with a little more olive oil, if desired. Serve immediately.

Serves 6

SECRETS OF SUCCESS:

Crushing the tomatoes by hand. The force and suction used to squeeze the tomatoes breaks the flesh and infuses the interior with the marinating juices.

Using your fingers. Rubbing oil on the bread with your fingers insures a thin even coating that can't be achieved with a brush.

STUFFED PASILLA CHILES WITH AVOCADO SALSA

Fog City Diner started a trend that's still gathering steam; it almost single-handedly brought back an idealized version of the old-fashioned diner. ✳ It doesn't matter that the outside shimmers with chrome and the rich interior looks like a private dinner club. ✳ Cindy Pawlcyn's food is eclectic and totally approachable, and the flavors span the globe. What you won't find is pretension. After all, how can you be a snob with goo on your fingers from the ribs or smudges of grease on your face from onion rings? ✳ Part of the menu also dabbles in other cuisines such as this recipe for grilled Stuffed Pasilla Chiles, kind of a takeoff on the Mexican chile rellenos. ✳ Pasillas, like all chiles, are unpredictable but they generally have only a mild kick. Pawlcyn stuffs them with five kinds of cheese, grills them, and presents them with avocado salsa.

Avocado Salsa

1 jalapeño
2 ripe avocados, pitted, peeled, and diced
½ small red onion, minced
3 scallions, minced
3 tablespoons roughly chopped fresh cilantro
6 tablespoons olive oil
2 tablespoons rice vinegar
Sea salt
Freshly ground black pepper

Stuffed Pasillas

6 pasilla (poblano) chiles
1 cup grated white Cheddar cheese
½ cup grated Fontina cheese
½ cup grated Monterey Jack cheese
½ cup grated Jarlsberg cheese
½ cup grated asiago or Parmesan cheese
12 fresh cilantro sprigs

—*To make the salsa:* Roast the jalapeño over a gas flame or under the broiler until blackened on all sides. Wrap a in paper bag; steam 10 minutes to loosen the skin. Peel, seed, and mince the jalapeño. Place in a medium bowl.

—Add the avocado, onion, scallions, and chopped cilantro.

—In a separate bowl, whisk together the oil and vinegar. Season to taste with salt and pepper. Pour over the salsa. Mix gently, being careful not to mash the avocado or it will look like guacamole. Cover with plastic wrap and set aside.

—*To make the stuffed pasillas:* Prepare the grill (medium heat). Cut all the way around the stem of each chile so that you can remove the stem and seed the base but keep it in one piece. Keeping the stem and top intact, trim off any seeds and membranes. Blanch the chiles for 2 minutes in a large pot of boiling salted water. Remove the chiles; refresh in ice water, then drain.

—Combine the cheeses in a bowl and mix well. Stuff each chile with about ½ cup of the cheese mixture. Do not overstuff or pack the cheese too densely. Replace the stem on top of the chile.

—Grill the stuffed chiles, turning frequently, until the cheeses are melted and the chilies are hot all the way through.

—Spoon the salsa onto each of 6 appetizer plates. Top with pasillas. Garnish with cilantro.

Serves 6

SECRETS OF SUCCESS:

Grilling the chiles. This not only adds a smoky quality, but it's less fattening than the traditional batter-fried chile rellenos.

Five cheeses. Generally these are stuffed with only one or two cheeses but the combination of Fontina, Jack, white Cheddar, Jarlsberg, and asiago make for a more interesting filling.

Cucumber Spread (Tsatsiki); Eggplant Spread (Melitzanosalata)

One of the best restaurants to open in the last few years has been Kokkari, one of only a handful of upscale Greek restaurants in the United States. ❃ The impressive $5-million interior feels like a grand living room with a massive fireplace, rustic beam ceiling, and a communal table for large parties. ❃ While the food is light and fresh, chef Jean Alberti uses his French training to add an edge of refinement to the lusty food. One of the classic ways to start is with a cucumber/yogurt spread called Tsatsiki and a roasted eggplant puree known as Melitzanosalata. He accompanies both with warm triangles of housemade grilled pita.

Cucumber Spread

1 pound Greek yogurt (see Note)
2 large cucumbers, peeled, seeded, and cut into ¼-inch pieces
Salt
4 tablespoons extra-virgin olive oil
¼ cup chopped fresh dill
1½ teaspoons white wine vinegar
2 garlic cloves, chopped
Pepper
Toasted pita bread triangles

Eggplant Spread

3 large firm eggplants
2 large ripe tomatoes, peeled, seeded, and diced (see page 363)
1 small onion, finely chopped
3 garlic cloves, finely chopped
1 scallion, chopped
¼ cup (or more) extra-virgin olive oil
1 tablespoon (or more) fresh lemon juice
Salt
Chopped fresh parsley for garnishing
Kalamata olives for garnishing
Toasted pita triangles

—*To make the cucumber spread:* Strain the yogurt in a cheesecloth-lined strainer over a large bowl in the refrigerator until it reaches the consistency of clotted cream, about 2 hours.

—Place the cucumbers in a colander. Sprinkle with salt. Drain for 1 hour to remove any excess water.

—Transfer the cucumbers to a medium bowl. Add 3 tablespoons of the olive oil, the dill, white wine vinegar, and garlic. Stir in the strained yogurt. Season to taste with salt and pepper. Drizzle with the remaining 1 tablespoon olive oil. Serve with toasted pita bread. Serves 6

—*To make the eggplant spread:* Pierce the whole, unpeeled eggplants with a sharp knife in several places. Grill slowly on a barbecue or a over gas burner until the skin is charred on all sides and the inside is very soft, about 10 to 15 minutes. Place the eggplants in a colander to drain off any excess liquid.

—When the eggplants are cool enough to handle, carefully peel off the black skin. Place the eggplants on a wooden board and cut off the stalks. Remove most of the seeds and finely chop the flesh to a puree-like consistency. Transfer to a large bowl.

—Add the tomatoes, onion, garlic, scallion, ¼ cup oil, and lemon juice and stir vigorously with a wooden spatula. Season to taste with salt. Adjust the amount of oil, salt, and lemon juice if necessary. Cover and refrigerate for at least 1 hour to allow the flavors to marry.

—Mix the puree with a fork just before serving and garnish with chopped parsley and a few olives. Serve with toasted pita. Serves 6

Note: *Greek yogurt is thicker and richer than commercial yogurt and can be found at some Middle Eastern markets in the Bay Area. Regular yogurt can be used but it will have a thinner consistency and tastes a little more acidic.*

SECRETS OF SUCCESS:

Draining the yogurt. Pouring the yogurt into cheesecloth and letting it drain richens and thickens the yogurt to a consistency of clotted cream.

Draining the cucumber. Adding salt to the diced cucumbers and letting them drain adds flavor but doesn't dilute the thick and creamy consistency of the spread.

Roasting the eggplant. The bland vegetable picks up a distinctive smoky flavor from the flames.

Vigorous mixing. This breaks down the fibers of the eggplant and blends the flavors of the dip. Do not use an electric mixture or food processor, however, or the spread will loose its character.

Roasted Polenta with balsamic sauce

One of the most popular—and magical—restaurants in the Napa Valley is Tra Vigne, and one of the most popular dishes there is the Roasted Polenta with Balsamic Sauce. ✻ The restaurant captures the spirit of the wine country like no other. There's even an outdoor patio, shaded by fig trees that make diners feel like they've been transported to the Mediterranean. ✻ The food crafted by Michael Chiarello promotes that feel too. The chef makes many of his own products including prosciutto, sausage, and olive oil. But like any good Italian cook, he knows the key to success is simplicity, as shown with this polenta dish. ✻ The polenta, perfumed with a little nutmeg and lightened with cream, is cooked until creamy. Then Fontina and Parmesan are added to the polenta before spreading on an oiled tray to cool. The balsamic is reduced to a sticky glaze, and the flavors are rounded out with butter stirred in just before serving. ✻ While the dish is great as it is, it can be embellished with sautéed mushrooms or grilled vegetables.

Oil for greasing
3 cups chicken stock
3 cups heavy cream
1 teaspoon salt, plus additional to taste
¼ teaspoon ground white pepper, plus
    additional to taste
Pinch of ground nutmeg
1 cup polenta
1 cup semolina
1 cup grated Parmesan cheese
½ cup grated Fontina cheese
2 cups balsamic vinegar
1 shallot, chopped
2 quarts chicken or veal stock
6 whole black peppercorns
2 bay leaves
8 tablespoons (1 stick) unsalted butter, plus
    additional for greasing

—Lightly oil a baking sheet. Combine the 3 cups of chicken stock, cream, 1 teaspoon salt, ¼ teaspoon white pepper, and nutmeg in a heavy pot. Bring to a boil. Gradually add the polenta and semolina, stirring constantly. Cook over medium heat, still stirring constantly, until the polenta pulls away from the sides of the pot, about 15 minutes. Remove from heat. Stir in ¼ cup of the Parmesan and the Fontina.

—Spread the polenta evenly on the prepared pan to a thickness of ¾ inch. Cool to room temperature, then cover and refrigerate until completely chilled.

—Meanwhile, combine the vinegar and shallot in a heavy large saucepan over high heat. Reduce to a syrupy consistency, being careful not to let the vinegar scorch, about 10 to 15 minutes. Add the 2 quarts of stock, peppercorns, and bay leaves. Bring to a boil; reduce to a syrupy consistency, turning down the heat near the end of cooking so that the sauce won't burn, about 1¼ hours. Strain the sauce into small saucepan.

—Preheat the oven to 500 degrees. Butter a large sheet pan.

—Cut the polenta into squares or triangles. Place on the prepared pan. Sprinkle with the remaining ¼ cup Parmesan and bake until golden brown, about 5 minutes.

—Bring the strained sauce to a simmer; reduce heat to low. Whisk in the butter a tablespoon at a time until fully incorporated. Season to taste with salt and pepper.

—Divide the sauce among serving plates. Top with polenta.

Serves 6

> **SECRETS OF SUCCESS:**
>
> *Heavy cream.* When the polenta cooks in the cream, it takes on a custard-like texture.
>
> *Reducing the sauce.* The balsamic vinegar is reduced to a syrup, making it dark, rich, and intensely flavored. Butter is then stirred in to soften the flavors.

POLENTA SOUFFLÉ WITH MUSHROOM SAUCE

Polenta seems too rough and tumble to be incorporated into a soufflé, but at Grand Cafe this unlikely combination has become a signature dish. ✻ To lighten the load, both polenta and a finer-grained cornmeal are used. When it's hot from the oven, the soufflé has a bread-like quality. It's unmolded and served with both a deeply flavored mushroom sauce and a tangy Cambozola sauce. ✻ The flavors are rustic, but the treatment and blend of ingredients are refined, a hallmark of Denis Soriano's cooking. Soriano, who rose to fame by cooking at Chez Michel, took over this fledgling kitchen and quickly made the food as impressive as the surroundings. ✻ The restaurant is located in a converted hotel ballroom so it has soaring forty-foot ceilings, an open kitchen, massive chandeliers, murals, expansive windows, and bigger-than-life bunny sculptures that add a sense of whimsy to the place. From the moment you enter until you spoon into the final bite of dessert, you'll feel like you've been transported to one of the grand brasseries of Paris.

Polenta Soufflé
Butter for greasing
1½ cups milk
2 cups cornmeal
½ cup polenta, preferably fine grain
½ cup (1 stick) butter
½ teaspoon salt
12 eggs, separated
2½ tablespoons baking powder
1 cup grated Parmesan cheese
2 tablespoons chopped fresh chives
½ teaspoon sugar
Mushroom Sauce (recipe follows)
Cambozola Sauce (recipe follows)
Minced fresh chives for garnishing

Mushroom Sauce
1 tablespoon plus 1 teaspoon butter
1 tablespoon vegetable oil
3 pounds mixed mushrooms (such as oyster, chanterelle, and shiitake), cleaned and finely chopped
1 garlic clove, minced
Salt and pepper
4 small shallots, finely diced
¼ cup port
4 cups veal or chicken stock
2 cups heavy cream
2 bay leaves

Cambozola Sauce
2 cups heavy cream
4 ounces Cambozola cheese, cut into small pieces
Freshly ground black pepper

—*To make the soufflé:* Preheat the oven to 300 degrees. Butter 10 soufflé dishes or ramekins.

—In a medium heavy-bottomed saucepan, scald the milk over medium-low heat. Stir in the cornmeal and polenta and cook, stirring frequently, until the mixture is thick and the polenta tastes cooked, about 15 to 20 minutes.

—Stir in the butter and ¼ teaspoon of the salt. Remove from heat. Transfer the polenta to a mixing bowl and cool to room temperature, stirring occasionally.

—When the polenta is at room temperature, add the egg yolks and beat with an electric mixer until fully incorporated, about 5 minutes. Add the baking powder and beat 5 more minutes. Stir in the Parmesan and chopped chives.

—In another mixing bowl with clean dry beaters, whip the egg whites, sugar, and remaining ¼ teaspoon salt until stiff. Fold a third of the whites into the polenta mixture to lighten; then gently fold in the remainder of the whites.

—Ladle the mixture into the prepared soufflé dishes. Arrange on a baking sheet. Bake about 40 minutes, until the soufflés are firm and golden brown.

—Unmold. Ladle the Mushroom Sauce around the soufflés; drizzle the Cambozola Sauce over. Garnish with minced chives. Serve immediately.
Serves 10

—*To make the mushroom sauce:* In a large sauté pan, melt the 1 tablespoon butter with the oil over medium heat. Add the mushrooms and the garlic and sauté until the mushrooms are tender, about 10 minutes. Season to taste with salt and pepper. Set aside.

—In another large sauté pan, melt the remaining 1 teaspoon butter. Add the shallots and sauté until translucent, about 2 minutes. Add the sautéed mushrooms and cook for about 2 minutes. Add the port and cook for about 2 minutes. Add the veal stock, cream, and bay leaves. Cover the pan and cook over medium heat for 20 minutes to blend the flavors. Remove the bay leaves before serving.
Makes 3 cups

—*To make the cambozola sauce:* Bring the cream to a simmer in a small saucepan. Remove from the heat; add the Cambozola in batches, stirring until melted after each addition. Season to taste with freshly ground black pepper.
Makes 2 cups

> **SECRETS OF SUCCESS:**
>
> *Two kinds of cornmeal.* Using both polenta for texture and cornmeal for lightness allows the ingredients to puff slightly during baking.
>
> *Two sauces.* The rich mushroom sauce and the Cambozola sauce make the appetizer more interesting.

POLENTA WITH FOUR CHEESES

In the Bay Area, polenta is almost as popular as potatoes when it comes to rounding out a restaurant plate. It's little wonder when you consider its versatility. It takes on an almost pudding-like consistency when hot from the pot. As it cools, polenta firms up so it can be cut into squares or triangles and then fried, baked, or grilled. ✱ At Aperto, a charming Italian restaurant on Potrero Hill in San Francisco, one of the best appetizers begins with polenta, softened with mascarpone cheese. The mixture is allowed to firm up before chef Chris Shepherd cuts it into triangles, bakes it to create a crisp shell, then tops it with three cheeses—tangy Gorgonzola, Parmesan, and pecorino. ✱ The hot triangles are arranged on a bed of arugula and diced tomatoes for a cool contrast to the hot, crispy polenta triangles.

Polenta
Olive oil for greasing
4 cups (or more) water
1 teaspoon salt, plus more to taste
1 cup coarse polenta
Ground white pepper
½ cup mascarpone cheese

Four-Cheese Topping
½ cup mascarpone cheese
½ cup Gorgonzola Dolce at room temperature
¼ cup grated Parmesan
¼ cup grated pecorino
¼ cup milk

Oil for greasing
4 Roma tomatoes, diced
4 ounces arugula
2 tablespoons olive oil
Salt and pepper

—*To make the polenta:* Lightly grease a cookie sheet with olive oil and set aside.

—In a heavy medium pot, bring the 4 cups of water and 1 teaspoon of salt to a boil. Slowly whisk in the polenta in a steady stream. Constantly stir the polenta with a wire whisk or wooden spoon for 5 minutes. Reduce the heat to low and cook until polenta is firm and fairly thick but the grains are tender, stirring often and adding more water if necessary, about 45 minutes. Season with additional salt and white pepper. Stir in the mascarpone cheese.

—Spread the polenta evenly to 1-inch thickness on the prepared pan. Refrigerate until cool and firm, at least 2 hours or overnight.

—*To make the four-cheese topping:* Mix the mascarpone, Gorgonzola, Parmesan, pecorino, and milk in a small bowl or blender. Using a hand mixer or blender, mix until well blended.

—Preheat the oven to 400 degrees. Lightly oil an oven-safe baking dish and place in the oven to heat for 5 minutes.

—Slice the polenta into equal-size squares. Then cut each square on the diagonal to form triangles.

—Remove the hot pan from the oven and carefully place the triangles, coarse side down, onto the pan. Do not allow the triangles to touch.

—Bake the polenta until the triangles are lightly browned and crisp, about 10 to 12 minutes.

—Toss the tomatoes and arugula with the olive oil. Season to taste with salt and pepper.

—Arrange the arugula-tomato mixture on a serving platter or on 4 individual plates. Place the polenta triangles browned side up on the greens and top with a dollop of the cheese mixture. Let the cheese melt for a few minutes before serving. Serve warm.

Serves 4

SECRETS OF SUCCESS:

The mascarpone in the polenta. Stirring in the soft cheese creates a creamy interior, making a more dramatic contrast to the crisp exterior.

The cheese topping. Mixing the four cheeses creates a complex creamy, tangy, and nutty flavor.

TWICE-BAKED GOAT CHEESE SOUFFLÉ

Back when California cuisine was just emerging, goat cheese became the lightening rod of ridicule and wise cracks. ✳ Today goat cheese has gone mainstream and is about as common as Gouda; but no dish is as uncommonly good as the Twice-Baked Goat Cheese Soufflé at Zax. ✳ The soufflé, which is baked in individual ramekins, cooled, then baked again right before serving, can be served alone or surrounded by lightly dressed greens such as arugula. It also shines with baby spinach dressed with an apple cider vinaigrette, apples, celery, and fennel. ✳ The soufflé puffs up again during the second baking, and the textures are seductive: a crisp, toasty exterior gives way to a light and tangy interior. The recipe was devised by a husband and wife team, Barbara Mulas and Mark Drazek, who produce some of the best California-Mediterranean food at their 49-seat restaurant, tucked away in an out-of-the-way location between North Beach and Fisherman's Wharf. ✳ Mulas and Drazek met in 1986 at the California Culinary Academy and they've been cooking together since, opening their restaurant in 1993. ✳ Barbara has an affinity for savory dishes. Mark is responsible for the desserts, including one of the best apple galettes in the Bay Area (see page 306). ✳ The modern storefront restaurant, decorated in soothing soft colors, features bright art work and a soffit ceiling that casts a warm glow over the dining room. It's a quiet understated backdrop to their vibrant food.

Butter for greasing, plus 3 tablespoons
1 cup dry bread crumbs
3 tablespoons cake flour
1 cup milk
10 ounces goat cheese
3 large egg yolks
Salt and pepper
1 cup egg whites (about 7 large)

—Preheat the oven to 425 degrees. Arrange a rack in the center of the oven.

—Butter eight 5-ounce ramekins, making sure to coat them well. Coat each ramekin with bread crumbs, turning them over to remove the excess. Reserve any remaining bread crumbs.

—Melt the 3 tablespoons of butter in a stainless steel sauté pan over medium-high heat. Whisk in the flour and cook for 20 seconds, whisking constantly. Whisk in the milk; cook until thickened to the consistency of a thin pourable pudding, whisking constantly, about 1 minute.

—Crumble 8 ounces of the goat cheese into a large mixing bowl. Pour the hot milk mixture on the cheese and mix well. Add the egg yolks and mix again. Season with salt and pepper.

—Using an electric mixer with clean dry beaters, beat the egg whites in a large bowl until stiff. Fold half the whites into the cheese mixture to lighten. Then gently fold in the remaining whites. Fill the prepared ramekins halfway with the soufflé mixture, using half of the mixture. Crumble the remaining 2 ounces of goat cheese over the soufflé mixture in the ramekins. Fill the ramekins with the remainder of the soufflé mixture. Sprinkle with the remaining bread crumbs.

—Place the ramekins in a baking dish and fill the dish halfway up the sides of the ramekins with boiling water. Bake on the center rack of the oven until golden, about 25 minutes.

—Remove from the oven and let sit in the water for 15 minutes.

—Using a towel to hold the ramekins, run a knife around the inside rims to loosen. Turn out the soufflés onto a baking sheet. The soufflés can be held at room temperature for up to 6 hours before baking again.

—When ready to serve, bake at 425 degrees until deep golden brown, about 5 to 7 minutes.

Serves 8

SECRETS OF SUCCESS:

Cake flour. Finer than all-purpose flour, it gives the Twice-Baked Goat Cheese Soufflé its airy refined texture. Since the soufflé is turned out on a baking sheet and reheated just before serving, the flour is the key element to the airy texture.

Bread crumbs. The ramekins are lined with bread crumbs, which helps to give the soufflés structure when they're turned out after the first baking. In addition, the crumbs give that dramatic contrast between the crunchy exterior and creamy interior.

HOUSE-SMOKED ATLANTIC SALMON WITH MASCARPONE CREAM

The problem with smoked salmon is that it can be too salty, smoky, or flabby. What's so good about the version served at Brannan's Grill in Calistoga is the mild balance of flavors. In addition, it can be prepared by the home cook because we have directions on how to turn your Weber-style grill into a cold smoker. ❖ The salmon is first brined in salt and vanilla for up to two days, which adds a delicate creamy, floral quality to the bright pink flesh. Two hours of gentle smoking with applewood chips imparts a mild aromatic quality, creating a magical synergy without overshadowing the natural flavor of the fish. ❖ Brannan's, which opened in downtown Calistoga a few years ago, serves American regional food from around the country. It's a concept perfected by owners Mark Young and Ron Goldin, who also own the casual Checkers restaurants in Napa and Sonoma counties. ❖ The restaurant is located in a 1906 vintage building, which blends the original architectural elements with artistic craftsman designs. On warm days—and there are lots of them in the upper reaches of Napa Valley—the windows can be thrown open to let in the balmy breezes.

Salmon
1 cup kosher salt
3 vanilla beans
Zest of 1 lemon
1 cup packed brown sugar
1 Atlantic salmon fillet, about 1½ pounds (bones removed)

Mascarpone Cream
4 shallots
1 tablespoon olive oil
1 cup mascarpone cheese at room temperature
Salt
Tabasco sauce

1 cup applewood chips (see Note)
Toast points

—*To make the salmon:* Using a food processor, grind the salt and
   vanilla beans until well blended. Add the zest and brown sugar
   and pulse briefly to combine.
—In the bottom of a large casserole, sprinkle a quarter of the salt
   mixture. Cut slashes ⅛-inch deep on the skin of the salmon. Place
   the salmon on top of the salt, skin side down. Cover the salmon
   completely with the remaining salt mixture. Cover with plastic
   wrap and refrigerate for 48 hours.

—*To make the mascarpone cream:* Preheat the oven to 400 degrees.
   Toss the shallots and the olive oil together in a small baking pan.
   Cover the pan and roast for 30 minutes or until soft. Transfer the
   shallots to a food processor and process until finely minced. Fold
   the shallots into the mascarpone. Season to taste with salt and
   Tabasco. Refrigerate until ready to use.
—Soak the applewood chips in a large bowl of warm water for 2
   hours. Drain.
—Prepare your home smoker or make your own by using a regular
   grill. To turn a regular grill into a smoker, place 6 briquettes in the
   bottom of the barbecue grill. Light them and allow them to
   become fully white in color.
—Using tongs, carefully place the hot briquettes in a coffee can or a
   small stainless steel bowl along with the soaked wood chips. Place
   this bowl inside a larger stainless bowl filled with ice.
—Remove the salmon from the salt mixture. Rinse in cold water. Pat
   dry with paper towels.
—Place the bowls filled with the hot briquettes and ice on the grate
   of the grill and arrange the salmon around it. Cover the grill and
   allow the fish to cold smoke for 2 hours, adding extra ice to the
   bowl if necessary.
—To serve, slice the salmon very thin and serve with the mascarpone
   cream and toast points.

Makes at least 24 appetizers

Note: *Applewood chips are available at local hardware and specialty food
   stores.*

SECRETS OF SUCCESS:

The vanilla. The beans used in the cure of
the salmon impart an exotic aromatic flavor to the fish.

Cold smoking. The smoke permeates and
gently flavors the meat.

SMOKED SALMON PIZZA

Wolfgang Puck's name is synonymous with pizza, but we're not talking about the ones found in the frozen food cases. This recipe is for his signature smoked salmon version. The hot, crisp crust is slathered with lemon crème fraîche and smoked salmon, then decorated with dollops of caviar. ❋ It was dishes like this that made him famous. It's one of the staples on the menu at Spago Palo Alto where Michael French is the chef/partner. French, who has been at the restaurant since it opened in late 1997, has worked for Puck for so long that the two are on the same wavelength. ❋ This compatibility shows in the food at the restaurant, which has a fresh California feel with nods to France, Italy, and Asia. ❋ Designed by Adam Tihany, who also did Le Cirque 2000 in New York, the interior has a modernist feel with an open kitchen and bright colors on the walls and ceiling beams. The expansive outdoor patio is located between the restaurant and the bar and gets constant use during the warm months and through much of the fall and spring.

Pizza

1 package dry yeast
¾ cup warm water (105 to 110 degrees)
1 teaspoon honey
2¾ cups all-purpose flour
2 tablespoons olive oil, plus additional for
   brushing
1 teaspoon salt
8 thin slices red onion
Lemon Crème Fraîche (recipe follows)
25 paper-thin slices of smoked salmon
1 tablespoon chopped fresh chives, chopped
2 tablespoons caviar

Lemon Crème Fraîche

2 cups crème fraîche
2 tablespoons chopped fresh chives
2 tablespoons fresh lemon juice
Salt and ground white pepper

—*To make the pizza:* In a small bowl dissolve the yeast with ¼ cup water and the honey. In a mixer fitted with a dough hook, mix the flour, olive oil, and salt until blended. Add the yeast mixture and the remaining ½ cup water. Knead in mixer on low speed about 5 minutes.

—Turn the dough out onto a lightly floured counter and knead until the dough is no longer sticky and has become elastic, about 4 minutes.

—Lightly oil a large bowl. Add the dough; turn to coat. Cover with a damp cloth. Let stand in a warm place until doubled in volume, about 30 minutes.

—Divide the dough into quarters. Work each in the palm of your hand to form a tight ball. Place the dough balls on a baking sheet. Cover with a towel and let stand in a warm place until doubled in volume, about 30 minutes.

—Preheat the oven to 500 degrees. Pull or roll each dough ball into very thin 8- to 10-inch rounds. Brush each with olive oil and top with two red onion slices.

—Working in batches, place 2 rounds on a pizza stone and bake until crisp and golden, about 8 minutes. Then place the other 2 rounds in to bake. Top each with Lemon Crème Fraîche, then smoked salmon. Sprinkle with chives and cut each pizza into 6 pieces. Place 1 dollop of caviar on each slice and serve.
Serves 4

—*To make the crème fraîche:* In a small bowl stir together the crème fraîche, chives, and lemon juice. Season to taste with salt and white pepper. Refrigerate until ready to use.
Makes about 2 cups

> **SECRETS OF SUCCESS:**
>
> *Making the crust.* Hot, thin, and crispy, it creates a texture and temperature contrast with the cool salmon and tangy Lemon Crème Fraîche.
>
> *The pizza stone.* It's the best way to achieve a crisp crust without a wood-fired oven.

TUNA TARTARE WITH SOY VINAIGRETTE

Tuna tartare, a mix of chopped raw fish and seasonings, has become a popular appetizer at trendy restaurants these days. In many cases the chefs add so much to the fish that its delicacy is obliterated. This version done by Scott Newman at Rubicon is different; it's as pared down as the restaurant's handsome interior. ❋ His recipe includes only a few complementary ingredients such as radish, shallots, and ginger that act to accentuate, not mask, the focus. And the soy vinaigrette consists of only two other elements to balance the salty liquid: lemon and olive oil. It's so good that this dish has become one of the most popular at the restaurant.

—In a large bowl, mix the tuna with the scallions, cilantro, shallots, ginger, and half of the julienned radishes.

—In a small bowl, whisk together the olive oil, soy sauce, and lemon juice until well blended. Stir half the vinaigrette into the tuna mixture and season to taste with salt and pepper.

—Sprinkle the serving platter with the remaining radishes and the daikon sprouts. Gently form the tartare mixture into a mound and place in the center of the platter. Drizzle the remaining vinaigrette over the tartare and serve with toast points.

Serves 4

1 pound top-quality fresh tuna, cut into
  ¼-inch dice
2 bunches scallions, thinly sliced
1 bunch fresh cilantro, stemmed, leaves cut into
  thin strips
3 shallots, finely diced
1 teaspoon finely chopped fresh ginger
6 radishes, finely julienned
1 cup olive oil
¼ cup soy sauce
¼ cup fresh lemon juice
Salt and finely ground black pepper
One 1-ounce package daikon sprouts
Toast points

SECRETS OF SUCCESS:

Selecting the tuna. We all like a bargain but the best fresh tuna is never cheap. Don't skimp on the quality or the taste and texture will be inferior.

A sharp knife. A good edge is essential to get a clean cut on the tuna. A dull knife will mash and tear the flesh and destroy the texture.

Hudhud Ghanoush (Turnip Spread)

Baba ghanoush is a traditional Middle Eastern dish made with eggplant, but Yahya Salih updates it with roasted turnips at his new cafe/take-out Ur, located next to the main restaurant, YaYa Cuisine in the Financial District. Salih named the spread Hudhud Ghanoush after his young son. ✿ The spread has an earthy mild taste and at first bite seems sweet from the date syrup, but after the second bite I became hooked. It's great on pita, very thin slices of bread, or crackers. It can also be used as a dip for vegetables, particularly celery. ✿ The creative cook can also substitute roasted potatoes, zucchini, or cauliflower for the turnips. And you can even use eggplant.

—Preheat the oven to 375 degrees.

—Place the turnips on a cookie sheet and bake for 30 to 45 minutes until very soft. Cool. When cool enough to handle, peel.

—Blend the turnips with the yogurt, tahini, lemon juice, and garlic in a food processor or blender until smooth. Stir in the date syrup. Season to taste with salt and pepper. Serve with pita bread and celery sticks, if desired.

Serves 6

Note: *Date syrup can be found in most Middle Eastern markets. To make a homemade version, boil 1 cup pitted dates in 1 cup water for about 5 minutes, then puree the mixture in a food processor.*

6 large turnips, trimmed
½ cup plain yogurt
⅓ cup tahini (raw or roasted)
Juice of ½ lemon
1 tablespoon chopped garlic
2 tablespoons date syrup (see Note)
Salt and pepper
Toasted pita
Celery sticks (optional)

SECRETS OF SUCCESS:

Roasted turnips. Using this vegetable in place of eggplant gives a twist to a traditional Middle Eastern preparation.

LOBSTER MARTINI

What's more American than Maine lobster and martinis? At Ricochet, the two classics are combined into an innovative and vibrant appetizer. ✳ There's a lot of razzle-dazzle in former chef David Wolfskill's Lobster Martini: Sweet chunks of seafood, refreshing strips of English cucumber, creamy cubes of avocado, tender baby lettuces, and bursts of tart lime segments. The dressing, however, brings these elements together. The vinaigrette, which includes vermouth, olives, and Champagne vinegar, is creamy and light because the ingredients are whirled in a blender. ✳ All the elements of the salad are then coated with the silken dressing, ensuring that everything is properly dressed. ✳ The Lobster Martini is an impressive appetizer to make at home because it's relatively easy and much of the work can be done ahead. If you don't want to use lobster, substitute shrimp or rock shrimp. ✳ The Lobster Martini has understandably become a popular signature dish at this West Portal restaurant. The dining room has a comfortable lived-in look and the bar area could double as a ski lodge with mirrors on the walls, bison heads, a fireplace, and brick walls.

Lobster

12 ounces cooked peeled lobster meat, or peeled shrimp or rock shrimp

4 ounces English cucumber, peeled and cut into sticks

1 ripe avocado, peeled, pitted, and cubed

4 ounces baby lettuces

About ⅓ cup Olive and Vermouth Vinaigrette (recipe follows)

1 lime, peeled and segmented (see page 363)

3 fresh dill sprigs, chopped

Salt

4 pimiento-stuffed olives for garnishing

4 lemon wedges for garnishing

Olive and Vermouth Vinaigrette

¾ cup extra-virgin olive oil

6 tablespoons Champagne vinegar

¼ cup dry vermouth

2 tablespoons brine from olive jar

1 small shallot, minced

¼ cup chopped green pimiento-stuffed olives

Salt and pepper

—*To make the lobster:* Place the lobster, cucumber, avocado, and lettuces in separate bowls. Toss each with some of the Olive and Vermouth Vinaigrette. Combine all dressed ingredients in one large bowl. Add the lime and dill. Toss with the remaining dressing as needed. Season with salt, if necessary.

—Divide the mixture among 4 plates or oversized martini glasses. Garnish each with an olive and a lemon wedge on the side.
Serves 4

—*To make the vinaigrette:* Combine the olive oil, vinegar, vermouth, and olive brine in a blender. Add the shallot and blend on high speed for 1 to 2 minutes. Add the olives and blend again. Season to taste with salt and pepper. Chill in the refrigerator until ready to serve.

—The additional dressing keeps well in the refrigerator for several days. Shake or stir before serving.
Makes about 2 cups

SECRETS OF SUCCESS:

The blender. Making the vinaigrette in a blender emulsifies the ingredients, giving it a silken, creamy texture. It retains the same silken consistency overnight in the refrigerator.

Lime segments. The bursts of tangy lime adds a startling "wake up" call. It helps to clean and refresh the palate for the next bite of rich lobster.

Applying the vinaigrette. It may seem like an unneeded step, but dressing each item individually ensures that each ingredient is properly seasoned. In addition, each item also retains its individual character.

TANDOORI PRAWNS WITH KIWI-MINT SAUCE

When people ask me for an out-of-the-way restaurant around Union Square, I always recommend Cafe Akimbo, located on the second floor of a building on Maiden Lane. ❈ It's not just that the feel of the place is so pleasant, with bright colors and a cool minimalist attention to details. It's because the food never ceases to offer surprises. ❈ Take the Tandoori Prawns with Kiwi-Mint Sauce, for example. Chef/owner Daniel Yang, who used to be a flight attendant, combines these unlikely flavors into an exciting dish, where the spiciness of the shrimp is tamed by the acidity of the fruit and the sweetness of the mint jelly. It's served on thinly sliced cucumbers, which provides a clean, fresh note. ❈ Because Yang has no formal training, he's not afraid to use what tastes good to him. His prawns are seasoned with taco seasoning mix as well as onion and garlic powder, ingredients that the professionally trained chefs wouldn't even consider. But Yang is a natural talent, and he pulls it off.

Prawns

One 3.5-ounce can tandoori masala (see Note)

3 tablespoons taco seasoning mix

1 tablespoon asafoetida powder (see Note)

8 jumbo prawns, shelled and deveined, with
     tails intact

Pinch of celery salt

⅛ teaspoon onion powder

¼ teaspoon garlic powder

¼ teaspoon low-sodium soy sauce

¼ teaspoon mirin

1 teaspoon plain yogurt

½ teaspoon canola oil

Kiwi-Mint Sauce

2 tablespoons mint jelly

1 tablespoon honey

1 tablespoon sugar

4 kiwi, peeled, cored, and diced

8 slices of English cucumber

—*To make the prawns:* Combine the masala, taco seasoning, and asafoetida powder in a small bowl. Set the spice mix aside.

—In a large bowl, toss the prawns with the celery salt, onion powder, and garlic powder. Drizzle with the soy sauce and mirin. Toss to combine. Set aside for 10 minutes.

—Add the yogurt, canola oil, and 1 teaspoon of the tandoori spice mix to the prawns (save the remaining spice mix for another use). Cover and refrigerate for 1 hour.

—*To make the sauce:* Place the mint jelly, honey, and sugar in a blender and mix well. Add the diced kiwi and process until the fruit is pureed but not overprocessed, about 20 to 30 seconds. Strain and discard the pulp. Set aside. (The sauce will keep in the refrigerator for 2 to 3 days.)

—Prepare the grill (high heat). Grill the prawns until just cooked, about 2 minutes per side.

—To serve, divide the cucumber slices between two plates. Drizzle the kiwi-mint sauce around cucumbers. Place a grilled prawn on each cucumber slice.

Serves 2 as an appetizer

Note: *The tandoori masala and asafoetida powder ingredients are available at Indian markets or natural foods stores.*

SECRETS OF SUCCESS:

Double marinating the prawns. They're first soaked in a soy and mirin marinade; then they're coated with the tandoori spices and a little yogurt.

Processing the kiwi. The sauce shouldn't be overprocessed; the seeds need to remain whole or the sauce can become bitter.

Black Mussel Soufflé

No other seafood restaurant in the city can compare with Aqua, and no other dish in the city can compete with the delicious Black Mussel Soufflé that's been on the menu from the day the restaurant opened. ❊ The texture is light and airy, but because of a wine and shallot reduction and the seasoned mussels stirred into the rich egg base, the flavors are intense. To add another layer of flavor, chef Michael Mina adds a sauce derived from cream and the reduced broth from the mussels. ❊ While many people are afraid to tackle a soufflé, this one is practically foolproof. Even if it falls, the flavors will be just as good. The soufflé may be made in individual dishes or in a single larger dish. ❊ Be forewarned that this recipe, while straightforward, will probably use every pot in the kitchen and take a good hour to prepare. It's well worth the effort, though. To minimize last-minute preparations, you can complete the shallots, mussels, and soufflé base an hour ahead. Whip the egg whites and fold them in right before baking. ❊ In addition to the expensive four-star food, there's a four-star ambiance at Aqua. In fact, with its curved walls, high ceilings, dramatic lighting, and impressive profusion of six-foot-high fresh flower arrangements, Aqua is probably the most beautiful restaurant in San Francisco.

Butter and flour for greasing soufflé molds
13 shallots
5 garlic cloves, minced
6 cups Chardonnay
¼ cup olive oil
1 pound Prince Edward Island black mussels, scrubbed and debearded
1 bunch fresh parsley, chopped
1¼ cups whole milk
½ cup (1 stick) unsalted butter
½ cup all-purpose flour
6 egg yolks
10 egg whites
Pinch of salt
Pinch of cornstarch
1½ cups heavy cream

—Preheat the oven to 375 degrees. Butter and flour 10 four-ounce soufflé dishes. (You may also use one large soufflé dish, if desired.)

—Mince 8 of the shallots and place in a large sauté pan. Add the garlic and 2 cups of the Chardonnay. Simmer over medium heat until the wine has cooked away and the mixture is almost dry, about 20 minutes. Remove from the heat; cool the shallot reduction.

—Mince the remaining 5 shallots. Heat the olive oil in a large pot over high heat. Add the shallots and sauté until translucent, about 1 minute. Add the mussels, the remaining 4 cups wine, and the parsley. Cover and simmer until the mussels open, about 5 minutes. Discard any unopened mussels. Strain the cooking liquid and set aside.

—Remove the mussels from their shells and finely chop. Set aside. Discard the shells.

—Bring the milk and butter to a boil in a large saucepan. Add the flour and stir constantly until a stiff batter forms. Reduce the heat and continue to cook and stir until the mixture is smooth and shiny, about 5 to 7 minutes.

—Pour the mixture into the bowl of an electric mixer and mix on low speed for 5 minutes, until the batter has cooled to room temperature. Add the egg yolks 1 at a time, beating well after each addition. Blend the shallot reduction and chopped mussels into the soufflé base.

—Using an electric mixer with clean dry beaters, whip the egg whites in a large bowl on high speed with the salt and cornstarch until they hold medium-firm peaks, about 5 to 7 minutes. Using a spatula, gently fold the whites into the soufflé base. Divide the mixture among the prepared soufflé molds.

—Bake until the soufflés are golden and rise about 1½ inches above the rim of the molds, about 25 minutes. If making one large soufflé, bake approximately 35 minutes.

—While the soufflés are baking, place the reserved mussel cooking liquid in a medium saucepan over medium-high heat and cook until reduced by half, about 10 to 15 minutes. Add the cream and simmer until the sauce has thickened, about 5 to 10 minutes.

—Serve the soufflés the moment they come from the oven, with the warm sauce on the side.

Serves 10

SECRETS OF SUCCESS:

Proportion of ingredients. The soufflé base has a higher ratio of eggs and butter to milk than most soufflé recipes.

Layers of flavor. Although light in texture, the soufflé has an extraordinarily intense flavor because of the reduction of wine and shallots added to the base. The addition of seasoned cooked mussels adds another level of flavor.

Briny juices. The cream sauce incorporates the mussel liquid to reinforce the seafaring flavors in the dish.

SICHUAN PEPPER CALAMARI WITH LEMON-GINGER DIPPING SAUCE

Anyone who eats out knows that just about every restaurant makes fried squid, but not like Ralph Tingle's Sichuan Pepper Calamari. ❋ For one thing he adds a dash of heat with Sichuan peppercorns to the coating, then he serves it with a piquant lemon-ginger sauce, which tastes better if made a day or two ahead. ❋ Most versions have a thicker batter, but Tingle lets the seafood shine by only lightly dusting the seafood in the flour and pepper. You can also add a little salt if you like, but the dipping sauce packs a lot of punch. ❋ With only 13 tables, Bistro Ralph, which opened in Healdsburg in 1992, has developed a national reputation thanks to Tingle, who worked in France and was the chef at Fetzer Vineyards before venturing out on his own.

—*To make the calamari:* Mix the flour, Sichuan pepper, and salt in a bowl. Toss the calamari in the mixture and then shake it in a strainer or colander to remove excess flour.
—Heat the oil in a deep pot to 375 degrees. Working in batches, fry the calamari until deep golden brown, about 2 to 3 minutes. Using a slotted spoon, transfer the calamari to paper towels and drain.
—Garnish with cilantro and serve with Lemon-Ginger Dipping Sauce.
Serves 6

—*To make the sauce:* Place the ginger in a food processor and grind to a pulp. Place the pulp in a clean towel and squeeze out the juice until you have ¼ cup. Whisk the ginger juice with the remaining sauce ingredients.

Calamari
2 cups all-purpose flour
¼ cup freshly ground Sichuan peppercorns
1 teaspoon salt
2 pounds calamari, cleaned and sliced
4 cups peanut or canola oil for frying
Cilantro sprigs for garnishing
Lemon-Ginger Dipping Sauce (recipe follows)

Lemon-Ginger Dipping Sauce
6 ounces fresh ginger, peeled and chopped
2 cups low-sodium soy sauce
¼ cup fresh lemon juice
¼ cup chopped fresh cilantro leaves
2 tablespoons toasted sesame seeds

SECRETS OF SUCCESS:

Hot oil. Be sure the oil reaches 375 degrees before frying, otherwise the flour won't cling properly.

The dipping sauce. Ginger juice combined with the lemon and soy creates an extraordinary flavor.

OYSTERS WITH CHILE, LIME, AND MINT GRANITA

It doesn't happen often, but once in a while a dish comes along that is so clever and makes such good sense that you wonder why everyone doesn't do it. ✳ I'm talking about the chile, lime, and mint granita that is spooned over fresh oysters at Le Colonial, the chic Vietnamese restaurant that took over the spot that once housed Trader Vic's. A spoonful of this intensely flavored ice not only keeps the oysters chilled, but as it melts it creates a delicious sauce that pools in the shell. ✳ The dish is also perfect for the environment of Le Colonial, which looks like a French-inspired tropical plantation. As you eat the oysters you practically feel the balmy nights and gentle breezes, which is quite a feat in San Francisco where a gusty chill seems to freeze any thoughts of summer.

—In a small pot, bring the water to a boil and add the mint. Reduce the heat and simmer until the liquid reduces by half.

—Remove from the heat and add the lime juice, sugar, and fish sauce. Stir the mixture until the sugar dissolves. Discard the mint sprigs. Add the chile-garlic sauce and mix well. Transfer the mixture to a stainless steel or glass pan and place in the freezer. Whisk the mixture every 10 to 20 minutes and continue to freeze until mixture is consistency of shaved ice, about 2 hours. The granita is best when made the day before. Break up crystals and whisk before serving.

—Top each oyster with a tablespoon of the granita and serve immediately.

Serves 4 to 6

2 cups water
2 fresh mint sprigs
½ cup fresh lime juice
¼ cup sugar
¼ cup fish sauce
1 teaspoon chile-garlic sauce
2 dozen oysters, shucked and arranged on a bed
   of crushed ice

SECRETS OF SUCCESS:

The granita. It keep the oysters chilled and adds a burst of flavor so you don't need any other sauce.

Stirring the mixture. Stirring and breaking up the mixture as it freezes helps to form lighter flakes.

ESCARGOTS IN POLENTA NESTS

It takes a clever and gifted man to create a truly innovative dish, and Roland Passot is just such a man. He took the classic escargots in garlic butter that was the rage in continental restaurants in the 1960s and paired it with the rage of the 1990s—polenta. ❋ Here's how it works: He sautés the snails with garlic, a splash of Pernod, and white wine. He then spreads cooked polenta on a cookie sheet, scores the top with a three-inch cookie cutter and presses five snails into the center of each. The polenta is then placed in the refrigerator to chill. ❋ When ready to serve Passot cuts out the snail-filled rounds and sautés the polenta cake to golden brown and arranges them on a pool of Roquefort sauce. ❋ It's a sophisticated idea, and it tastes even better than it looks. This is only one of the impressive dishes Passot has pioneered at this new 175-seat branch of his French restaurant, which has the high-ceiling feel of a grand Parisian brasserie. The creative ideas continue with dessert, such as a rich Chocolate Fondant with Orange–Black Pepper Crème Fraîche (see page 342).

Escargots
6 tablespoons (¾ stick) unsalted butter
20 pieces French Helix snails
4 shallots, minced
2 teaspoons chopped garlic
¼ cup Pernod
¼ cup dry white wine
1 bunch fresh Italian parsley, finely chopped
1 bunch fresh chives, finely chopped
1 sprig fresh thyme, finely chopped
Salt and pepper

Polenta Nests
Oil for greasing
1 cup water
1 cup heavy cream
1 tablespoon chopped garlic
2 sprigs fresh thyme, finely chopped
Salt and pepper
1 cup coarsely ground cornmeal
¼ cup (½ stick) unsalted butter
2 tablespoons grated Parmesan cheese

Roquefort Sauce
1 cup chicken stock
1 cup heavy cream
¼ cup crumbled Roquefort or other blue cheese
½ cup toasted pine nuts
1 bunch fresh chives, finely chopped
Salt and pepper

2 tablespoons vegetable oil
2 Roma tomatoes, finely diced

—*To make the escargots:* In a sauté pan over medium heat, melt the butter until foamy but not brown. Add the snails and sauté for 1 to 2 minutes. Add the shallots and sauté until translucent, about 3 minutes. Add the garlic; sauté 1 minute. Add the Pernod and wine. Stir in the parsley, chives, and thyme. Season to taste with salt and pepper. Remove from heat.

—*To make the polenta:* Oil a large baking sheet. In a heavy-bottomed saucepan over high heat, bring the water and cream to a boil. Add the garlic and thyme. Season generously with salt and pepper. Add the cornmeal in a slow, steady steam, whisking continuously. Reduce the heat to a simmer and stir with a wooden spoon until thick and the polenta begins to pull away from the sides of the pan, about 10 minutes. Add the butter and cheese and stir until melted.

—Remove the pan from the heat and spread the polenta onto the prepared sheet to 1½-inch thickness. Press a 3-inch cookie cutter into the polenta to mark it so it can be cut out into 4 circles later. While the polenta is still warm, place 5 snails in the center of each of the scored circles, pressing the snails about 1 inch into the polenta. Cover and refrigerate until cool, about 2 hours.

—*To make the Roquefort sauce:* In a small saucepan over medium heat, bring the chicken stock to a boil. Add the cream and boil 3 minutes. Reduce the heat and add the cheese, whisking until melted. Stir in the pine nuts and chives. Season to taste with salt and pepper. Remove from heat. Cover to keep warm.

—Preheat the oven to 400 degrees. Cut out the circles in the polenta with the cookie cutter. In a large ovenproof sauté pan, heat the oil over medium-high heat. Place the polenta circles snail side down in the pan and cook until golden, about 5 minutes. Flip and cook other side until golden, about 5 minutes.

—Transfer the pan to the oven and bake until warmed through, about 5 minutes.

—Transfer each polenta circle to a plate; drizzle with the Roquefort sauce. Sprinkle with the tomatoes.

Serves 4

> **SECRETS OF SUCCESS:**
>
> *The polenta cake.* The addition of cream and cheese helps to enrich the polenta. It's a clever idea to use rounds of firm polenta as a nest for the snails.
>
> *The Roquefort sauce.* This tangy addition adds a unifying element to the snails and polenta.

MINCED CHICKEN IN LETTUCE CUPS

Cecilia Chiang, who owned the pioneering Mandarin restaurant in Ghirardelli Square for thirty years, invented this recipe for Minced Chicken in Lettuce Cups served at Betelnut, a restaurant that specializes in food from all over Asia including Vietnam, Thailand, and Singapore. ❋ It's a take off on the minced squab that was the signature dish at her other restaurant. For Betelnut, which was designed to look like a sexy back-alley speakeasy in Shanghai, she wanted to use less expensive ingredients so she replaced the squab with chicken. The dark meat in particular has a similar flavor and texture. ❋ It's a wonderful blend featuring minced chicken, crunchy water chestnuts, black mushrooms, Chinese sausage, and toasted pine nuts. She seasons the mixture with ginger, soy sauce,

and oyster sauce and serves the warm stir-fry in crisp, cold iceberg lettuce cups. If you really want to splurge, replace one-fifth of the chicken with squab. ❋ I particularly like to add a little dollop of plum sauce to the lettuce leaf before adding the hot chicken mixture. To eat, just pick up the lettuce leaf and eat as you would a taco. The combination of the hot, fragrant chicken and the crisp, cold lettuce is a true culinary delight.

1 head iceberg lettuce

¼ cup dried black mushrooms

½ pound boneless skinless chicken thighs, finely minced

1 tablespoon light soy sauce

1 egg white

1 teaspoon cornstarch

1 tablespoon vegetable oil

1 teaspoon finely minced fresh ginger

½ cup finely minced water chestnuts

2 tablespoons finely minced Chinese sausage (see Note)

1 tablespoon oyster sauce

2 scallions, finely chopped

Pinch of ground white pepper

Asian sesame oil

1 tablespoon pine nuts, toasted

Plum sauce

—Remove the core from the lettuce and gently separate the leaves. Use a knife or scissors to cut the leaves into the desired cup shape. Refrigerate.

—Place the mushrooms in a small bowl. Add enough hot water to cover. Soak until soft, about 1 hour. Drain, reserving the mushroom liquid. Discard the stems of the mushrooms; finely chop the caps.

—In a large bowl, combine the chicken, soy sauce, egg white, and cornstarch.

—In a wok or skillet over high heat, heat the vegetable oil. Add the chicken mixture and ginger and cook until the chicken loses its translucency, about 3 minutes. Add the rehydrated mushrooms, water chestnuts, and sausage. Reduce heat to low. Stir in the oyster sauce, scallions, and white pepper. If mixture seems too dry, add enough of the reserved mushroom liquid to moisten. Remove from the heat. Drizzle with sesame oil to taste. Spoon the mixture onto a serving platter. Sprinkle with the pine nuts. Serve with the chilled lettuce cups and plum sauce.

Serves 4

Note: *Chinese sausage is available at Asian markets.*

SECRETS OF SUCCESS:

The egg white. Adding egg white to the chicken before frying in a hot wok gives that moist, velvety coating so admired in Chinese cooking.

The lettuce cups. Trim the leaves with scissors into round cups and make sure they are well chilled to enhance the contrast with the hot chicken.

Sautéed Chicken Liver Salad

There's something totally satisfying about Le Charm's Sautéed Chicken Liver Salad. The taste and texture are almost perfect. The livers are crisp outside and coated with a rich sauce made with a blend of Port and Cabernet Sauvignon. ❇ The hot crispy, creamy nuggets are then spooned over chilled mixed greens and served with slices of toasted baguette. The livers have such a creamy texture that you can spread them on the bread, if you like. ❇ This bargain-priced French bistro is owned by Alain Delangle and his wife, Lina Yew. The couple started out in this location with a catering business, and Yew, who was a pastry chef at Fleur de Lys, brought Hubert Keller to look at the space. He immediately saw the potential as a restaurant, even though it's not in a glamorous location, and he suggested they serve meals, too. They took his advice, but they soon became so busy that the catering fell by the wayside.

Beef Sauce

1 tablespoon butter
1 onion, diced
1 carrot, diced
1 tomato, diced
½ bunch fresh thyme
3 ounces red port
¼ cup Cabernet Sauvignon
1½ cups beef demi-glace (see Note)
Salt and freshly ground pepper

Vinaigrette

2 tablespoons sherry vinegar
1 tablespoon balsamic vinegar
2 teaspoons diced shallots
1 cup olive oil
Salt and freshly ground pepper

Salad

1 pound chicken livers
Salt and freshly ground pepper
2 teaspoons olive oil
1 tablespoon butter
¼ cup diced shallots
2 teaspoons sherry vinegar
½ cup beef sauce (from above)
¼ cup chopped fresh parsley
¾ pound mixed greens
18 toasted baguette slices

—*To make the beef sauce:* Melt the butter in a large skillet over medium-high heat. Add the onion and carrot. Sauté about 5 minutes. Add the tomato and thyme and sauté until tender, about 10 minutes. Add the port and wine. Bring to a boil. Reduce slightly. Add the beef demi-glace. Simmer over medium heat until slightly reduced, about 10 minutes. Season to taste with salt and pepper. Using a hand blender, blend the sauce until almost smooth. Pass it through a fine strainer. Set aside.

—*To make the vinaigrette:* In a small bowl, whisk together both vinegars and the shallots. Slowly drizzle in the oil, whisking constantly until well blended. Season to taste with salt and pepper.

—*To make the salad:* Season the livers with salt and pepper. In a large sauté pan over high heat, heat the olive oil until very hot. Add the livers and sear, without stirring, until the livers are slightly caramelized, about 2 minutes. Gently turn them over; add the butter to the pan, then the shallots. Reduce the heat to medium-high.
—Sprinkle on the sherry vinegar, then the ½ cup beef sauce. Reserve the remaining beef sauce for another use. Cook until the livers are cooked through and glazed with sauce, about 2 minutes. Remove from heat and stir in the parsley.
—Toss the greens with the vinaigrette in a large bowl. Divide among 6 salad plates. Place livers atop greens, then arrange 3 baguette slices around the perimeter of each plate. Serve warm.

Serves 6

Note: *Demi-glace is available at specialty foods stores.*

SECRETS OF SUCCESS:

Heating the skillet. Be sure the pan is very hot, so the livers crispen and caramelize. They should stay slightly crunchy, even after the sauce is added.

The sauce. Port and Cabernet Sauvignon add a rich and mildly sweet smoothness to the sauce.

DUCK LIVER FLAN WITH GREEN PEPPERCORNS

When I think of Bay Wolf in Oakland, I think of duck. Owner Michael Wild has a passion for the bird and you'll always find up to a half-dozen preparations on the menu. He even uses duck eggs for some desserts. ✷ My favorite dish is the duck flan with Marsala. Baked in a terrine, it's a smooth, spreadable paté topped with green peppercorns. Serve it with toasted or grilled bread, pickled onions, and cornichons, to help cut the richness of the flan. ✷ Bay Wolf, which has been in business for more than twenty-five years, was an Oakland pioneer in serving fresh-from-the-farm produce. Located in a Victorian house, the restaurant has two homey dining rooms separated by a bar at the entrance. There's also a front deck, making it a pleasant spot during the day and the sometimes warm Oakland nights.

Olive oil for greasing
1 cup Marsala
3 tablespoons pickled green peppercorns, rinsed thoroughly
1 pound duck livers, bile sacks removed
2 ½ cups heavy cream
4 eggs
1 tablespoon (or more) salt
1 teaspoon finely chopped fresh thyme
1 teaspoon sugar
½ teaspoon (or more) ground white pepper
Accompaniments such as toasted or grilled bread, pickled onions, and cornichons

—Preheat the oven to 350 degrees. Arrange a rack in the lower third of oven.

—Brush a bread pan (4½-by-10 inch or similar size) or terrine mold with olive oil and line with a piece of parchment or wax paper. The paper should extend at least half an inch over the side of the pan. Place the pan in a larger pan with sides at least 2 inches high.

—Boil the Marsala and the rinsed peppercorns in a small skillet over high heat until reduced by half, about 10 minutes. Strain and set the liquid aside. Spread the peppercorns on the bottom of the paper-lined pan.

—Puree the livers in a food processor until totally smooth, about 3 minutes. Add the cream and eggs and process just long enough to clean the sides of the bowl of the liver paste.

—Pass the mixture through a fine-meshed sieve and add the reduced Marsala. Stir in the 1 tablespoon salt, thyme, sugar, and ½ teaspoon white pepper. Taste and adjust seasoning if necessary.

—Pour the mixture into the prepared pan. Add enough hot water to the larger pan to come ½ inch up the sides of the terrine mold. Bake on the lower rack until just set, about 45 minutes to 1 hour. Let stand at room temperature until cool; refrigerate until well chilled.

—To remove the flan, invert onto a plate or small plastic board and tug on the parchment until the flan releases.

—Serve with toasted or grilled bread, pickled onions, and cornichons.

Serves 8 to 10

Note: *The flan can be baked in individual ramekins, if desired. In that case, place in a water bath and reduce cooking time by half. These should be served in the ramekins, as they are too difficult to unmold, so you don't need to line them with parchment.*

SECRETS OF SUCCESS:

The fine-meshed sieve. The livers are pureed until smooth and then passed through a sieve to create a velvety, spreadable flan.

The peppercorns and Marsala. Marsala is reduced with the green peppercorns to form a topping that adds flavor and textural contrasts to the smooth paté.

LEMONGRASS BEEF SKEWERS

The An family have made their reputation on crab, probably the best in San Francisco, and on garlic noodles prepared in a separate kitchen by Helene An or one of her children. ✻ Their empire started at Thanh Long and has expanded to Crustacean in San Francisco and a wildly popular branch in Beverly Hills. ✻ Unfortunately, people don't know what they're missing when they head straight to the crab. One of the best starters around is the Lemongrass Beef Skewers. ✻ Thin slices of beef are marinated twice, first in pineapple juice, then in soy sauce, shrimp paste, lemongrass, and toasted sesame seeds. This marinade is also brushed on during grilling, which adds even more character to the meat. ✻ At home you can make a meal of these wonderful appetizers, or serve them before a grilled main course. ✻ In late 1998 the family remodeled Thanh Long, adding more seats and sprucing up the interior with restful murals, comfortable chairs, and banquettes. There's a wine list that has some interesting selections to accompany the Asian-inspired dishes.

3 pounds beef sirloin tips, thinly sliced
½ cup pineapple juice
3 tablespoons vegetable oil
1 onion, chopped
1 tablespoon minced garlic
½ cup soy sauce
½ cup toasted sesame seeds
¼ cup fish sauce
½ tablespoon shrimp paste (see Note)
2 teaspoons fresh minced lemongrass
2 teaspoons powdered lemongrass root
   (see Note)
Bamboo skewers

—Toss the beef, pineapple juice, and 2 tablespoons of the vegetable oil in a large bowl. Cover and refrigerate for at least 30 minutes and up to 4 hours.

—Heat the remaining 1 tablespoon oil in a medium skillet over medium heat. Add the onion and garlic and sauté until tender, about 5 minutes. Stir in the soy sauce, sesame seeds, fish sauce, shrimp paste, minced lemongrass, and lemongrass powder. Bring to a boil. Add to the bowl with the beef and toss to combine. Cover and refrigerate at least 30 minutes and up to 4 hours.

—Prepare a grill (medium heat). Remove the beef from the marinade. Reserve the marinade. Thread one slice of beef on each skewer. Grill the beef until cooked through, brushing occasionally with reserved marinade during the first part of cooking, about 2 to 3 minutes per side.

Serves 8 to 10

Note: *Shrimp paste is available at Asian markets. To make at home, mash cooked shrimp with a small amount of water. Powdered lemongrass root is available at Asian markets.*

SECRETS OF SUCCESS:

Tenderizing with pineapple. This juice has an enzyme that works as a natural tenderizer for the beef.

A second marinade. Garlic, onions, soy sauce and fish sauce form the base for an additional marinade. It's also used to keep the beef moist during grilling.

SALADS AND SOUPS

Leek and Corn Veloute with rock shrimp

Roland Passot is considered one of the best French chefs in the city, and what he produces at his restaurant—called La Folie—is anything but simple. In the classic French style, Passot blends lots of elements to produce fresh and exciting combinations. ✳ A native of Lyons, Passot came to the United States more than twenty years ago to work with Jean Banchet at the famous Le Français near Chicago. ✳ But Passot is now a Californian at heart, and his Leek and Corn Veloute with Rock Shrimp is amazing for its simplicity and full-rich flavors. For this dish he sautés shallots and leeks in butter before tossing in fresh corn, cream, chicken stock, and vermouth. A blender and strainer ensure a silken texture, and rock shrimp, sautéed quickly in butter, add an exciting element to the center of the bowl. ✳ If you prefer, cooked lobster or poached oysters are great substitutes for the shrimp. If using oysters, poach them in the vermouth for 1 minute before adding to the soup. ✳ And here's our own little secret. Because of the combination of ingredients—and the vermouth—canned chicken broth works just fine. Just tell your friends it's from Roland Passot and they'll think you've spent days in the kitchen.

½ cup plus 2 tablespoons unsalted butter
5 shallots (about 1 pound), chopped
4 leeks (white part only), washed and thinly sliced
3 ears of corn, kernels cut from the cob, or 1½ cups frozen kernels
1 cup extra-dry vermouth
4 cups heavy cream
4 cups chicken stock
Salt and pepper
½ pound rock shrimp, peeled

—In a medium saucepan over medium heat, melt the ½ cup butter. Add the shallots and leeks and cook until translucent, about 5 minutes. Add the corn kernels and cook until the corn is crisp-tender, about 15 minutes. Remove 6 tablespoons of the mixture from the pan and reserve for garnish.

—Add the vermouth to the pan. Bring to a boil and reduce by half, about 10 minutes. Add the cream and bring to a boil, stirring constantly. Add the chicken stock, return to a boil, and simmer until the soup thickens slightly, about 15 minutes. Working in batches, puree the soup in a blender until smooth. Pass the soup through a fine strainer. Season to taste with salt and pepper.

—Melt the remaining 2 tablespoons butter in a medium sauté pan over medium-high heat. Season the shrimp with salt and pepper. Add to the pan and sauté until just cooked through, about 2 minutes.

—Ladle the soup into bowls. Top with shrimp. Garnish with the reserved corn and leek mixture.

Serves 4 to 6

SECRETS OF SUCCESS:

The vermouth. This secret ingredient is almost undetectable in the finished soup, but it adds richness and a complex depth of flavor.

Straining the soup. In many recipes a chunky soup is fine, but in this version you want the silken texture to set off the seafood. The liquid needs to be blended smooth and passed through a fine strainer.

GARLIC AND SAFFRON SOUP

When you think of Fleur de Lys, probably the fanciest restaurant in the Bay Area, you think of intricate recipes, complicated combinations, and spectacular presentations. While that's true, one of my favorite dishes—the Garlic and Saffron Soup—takes only about 40 minutes to prepare at home. ❋ This rustic soup, created by chef/owner Hubert Keller, has a smooth refined texture and is based on the Provençal Soupe d'Ail Doux, or Sweet Garlic Soup. Keller, who is a native of Alsace and has worked with several three-star French chefs, adds a twist, of course: the saffron. This gives a pleasing yellow color and a haunting herbal background to play against the garlic. ❋ Keller uses vegetable stock, but at home you can use either water or a mild chicken broth, if you like. ❋ To make the soup even more substantial, he suggests placing a slice of toasted baguette in the bowl and topping it with a warm poached egg. Then ladle the hot soup around the perimeter. ❋ Coaxing robust flavors out of food is one of Keller's trademarks. His style is refined, but every item on the plate is treated like it's the star, down to the tiniest mince of carrot. ❋ At Fleur de Lys, Keller offers both a fixed price and an à la carte menu. He also pioneered a multicourse vegetable tasting menu that other chefs have since copied. He's even prepared to make a no-fat dinner if customers call ahead. It's this type of accommodation that has made Fleur de Lys the top restaurant in the city.

3 or 4 whole heads of garlic, separated into cloves and peeled

1 tablespoon extra-virgin olive oil

2 small leeks, white part only, cut in half lengthwise and thickly sliced

1 quart vegetable broth or water

Salt and freshly ground pepper

¼ cup peeled and finely diced white potato

1 large pinch saffron threads

¼ cup heavy cream or half-and-half

3 tablespoons peeled, seeded, and diced tomato (optional, see page 363)

2 tablespoons finely sliced fresh chives for garnishing

—Blanch the garlic 1 minute in a medium pot of boiling water. Remove the garlic and repeat the process 2 more times, changing water after each batch.

—Heat the oil in a heavy-bottomed saucepan over medium heat. Add the leeks and cook until soft, stirring often, about 6 minutes.

—Add the broth and blanched garlic. Season to taste with salt and pepper. Bring to a boil. Add the potato and saffron threads, reduce the heat, and simmer until the potato is soft, about 7 or 8 minutes. Stir in the cream and return to a boil.

—Remove the soup from the heat and cool slightly. Working in batches, puree the soup in a blender or food processor until smooth. Return the soup to a clean saucepan and heat through. Adjust the seasonings, if necessary. Stir in the tomato, if desired.

—Ladle the hot soup into warm soup bowls, sprinkle with the chives, and serve.

Serves 4

Note: *You can give this soup an unusual touch by placing a warm poached egg on a slice of toasted baguette in each soup bowl, a common addition to peasant-style soups from the South of France.*

> **SECRETS OF SUCCESS:**
>
> *A pinch of saffron.* While it adds a pleasing color, it also lends an herbal complexity to the soup.
>
> *Blanching the garlic.* This step removes the sharpness and pungency without diminishing the flavor.

BEET BORSCHT

Beet borscht isn't considered sexy, but beets weren't considered a delicacy either until a few years ago when they started showing up at trendy restaurants in salads, soups, and side dishes. Now they come in every color—white, yellow, red, and striped—and they're everywhere. ❋ This newfound popularity might even convince some people to give this Russian soup another try. Armed with the light, refreshing version created by Katia Troosh at her namesake restaurant in the Richmond, you won't have a hard time making converts. ❋ The soup is different from many versions because of its lightness, but it still has an intense flavor. Red cabbage and other vegetables complete the soup, so the flavors and textures are anything but mundane. ❋ While Katia serves traditional Russian cuisine at her comfortable thirty-seat restaurant, she tries to lighten the recipes whenever possible, as shown in her borscht. The flavors are so robust you can use water and beef bouillon cubes instead of homemade beef stock as the base for the soup. No one will know the difference.

10 cups water, plus additional for cooking beets
5 beef bouillon cubes (preferably Knorr)
1 small onion, halved
¼ bunch fresh dill sprigs with stems
¼ bunch fresh parsley with stems
3 medium carrots, peeled
2 medium beets
1 tablespoon oil
1 small onion, thinly sliced
1 tablespoon all-purpose flour
1 tablespoon tomato paste, or 2 to 3 tablespoons canned tomato sauce
3 medium potatoes, peeled and cubed
2 celery stalks, chopped
1 small head red cabbage, finely chopped
1 tablespoon fresh lemon juice
Salt
Sour cream
Chopped fresh dill for garnishing

—Combine the 10 cups water, bouillon cubes, halved onion, dill sprigs, and parsley in a large pot. Bring to a boil; reduce heat and simmer 30 minutes. Add the carrots and simmer until just tender, about 5 to 7 minutes. Transfer the carrots to a cutting board. Strain the broth through a fine sieve and reserve. Thinly slice the carrots and reserve.

—Place the beets in a small pot and add just enough water to cover. Simmer over medium heat until the beets are tender, about 45 minutes. Remove the beets, reserving the liquid, and set aside to cool. When cool enough to handle, peel the beets and cut into small cubes.

—In a medium sauté pan, heat the oil over medium-high heat. Add the sliced onion and sauté until soft, about 5 to 7 minutes. Sprinkle the onion with the flour and stir until well blended. Stir in the tomato paste; remove from the heat and set aside.

—Return the reserved broth to a large saucepan over medium-high heat and bring to a simmer. Add the potatoes; cook for 2 minutes. Add the onion-flour mixture; cook for 2 minutes. Repeat adding and cooking for 2 minutes before each next addition with the carrots, beets, celery, and finally the cabbage.

—Remove from heat. Stir in the lemon juice. Stir in the reserved beet-cooking liquid. Season to taste with salt.

—Ladle the soup into bowls. Serve with a dollop of sour cream and a sprinkling of chopped dill.

Serves 6

SECRETS OF SUCCESS:

Cooking the beets. The beets are cooked in only a little water, which is used to give the finished soup an intense red color.

Beef bouillon cubes. Because of the intensity of the beets, the beef bouillon cubes work well; in fact they add a pleasant meaty background.

Cooking the vegetables. Each vegetable is added individually to the finished soup so they retain their flavor and texture and prevent the soup from tasting one-dimensional.

UDON NOODLE SOUP WITH SMOKED TROUT

David Vardy has a unique personal vision of East-West cooking at O Chame in Berkeley. While he wouldn't claim to be a Japanese chef, his sensibilities are as traditional as his top-level Tokyo counterpart. ✳ At his restaurant he has become known for his noodle dishes, and what he creates is superior to any of the noodle houses in San Francisco's Japantown. The broth, made with dried fish flakes, has a subtle smokiness that pairs well with myriad toppings. ✳ One of the most popular combinations is the fleshy udon noodles with smoked trout. The bland noodles, the peppery daikon sprouts, and the flaky smoked fish combine for a bracing and restorative combination. ✳ At the restaurant, the large udon (wheat) and the more delicate soba (buckwheat) noodles are served in large pottery bowls, shimmering in the bonito-based broth. Combinations include shrimp with wakame seaweed, grilled chicken breast with spinach, and beef with burdock root and carrots. ✳ The room has a similar cross-cultural orientation, and it translates into a peaceful setting that has a soothing effect after a long day. The focal point of the room is an Oriental carpet at the entrance, centered under a long table that holds a vase with an arrangement of grasses and blooms, platters of wonderful cookies, and a few baked goods. ✳ The terra-cotta-colored stucco walls are subtly etched with a dragon and other Asian scenes. The Japanese country feel is further enhanced with the straight-back rough wood chairs and a round window inset with bamboo.

This traditional Japanese noodle dish is versatile. A number of toppings, including grilled chicken, shrimp, or thinly sliced beef, can be substituted for the trout. Other julienne vegetables such as daikon, carrots, or cabbage can also be added. All the ingredients, except the smoked trout, are readily available at Japanese grocery stores.

2 quarts water
1 piece (about 3x4 inches) dried Dashi Kombu (kelp)
3½ ounces shaved dried bonito flakes
¼ cup mirin
2 tablespoons Japanese soy sauce
¾ tablespoon (or more) sea salt
1 pound dried udon noodles
4 smoked trout fillets
1 bunch daikon radish sprouts (about 4 ounces)
2 scallions, thinly sliced

—Place the water and Dashi Kombu in a 8- to 10-quart pot. Set over medium-low heat and slowly heat the water until almost ready to boil, about 50 minutes.

—Using tongs, remove the Dashi Kombu and discard. Add the bonito flakes and bring to a simmer over medium heat, skimming any scum that might form on the surface. Do not boil. Remove from the heat and let stand for 30 seconds.

—Strain the broth through cheesecloth or a fine sieve, pushing hard on the bonito to release all the liquid. Discard the bonito.

—Return the strained liquid to the pot and add the mirin, soy sauce, and ¾ tablespoon of salt. Bring to a simmer and cook for 2 minutes to blend the flavors. Add more salt, if needed. The stock can be used immediately or refrigerated and reheated when needed.

—When ready to serve, cook the udon in a large pot of boiling unsalted water until tender, about 12 to 15 minutes. Drain. Rinse with cold water.

—Divide the noodles among four bowls. Top with the trout fillets, either whole or cut into bite-sized pieces, daikon sprouts, and scallions. Gently pour 1 ½ to 2 cups of hot broth over the noodles and serve immediately.

Serves 4

SECRETS OF SUCCESS:

Simmering the seaweed. The Dashi Kombu, a type of seaweed, gives the water a silken texture by releasing a sticky substance the consistency of aloe. If boiled this texture will be destroyed.

Simmering the bonito. Much like a French fumet, the fish flakes should not boil. The water needs to be brought to a simmer and immediately removed from the heat.

Cooking the noodles. The noodles are cooked like Western pasta, but you don't want them to be al dente. They should be cooked through and tender. Do not put any salt or oil in the water during cooking.

POLENTINA SOUP

No matter what comes out of Alice Waters' kitchen, one thing is certain: you taste the main ingredient. In the case of Polentina Soup, often served at the Cafe at Chez Panisse, it's cornmeal. ❈ Making soup out of polenta could seem boring, but when you season it with onions, garlic, chicken stock, sautéed greens, and Parmesan it's a warming way to begin any meal, or a fast answer to a weeknight supper. ❈ Either way, the polenta stars. Once you make the soup base, you can embellish it just about any way you like. It's a perfect vehicle for leftover chicken, pork, or vegetables. ❈ The soup is served from time to time in the Cafe, upstairs from the main restaurant, where you get more casual food made with the same quality of ingredients you'll find downstairs.

—In a large saucepan, melt the butter over medium-high heat. Add the onion and sauté until soft, about 5 to 7 minutes. Add the stock, garlic, thyme, parsley, sage, and bay leaf. Bring to a boil over high heat. Whisk in the cornmeal, using more cornmeal for a thicker soup and less for a thinner soup. Season with salt to taste. Reduce the heat to medium-low and simmer until the cornmeal is tender but the mixture is still soupy, stirring frequently, about 15 to 20 minutes.

—Heat the oil in a large skillet over medium heat. Add the spinach and stir just until wilted, about 3 minutes. Remove from heat.

—Remove the bay leaf from the soup. Whisk the soup so the cornmeal doesn't settle to the bottom of the pan. Ladle into bowls.

—Garnish with the spinach and a few shavings of Parmesan.

Serves 4

1 tablespoon unsalted butter
½ white onion, sliced
1 quart chicken stock
2 garlic cloves, sliced
3 fresh thyme sprigs, chopped
2 fresh parsley sprigs, chopped
2 fresh sage leaves, chopped
1 bay leaf
¼ to ½ cup coarse cornmeal
Salt
1 teaspoon olive oil
Half a bunch of spinach, washed and trimmed
Parmesan cheese shavings

SECRETS OF SUCCESS:

The amount of polenta. The consistency is determined by the amount of cornmeal; stir in ¼ to ½ cup of polenta for each quart of liquid.

CHESTNUT SOUP WITH LEEKS AND APPLES

Richard Reddington might not be as well known as Hubert Keller or Roland Passot, but his star is on the rise. Just taste his Chestnut Soup with Leeks and Apples if you need convincing. Like any great cook, Reddington, who worked at Chapeau in the Richmond District until 1999, is able to coax complexity out of only a few ingredients. And this soup is easy for the home cook because it requires no stock and only a few ingredients—mainly chestnuts, leeks, apples, celery root, and cream. If you can't find fresh chestnuts, canned work just fine, and the celery root is readily available at most supermarkets. ✻ The soup is an adaptation of one that Reddington learned working with Daniel Boulud at Daniel in New York.

—Melt the butter in a large saucepan over low heat. Add the leeks and onion and cook until soft and translucent, about 20 minutes. Add the apples and celery root and continue to cook over low heat until the apples begin to fall apart, about 30 minutes. Add the chestnuts and enough water to cover. Increase the heat to medium-high. Simmer until the chestnuts are very tender, about 20 minutes. Stir in the cream and season to taste with salt and pepper. Return the soup to a boil; remove from heat. Cool slightly. Puree in a blender until smooth. Strain. Rewarm, if necessary.

2 tablespoons unsalted butter
2 leeks, finely chopped
1 onion, finely chopped
2 apples, peeled and diced
2 medium-sized celery roots, peeled and diced
½ pound roasted and peeled fresh or canned
   chestnuts
Water
1 cup heavy cream
Salt and pepper

Serves 4

SECRETS OF SUCCESS:

Sweating the vegetables. Don't rush the process of slowly cooking the leeks and onions, which is known in professional kitchens as sweating. Cooking slowly gently releases the vegetables' sweet flavor.

An unexpected combination. The play of the distinctive chestnuts and the celery root mediated by the apple is extraordinary.

CLAM CHOWDER

Clam chowder is offered in just about every seafood restaurant along Fisherman's Wharf, but there's something special about the Waterfront Cafe's version perfected by Bruce Hill. This rich, smooth soup gets extra character from fennel. Bacon adds smoky nuances to the background, with big chunks of clams in the foreground. ❊ It's a perfect warming blend for the chilly San Francisco climate. On cool days you can sit inside the sophisticated nautical-meets-men's club environment. On warmer days there's a patio protected by a see-through windscreen that overlooks the Bay Bridge and Treasure Island.

—Heat the oil in a heavy-bottomed saucepan over medium-low heat. Add the celery, fennel, onion, leek, and garlic. Cover the pan and cook until the vegetables are tender but not browned, stirring occasionally, about 15 minutes. Add the wine. Increase the heat to medium and bring to a boil. Boil until the liquid is reduced by half, about 10 minutes. Add the clam juice, uncooked potatoes, thyme, and bay leaves. Reduce heat to low. Cover and cook until the potatoes begin to fall apart, about 20 minutes. Pass the chowder through a fine strainer. Puree the strained chowder until smooth.

—Transfer the chowder to a clean saucepan and stir in the cream. Season to taste with salt and pepper. Heat the chowder to a simmer. Remove from heat. Ladle the chowder into four soup bowls and garnish with the clams, cooked potatoes, bacon, and parsley, dividing evenly among the bowls.

Serves 4

¼ cup olive oil
⅔ cup chopped celery
½ cup chopped fennel
½ cup chopped yellow onion
½ cup chopped leek
2 garlic cloves, crushed
2 cups dry white wine
4 cups bottled clam juice
¾ cup peeled and chopped russet potatoes
4 fresh thyme sprigs
4 bay leaves
1½ cups heavy cream
Salt and pepper
8 ounces fresh cooked shelled clams
½ cup ⅛-inch-diced potatoes, boiled and drained
4 ounces bacon, diced and cooked until crisp
2 tablespoons chopped fresh Italian parsley

SECRETS OF SUCCESS:

Adding the bacon. This gives a meaty smoky nuance to the creamy chowder.

Straining and blending. This two-step process makes the chowder extra smooth and creamy. The clams, bacon, and parsley add texture.

FENNEL AND MINT SALAD

Fennel has become the darling of the chef set; even five years ago it was rare on the menu and now it's almost as common as parsley. It has a lot to offer, especially when served raw in a salad. Scores of variations of fennel salad abound, but the best is at Zinzino, a charming Marina-area trattoria where chef Andrea Rappaport pairs the licorice-flavored bulb with a minimum of ingredients: lemon juice, mint, olive oil, salt, pepper, and Parmesan cheese. Who would have thought that so few ingredients could be so good? ❊ At home, try this refreshing salad before a hearty braised or stewed dish. ❊ Zinzino has become a pleasant place to hang out. A babbling fountain runs down one wall, adding a soothing note to the experience, a contrast to the always bustling cooks toiling in the open kitchen.

—Using a mandoline, cut the fennel bulbs into paper-thin slices. Transfer the fennel to a medium mixing bowl.
—Drizzle the fennel with the olive oil and lemon juice. Sprinkle with the salt and pepper. Mix gently but thoroughly.
—Stack the mint leaves on top of each other, roll them up lengthwise, and slice them very thinly with a sharp knife. Set aside.
—Using a vegetable peeler or mandoline, shave off thin slices of cheese.
—Divide the fennel mixture among 4 salad plates. Sprinkle with the mint, then top with shavings of cheese. Spoon any extra dressing over the salad.

Serves 4

2½ medium-size fennel bulbs, trimmed
½ cup extra-virgin olive oil
Juice of 2 lemons
2 teaspoons salt
½ teaspoon freshly ground black pepper
8 fresh mint leaves
One 4-ounce chunk Parmigiano-Reggiano cheese

SECRETS OF SUCCESS:

Shaving the fennel. Use a mandoline to get paper-thin slices; this allows the fennel to absorb the dressing.

Good-quality cheese. Use only the real Parmigiano-Reggiano, prized for its tangy nutty flavor.

MIXED GREEN SALAD WITH GRAPEFRUIT AND WARM SHRIMP

Fabrizio Laudati concentrates on the classics at his charming 42-seat neighborhood restaurant, Baraonda, on Russian Hill. Yet his talent is in adding an innovative twist to many of these dishes, as he does in this salad where the contrast of hot shrimp, cool greens, and vibrant grapefruit is irresistible. ✳ It's perfect for the home cook because the pieces can be assembled ahead and finished at the last minute for an impressive appetizer to begin an elegant dinner.

Shrimp
¼ cup extra-virgin olive oil
¼ cup grapefruit juice
2 garlic cloves, minced
Salt and ground white pepper
12 ounces uncooked medium shrimp, peeled and
     deveined
1 tablespoon butter

Vinaigrette
¼ cup extra-virgin olive oil
2 teaspoons balsamic vinegar
2 teaspoons grapefruit juice
3 garlic cloves, minced
Salt and ground white pepper

Salad
3 ounces mixed baby greens
2 heads Belgian endive, separated into spears
2 pink grapefruit, peeled and cut into segments
     (see page 363)
1 teaspoon minced fresh Italian parsley

—*To make the shrimp:* Combine the oil, grapefruit juice, and garlic in a medium bowl. Season to taste with salt and white pepper. Add the shrimp; toss to coat. Transfer the mixture to a plastic freezer bag. Seal. Refrigerate at least 6 and up to 24 hours.

—*To make the vinaigrette:* In a mixing bowl combine the oil, vinegar, grapefruit juice, and garlic, whisking until well blended. Season to taste with salt and white pepper.

—*To make the salad:* Place the greens, endive, and grapefruit segments in separate bowls (reserve any of the juices from the grapefruit segments). Toss each gently with some of the vinaigrette.

—Heat a skillet large enough to hold all the shrimp over high heat. Add the shrimp and marinade and stir until the shrimp are pink and curled, and the sauce reduces slightly, about 3 minutes. Add the butter and toss until butter melts. Remove from heat. Add the reserved juices from the grapefruit segments to the skillet and stir to blend.

—Place 3 or 4 spears of endive in a starburst fashion around the edge of each of 6 plates. Add a grapefruit piece on top of each spear. Pile a mound of greens in the center. Top with two hot shrimp and another grapefruit piece. Drizzle with a little of the sauce. Sprinkle with the minced parsley.

Serves 6

SECRETS OF SUCCESS:

The grapefruit. This ingredient adds an exciting element to the salad. The flavor is echoed in the dressing and on the shrimp.

The temperature contrast. The hot shrimp paired with the chilled fruit and greens are enticing.

INSALATA ROSSA

Jack Krietzman is a passionate Italian cook, reflected in what he cooks at his Marin outpost, Cucina Jackson Fillmore. The restaurant is named after his popular restaurant in the city, Jackson Fillmore. ✳ At Cucina, Krietzman has designed a stage for his cooking, featuring an open kitchen so his customers are always in his range of vision. The compact restaurant is stylishly simple, with large windows that overlook downtown San Anselmo. ✳ One area that sets his cooking apart is the warm salads. My favorite is the Insalata Rossa, a simply amazing combination of coarsely chopped radicchio blended with onions, Italian parsley, and an olive oil dressing flavored with tomato and basil. The salad is crowned with shards of paper-thin slices of Pecorino Romano cheese that brings all the elements in line.

—*To make the dressing:* Whisk the oil, tomato, basil, and garlic in a small bowl to blend. Season to taste with salt and pepper.

—*To make the salad:* Combine the radicchio, scallions, parsley, salt, and pepper in a large pot set over medium heat. Add the dressing. Using your hands and a wooden spoon, keep the salad moving, quickly wilting but not cooking the radicchio. (It shouldn't be too hot to handle.)

—Season with more salt and pepper, if desired. Mound salad on 4 salad plates. Top with the cheese.

Serves 4

Dressing
¾ cup extra-virgin olive oil
½ cup diced tomato (in ¼- to ½-inch dice)
6 to 8 large fresh basil leaves, coarsely chopped
1 teaspoon minced garlic
Salt and pepper

Salad
6 cups loosely packed coarsely chopped radicchio
½ cup thinly sliced scallions
¼ cup chopped fresh Italian parsley
½ heaping teaspoon (or more) kosher salt
¼ teaspoon (or more) fresh ground pepper
1 to 1 ½ cups Pecorino Romano cheese, in thin shards

SECRETS OF SUCCESS:

Warming the radicchio. Using your hands to toss the vegetables in the cooking pot ensures that everything warms and wilts, but doesn't cook.

Shaving the cheese. Sprinkled on the warm mounded salad, the cheese smoothes out any bitter edges and perks up the flavor. If you don't have a mandoline, then use a coarse grater, making the shards as long as you can.

MARINATED MOZZARELLA, WALNUT, AND CELERY SALAD

You would think this simple, sensational blend was right out of Italy: Marinated mozzarella, toasted walnuts, and thin slices of celery in a simple dressing studded with red pepper flakes. The tangy cheese, crunchy nuts, and cooling celery create a dynamic mix of flavors. ❈ The recipe has an Italian flair, no surprise since it was created by Carol Field, the author of several impressive Italian cookbooks including *Italy in Little Bites*. ❈ Field is a consultant to Mazzini in Berkeley, which was opened in 1998 by Jim and Laura Maser. He also owns Picante Cocina Mexicana and is part owner of Cafe Fanny with Alice Waters. However, the connections go even deeper, as Laura Maser is Waters's sister. ❈ At Mazzini, which feels like an upscale trattoria, simplicity is the key. It does feel just like Italy.

—Heat the olive oil in a small sauté pan over low heat. Add the garlic, red pepper flakes, and black pepper. Cook for 5 minutes to blend flavors. Cool. Stir in the salt.

—Put the cheese in a medium bowl. Pour the marinade over. Toss to coat well. Cover and refrigerate at least overnight or up to several days. For a quicker turnaround, the mozzarella can also be marinated at room temperature for several hours.

—Remove the cheese from the marinade. Reserve the marinade. Combine the marinated mozzarella with the celery and walnuts in a large bowl. Add enough of the reserved marinade to make the mixture glisten. Season to taste with more salt and marinade, if necessary. Let stand at room temperature for 1 hour before serving.

Serves 6 to 8

1 cup olive oil
2 medium garlic cloves, minced
½ teaspoon dried red pepper flakes
20 grinds of fresh black pepper
½ teaspoon (or more) salt
1 pound fresh mozzarella, cut into 1-inch cubes
6 celery ribs, thinly sliced on the diagonal
6 to 8 ounces walnut pieces, toasted

> **SECRETS OF SUCCESS:**
>
> *Heating the marinade.* Gently heating the oil used to marinate the mozzarella releases the flavor of the garlic and red pepper flakes.
>
> *Resting the salad.* Allowing the salad to stand at room temperature before serving also helps to marry the flavors.

FRISEE SALAD WITH POACHED EGGS AND WARM BACON DRESSING

Not content with wowing people with one restaurant—Fringale—Gerald Hirigoyen decided to try it with two. At Pastis, he offers more elaborate dishes as well as some classics such as this Frisee Salad. ❋ The salad is served all over France, and is now becoming popular in the United States. It's a combination that can't be beat: bacon and eggs in a salad. ❋ When the yolk is pierced and runs into the cool, lacy greens and mixes with bacon and vinegar, it's like manna from heaven. ❋ When done right, this is one of the best salads you'll find. It's done right at Pastis, and you can do it right at home by following this recipe.

4 small heads frisee lettuce

Four ½-inch-thick slices pancetta (about 8 ounces total), unrolled, cut into 1/2-inch-wide strips

Twelve ½-inch-thick diagonally cut baguette slices

4 tablespoons olive oil

4 tablespoons sherry or red wine vinegar

4 eggs

2 tablespoons chopped fresh chives

Salt and freshly ground black pepper

—Preheat the oven to 450 degrees.

—Gently dip the frisee into a large bowl of water, repeating with clean water until the water stays clear. Spin or pat dry. Remove and discard the green outer leaves and trim and discard the tough core from the white inner leaves. Place the frisee in a large bowl and refrigerate.

—Place the pancetta in a small saucepan. Add enough water to cover. Bring to a boil, then remove from the heat. Drain the pancetta, rinse with cold water, drain again. Set aside.

—Brush the baguette slices on both sides with 2 tablespoons of the olive oil. Arrange on a baking sheet and bake until toasted, about 1 to 2 minutes. Turn the slices over and bake until the edges on the other side are golden brown, about 2 minutes. Remove from the oven and set aside.

—Heat the remaining 2 tablespoons of olive oil in a small sauté pan over medium heat. Add the pancetta and sauté until golden brown, about 5 minutes. Add 2 tablespoons of vinegar and stir for 45 seconds, scraping any browned bits from the bottom of the pan. Remove from the heat.

—Fill a large saucepan three-quarters full of water and bring to a boil. Add the remaining 2 tablespoons of vinegar and return to a boil. Reduce the heat to medium-low so that the water is just at a simmer. Working quickly, break the eggs one at a time into a saucer and slide them into the water. Poach the eggs until the whites appear cooked but the yolks are still mostly liquid, about 3 minutes. Using a slotted spoon, remove the eggs from the water and place on small plates.

—Pour the warm vinegar and pancetta mixture over the frisee. Add the chives and toss well. Divide the salad equally among 4 plates. Carefully place a drained egg on top of each salad and sprinkle the egg with salt and pepper. Garnish with the toasted baguette slices and serve immediately.

Serves 4

SHAVED PORTOBELLO WITH FENNEL AND RADISHES

Nancy Oakes, chef/owner of the wildly popular Boulevard, loves the Shaved Portobello with Fennel and Radishes salad. She says, "It allows the celery and radishes, often ignored, to step out on the town with their more glamorous friends endive, fennel, and portobello mushrooms." ❉ One of the differences in this bright winter salad is that all the ingredients are sliced very thin, making for a delicious melding of tastes and texture. It also makes it easy to eat. The vegetables are crowned with shavings of Manchego cheese and dressed with a roasted lemon vinaigrette, another unusual addition. ❉ It's a spectacular dish that you won't find anywhere else. Oakes is one of the most original cooks in the Bay Area, and the Belle Epoque restaurant designed by Pat Kuleto is an appropriate stage for her talents.

Salad

1 large head fennel
12 large red radishes
5 stalks celery (preferably with pale green leaves)
1 head frisee
3 heads white or red endive
1 large portobello mushroom, stemmed, gills
    removed
½ pound Manchego cheese
Roasted Lemon Vinaigrette (recipe follows)
Salt and pepper
½ cup chopped fresh mixed herbs such as Italian
    parsley, tarragon, and chervil (optional)

Roasted Lemon Vinaigrette

3 lemons
1 tablespoon sugar
1 tablespoon white balsamic vinegar
10 yellow cherry tomatoes
1 cup olive oil
Salt and freshly ground black pepper

—To make the salad: Fill a large bowl with ice and add water to cover.

—Lay the fennel on a cutting board; let it lay flat naturally. Cut in half lengthwise.

—Using a Japanese or French mandoline, slice the fennel as thin as possible. Put into the ice water. Next slice the radishes into rounds and add to the ice water. Repeat with the celery stalks. Add the celery leaves to the ice water as well. Trim the frisee by cutting off all the tough green leaves down to the white part. Then cut away the root. Add the frisee to the ice water. Peel the large leaves from the endive; try to get 18 large leaves. Set aside. Cut the remaining center leaves of the endive in half lengthwise. Carefully cut a "V" shape out of the root bottom—which is bitter—and discard. Lay the center endive pieces on a cutting board flat side down. Thinly slice crosswise. Add to the ice water. Allow the vegetables to remain in the ice water for 10 minutes. Drain and spin in a lettuce dryer.

—Using the mandoline, slice the portobello mushroom and Manchego cheese very thin.

—To serve, place three large endive leaves on each of 6 salad plates forming a loose triangle. Drizzle with a little of the Roasted Lemon Vinaigrette.

—Put the drained vegetables in a large bowl. Drizzle with enough remaining Roasted Lemon Vinaigrette to coat. Toss. Season to taste with salt and pepper. Add the herbs, if desired. Add the shaved cheese and portobello mushroom. Toss to combine. Place a handful of salad in the middle of the endive triangle on each plate.

Serves 6

—To make the vinaigrette: Pierce each lemon with a paring knife. Place the lemons in a microwave safe container and cover with plastic wrap. Cook in the microwave on high for 10 minutes. Remove the cover and cool. (If you do not have a microwave, pierce the lemons and wrap in several layers of aluminum foil making sure no liquid can escape. Place in a pan and roast in a 325 degree oven for 45 minutes.)

—When the lemons are at room temperature, gently squeeze them to release the juices, but not so hard as to force out the seeds. Put the juice in a blender; add the sugar, balsamic vinegar, and tomatoes. Puree until smooth. Transfer to a medium bowl. Gradually whisk in the olive oil until the vinaigrette is well blended. Season to taste with salt and ground pepper.

Makes about 1½ cups

Note: *Any leftover dressing keeps well in the refrigerator for up to a week and can be used to dress salads or to pour onto grilled chicken, fish, or pork.*

SECRETS OF SUCCESS:

The dressing ingredients. The roasted lemon adds a mellow flavor. The acidic tomatoes help to emulsify the dressing. The white balsamic adds a smooth richness, and the sugar helps to balance the acid.

Shaving the ingredients. This allows the dressing to cover more surface, intensifying and unifying the flavors.

An ice water bath. This ensures that the vegetables will be cold and crisp, which helps them retain their individual character.

Medjool Date and Celery Salad

"Dates and celery?" questioned a friend when she saw this combination on the menu at 42 Degrees, a trendy Mediterranean restaurant next to the Esprit outlet South of Market. ❊ By that time, however, I knew Jim Moffat's talents enough to know that it would be delicious. He loves lusty combinations, and he's not afraid to take chances. With the celery and date salad he's created yet another stellar dish. The ingredients can be prepared in a flash, but the results will cause quite a splash. The sweetness of dates and the crunchiness of celery combine for a truly remarkable taste sensation. ❊ The celery is cut on the diagonal and combined with Italian parsley, salt, pepper, olive oil, and aged balsamic vinegar. Then well-aged Parmesan is shaved over the top to add a salty component. Ripe figs can be used in place of the dates, if you like. ❊ This simple rustic preparation belies the trendiness of the warehouse-sized space where everyone seems to wear black. The mezzanine upstairs, connected to the dining room by an open curved staircase, affords a view of the action, as well as the live musicians that play nightly.

3 celery stalks, thinly sliced on the diagonal
1 bunch fresh Italian parsley, leaves removed, stems discarded
2 tablespoons extra-virgin olive oil
2 teaspoons aged balsamic vinegar, plus more to drizzle
Kosher salt and freshly ground black pepper
36 large slivers Parmigiano-Reggiano cheese
24 Medjool dates, quartered

—Combine the celery and parsley in a medium bowl.

—Whisk together the oil and 2 teaspoons of balsamic vinegar. Season generously with salt and pepper. Add to the celery mixture and toss to coat.

—Place 16 date quarters in the center of each of 6 salad plates. Place 6 cheese slivers over the dates. Place a mound of celery salad on top. Drizzle additional balsamic vinegar around the salad.

Serves 6

SECRETS OF SUCCESS:

The balsamic vinegar. For best results you need to have vinegar that has been aged at least ten years. If you've never tasted the real thing you'll be amazed at the difference. It has a syrupy consistency and a haunting sweet/acidic flavor.

Use real Parmesan. Many countries make Parmesan cheese but only Italy makes Parmigiano-Reggiano, which has an unsurpassed sharp, nutty flavor.

CELERY SALAD

It's an almost pedestrian combination—red onions, carrots, and celery—but it's a spectacular one in the hands of Ping Sung, the chef/owner of Eliza's. ❋ With the added attractions of pickled ginger, dry mustard, and sesame oil drizzled on just before serving, the balance of flavors is refreshingly sophisticated. ❋ Sung and his wife, Jan, have created two moderately priced neighborhood Chinese restaurants—one on Oak Street near San Francisco's Civic Center and another on 18th Street on Potrero Hill—that have become citywide destinations because of the owners' innovative cooking style. Later this year, the Sungs plan to open a much larger and grander space on California Street. ❋ However, that's not to say their current space is lacking. The restaurant first distinguished itself by the use

of Wedgwood cups for tea and by the artfully presented food served on colorful plates. In addition, the Sungs collect art glass, which they display in both restaurants. Even the lights, with hand-blown globes and whimsical shapes, are custom-designed. ❋ These colorful elements create an appropriate stage for Sung's cooking, which goes well beyond the expected potstickers and sizzling rice soup. This simple celery salad adds an extraordinary change of pace and cools and refreshes the palate. At home, it's a great accompaniment to roast chicken or a spicy curry dish. It can be made in minutes once you have the ingredients, available at specialty stores and Asian markets throughout the Bay Area.

½ pound celery, preferably the tender inner ribs
½ medium carrot
¼ small red onion, thinly sliced
1 tablespoon slivered Chinese pickled ginger (see Note)
¼ cup distilled white vinegar
½ teaspoon salt
¼ teaspoon prepared Chinese mustard
¼ teaspoon freshly ground black pepper
½ teaspoon sugar
1 teaspoon Asian sesame oil
2 fresh cilantro sprigs for garnishing

—Remove the strings from the celery, then cut the ribs into thin julienne strips (⅛-inch thick by 2 inches long); you should have about
2 cups. Cut the carrot into the same size julienne. Combine the
celery, carrot, onion, and ginger in a medium bowl.

—Whisk together the vinegar, salt, mustard, pepper, and sugar. Pour
over the vegetables and toss to coat.

—Portion the salad onto plates. Drizzle 1 tablespoon of the remaining dressing in the bottom of the bowl over each salad, and sprinkle each with ½ teaspoon sesame oil. Garnish with cilantro.

Serves 2

Note: *Pickled ginger is available at Asian food markets or upscale
supermarkets.*

SECRETS OF SUCCESS:

The main ingredient. The captivating
aspect of this recipe is that celery is
allowed to star rather than play a supporting role, as it does in most recipes.

The method. Cutting the celery in julienne
strips helps to expose more surface to the
dressing, making the entire salad taste
better.

The flavors. Slivers of pickled ginger add a
refreshing note, as does a sprinkling of
sesame oil just before serving.

STRAWBERRY WATERCRESS SALAD

Pairing fruit and savory ingredients is a difficult challenge, and frankly, not many chefs are good at it. Without the proper balance the flavors clash and the dish becomes one-dimensional. ❋ Fortunately Jennifer Cox, chef of Montage in the Sony Metreon, has the gift. There are several examples on her seasonal menu, but my favorite is a pairing of juicy strawberries and peppery watercress accented with toasted almonds and creamy fromage blanc, a mild soft white cheese with a slightly tangy edge. ❋ Montage looks kind of like a 1990s version of a supper club. There's not a straight wall in the entire restaurant. Three rows of booths separated by five-foot-high partitions appear to stair-step up, thanks to the soffit ceiling. The artwork on the curved walls consists of gold-framed video screens that project moving abstract images and famous artwork from the Museum of Modern Art, located close to the Metreon. ❋ This huge shopping complex—with a host of restaurants, video games, virtual bowling, and high-tech shops such as Microsoft's first retail store—is Sony's answer to our digital society. Fortunately this cool countenance doesn't translate to Cox's food. You could grab a vitamin shake or pop a pill, but Cox's refreshing, soulful California style is soothing after a grueling day of virtual reality.

Salad
½ pound watercress, trimmed
1 pint fresh strawberries, stemmed and cut into
    ¼-inch slices
½ cup (or more) Balsamic Vinaigrette (recipe
    follows)
Salt and pepper
1 cup fromage blanc (see Note)
½ cup sliced almonds, toasted
Balsamic Syrup (recipe follows)

Balsamic Vinaigrette
2 tablespoons Balsamic Syrup (recipe follows)
¼ cup good-quality balsamic vinegar
½ teaspoon Dijon mustard
2 teaspoons kosher salt
⅔ cup plus 1½ teaspoons mild olive oil

Balsamic Syrup
Any extra syrup can be stored in the refrigerator
and used on grilled vegetables.

1 cup good-quality balsamic vinegar
½ cup finely minced shallots

—*To make the salad:* Put the watercress and strawberries in separate bowls. Divide the Balsamic Vinaigrette between the bowls and toss to coat. Season to taste with salt, pepper, and more Balsamic Vinaigrette, if desired.

—Divide the watercress among 6 salad plates. Top with the strawberries. Generously dot the salad with the cheese. Sprinkle on the almonds. Drizzle on a small amount of the Balsamic Syrup.
Serves 6

—*To make the vinaigrette:* Whisk the Balsamic Syrup, vinegar, mustard, and salt in a medium stainless steel bowl. Gradually whisk in the oil until the mixture is emulsified. Whisk to blend.
Makes about 1 cup

—*To make the syrup:* Combine the balsamic vinegar and shallots in a medium non-reactive saucepan over low heat. Gently simmer until the liquid is reduced to about ⅓ cup, increasing the heat slightly at the end, but watching carefully to avoid scorching, about 30 minutes.

—Strain the syrup, pressing out as much liquid as possible from the shallots.

Note: *Fromage blanc is a soft fresh white cheese available at cheese stores and many upscale markets.*

SECRETS OF SUCCESS:

Pairing fruit and greens. The combination of watercress and strawberries sets up a refreshing, startling contrast.

Balsamic reduction. The dressing, made from reduced balsamic vinegar, has a natural infinity to strawberries.

WARM MOROCCAN BEET SALAD WITH TANGERINES AND HONEY

Jody Denton, the chef of Zibibbo in Palo Alto, has come up with yet another way to showcase beets. They're spiced with cinnamon, allspice, and cloves and bathed in a sauce of tangerine, lime, honey, and mint. It's an extraordinary combination. ✽ Denton, who is also the chef at LuLu in San Francisco, is having fun these days experimenting with Mediterranean flavors at Zibibbo. The warmer Peninsula climate begs for a tapas-style menu, particularly when people can sit outside on the covered patio. ✽ Inside is just as exciting; the loft-like interior has a big-city feel. And the food, too, can compete with any in San Francisco; the Moroccan beet salad is only one example.

3 or 4 bunches baby beets, such as red, golden, candystripe, or chiogga, with greens still attached

3 tablespoons extra-virgin olive oil

Salt and freshly ground black pepper

3 tablespoons water

1/8 teaspoon ground cinnamon

2 allspice berries, crushed

1 whole clove, crushed

2 tablespoons dried currants

1 tablespoon honey

1 tablespoon tangerine zest

1/4 cup tangerine juice

1/2 cup tangerine segments (see page 363)

1 tablespoon chopped fresh mint

2 teaspoons fresh lime juice

—Preheat the oven to 350 degrees.

—Remove the green beet tops. Trim and discard the woody stems. Wash the remaining greens thoroughly and reserve. Wash the beets thoroughly.

—Place the beets in a large baking pan. Toss the beets with 1 tablespoon of the olive oil. Season with salt and pepper. Add the water to the pan. Cover and roast until the beets offer little resistance when poked with a small knife or wooden skewer, about 45 minutes. When cool, peel the beets by rubbing them with a kitchen towel. Set aside.

—Heat the remaining 2 tablespoons oil in a large sauté pan over medium heat. Add the roasted beets, cinnamon, allspice, and clove. Gently toss the beets with the spices until fragrant, about 1 minute. Add the currants, honey, and tangerine zest and increase the heat to high. Toss until the honey just begins to caramelize, being careful not to let it burn, about 1 to 2 minutes.

—Add the tangerine juice and boil until the liquid is reduced to a thick syrup. Mix in the reserved beet tops and stir until wilted, about 30 seconds. Transfer the mixture to a serving bowl. Add the tangerine segments, mint, and lime juice. Season to taste with salt and pepper. Serve warm.

Serves 4 to 6

SECRETS OF SUCCESS:

The spicing. The use of sweet spices with the earthy beets sets up a dramatic and delicious contrast.

The tangerine. The use of both juice and zest brings out a sweetness in the beets, balanced by the tartness of lime juice.

Using the beet tops. These pungent greens are often thrown away, but they make a brilliant addition to the blend.

WARM ARTICHOKE, POTATO, AND POACHED LEMON SALAD

When we ordered the Warm Artichoke, Potato, and Poached Lemon Salad at Black Cat, my friend couldn't quite accept the fact that someone would actually eat a whole lemon—peel, pith, and all. ✽ But that's one of the highlights of this simply delicious salad at the North Beach restaurant celebrating the cuisines of four cultures: Chinese, Italian, seafood, and the old-time American grill. ✽ For the salad, chef Reed Hearon boils small fingerling potatoes and sets them aside. Then he cooks artichokes and lemons together. The ingredients are drained, then lightly coated with a straightforward vinaigrette made from olive oil and the warm juices from one of the poached lemons. It's simple, yet delicious. ✽ The most time-consuming task is preparing the artichokes. They must be trimmed and stored in lemon water so they won't discolor before cooking. ✽ Hearon, who also owns Rose Pistola, opened the Black Cat in 1998, but it looks as if it has been around for years. At no other restaurant in the city can you find such a diverse collection of dishes. It's a smorgasbord of flavors, but the simplicity of the warm salad celebrates the best of California freshness.

4 lemons
4 medium-size artichokes
Salt
8 small fingerling potatoes
8 fresh parsley sprigs, coarsely chopped
¼ cup extra-virgin olive oil
Freshly ground pepper

—Fill a large mixing bowl with cold tap water and add the juice of 1 lemon.

—Working with 1 artichoke at a time, remove the leaves and pare the woody stem with a vegetable peeler. Cut the heart (with stem) in half lengthwise and scoop out the fuzzy choke. Immediately place the artichoke heart halves in the lemon water to keep them from discoloring.

—Bring a large pot of generously salted water to a boil. Drain the artichoke hearts and add them, along with the remaining 3 whole lemons. Simmer until the artichokes are tender, about 20 minutes. Drain.

—Meanwhile, simmer the potatoes in another large pot of salted water until they are tender, about 15 minutes. Drain, peel if desired, and cut in half lengthwise.

—Combine the warm potatoes, artichoke hearts, and the parsley in a serving bowl. Cut each lemon in half. Add 4 of the halves to the salad.

—Squeeze the juice from the remaining 2 halves into a small bowl. Add the olive oil. Season to taste with salt and pepper and stir to emulsify. Pour this vinaigrette over the vegetables and toss gently to coat. Add more salt and pepper, if needed. Divide the salad equally among salad plates.

Serves 4

SECRETS OF SUCCESS:

The ingredients. The combination of creamy potatoes, artichoke hearts, and lemons is irresistible.

Poaching the lemon. Cooking takes away much of the bitterness from the skin and pith, so you can eat the whole fruit.

WARM EGGPLANT SALAD WITH GOAT CHEESE

Pierre Morin is a classic French chef who creates simple, satisfying combinations at his cute restaurant, Anjou, hidden away in an alley off Union Square. ❋ Few dishes are as exciting as his Warm Eggplant Salad with Goat Cheese. Cubes of eggplant steep in vegetable broth, infusing the flesh with flavor and creating a velvet-like texture. Goat cheese is then crusted in nuts and quickly fried to give the contrast of crunchy/creamy and cool/hot. A drizzle of tangy red wine vinaigrette completes the dish with an explosion of flavor. You can use any vinaigrette, but the best is made with three parts oil to one part vinegar, with salt, pepper, and Dijon mustard to taste. ❋ Morin hails from Anjou, a province of France known for its variety of cheeses and vegetables, so the man knows his goat cheese. His cooking style evolved over many years of cooking all over the world with the French Navy. He found his way to San Francisco cooking for Kennedy's White House chef, Rene Verdon, at Le Trianon. ❋ He uses all of that experience to create a casual full-flavored cuisine that bows to California freshness. The restaurant combines brick walls with gleaming brass on the two-level interior. A partly open kitchen on the lower level adds a warm inviting feel to this out-of-the-way place.

Salad

11 ounces fresh goat cheese (preferably 45% matiere grasse)

1 egg, beaten

2 drops plus 1½ cups olive oil

2 drops plus 2 quarts water

Salt and freshly ground pepper

⅓ cup all-purpose flour

2½ ounces chopped blanched almonds

2 stalks of celery, sliced

1 carrot, sliced

1 onion, sliced

1 large garlic clove, cut in half

4 fresh thyme sprigs

4 fresh parsley sprigs

3 bay leaves

2 eggplants, peeled and cut into ½-inch cubes

Juice of 2 lemons

½ red onion, thinly sliced

½ cup Red Wine Vinaigrette (recipe follows) or any other vinaigrette

2 teaspoons chopped fresh parsley

12 cherry tomatoes, halved

Red Wine Vinaigrette

½ cup extra-virgin olive oil

Salt and pepper

1 tablespoon (or more) red wine vinegar

1 teaspoon Dijon mustard

—*To make the salad:* Slice the goat cheese into 6 equal portions, cutting with a knife moistened with hot water or with a cheese slicing wire.

—Beat the egg with the 2 drops of olive oil and 2 drops of water in a small bowl. Season with salt and pepper. Roll the cheese portions in the flour, dip into the egg mixture, then roll in the almonds until evenly coated. Refrigerate until just before serving.

—Combine 2 quarts of water with the celery, carrot, onion, garlic, thyme, parsley, and bay leaves in a large pot. Bring to a boil over high heat. Reduce heat and simmer 20 minutes. Strain. Return the liquid to the pot and bring to a boil over high heat. Add the eggplant, ½ cup of olive oil, and lemon juice. Cook, stirring frequently, until the eggplant is tender, about 5 to 8 minutes. Remove from heat. (The eggplant can be prepared to this point 1 day ahead. Warm over low heat before serving.)

—Heat the remaining 1 cup of olive oil in a deep pan over medium-high heat. Working in batches, gently place the goat cheese into the hot oil and cook until evenly browned, about 2 minutes per side. Using a slotted spoon, transfer the goat cheese to paper towels and drain.

—Strain the eggplant, discarding the liquid. Divide eggplant evenly among six appetizer plates. Garnish with the red onion. Drizzle with Red Wine Vinaigrette. Place one portion of cheese on top of each mound of eggplant. Sprinkle with parsley and cherry tomatoes.
Serves 6

—*To make the vinaigrette:* Season the oil with salt and pepper. Let stand for at least 10 minutes. Whisk the vinegar and mustard in a small bowl. Gradually whisk in the oil until the dressing has a creamy consistency. Whisk in more vinegar, if desired.

SECRETS OF SUCCESS:

Poaching the eggplant. Simmering the cubes in the vegetable stock adds loads of flavor and gives the flesh a soft, seductive texture.

Making it ahead. The cheese can be cut, coated, and refrigerated overnight. The eggplant can be cooked the day before and left in the vegetable broth. It then has to be reheated before serving.

WARM GOAT CHEESE SALAD

In the 1970s the connection between goat cheese and California cuisine became a running joke, and when you added it to a salad, it was the ultimate cliché. Never mind that this has been a staple of the French brasserie for generations. And new generations of Californians are discovering how wonderful the combination can be at Baker Street Bistro, the charming neighborhood bistro near the Marina. ✼ For this delicious salad, rounds of goat cheese are crusted in crushed walnuts and thyme. It's warmed and then placed on a nest of mixed baby greens, delicately dressed with a red wine vinaigrette with a touch of balsamic vinegar and Dijon mustard. ✼ The recipe is done to perfection by Jose Sanchez, who trained with Fredy Girardet in Switzerland for five months before taking work in Europe and Tokyo. He took over the kitchen at Baker Street Bistro in 1997. ✼ When you enter the cramped quarter, which now spreads out over two small storefronts with a postage-stamp-sized kitchen in the center, you'll be greeted by Jacques Manuera, who opened this bargain-priced place in 1991.

15 ounces fresh goat cheese
1 teaspoon minced fresh thyme
Salt and pepper
½ cup coarsely ground walnuts
3 tablespoons red wine vinegar
2 teaspoons balsamic vinegar
1 teaspoon Dijon mustard
½ cup vegetable oil
12 slices ¼-inch thick French bread
8 tablespoons olive oil, plus additional for greasing
1 tablespoon minced fresh parsley
1 pound mixed salad greens
2 cups halved cherry tomatoes or chopped tomatoes
1 tablespoon minced fresh mixed herbs (such as tarragon, parsley, and marjoram)

—Preheat the oven to 350 degrees.

—Divide the cheese into 6 portions (about 2½ ounces each) and shape into flat rounds (about ⅜-inch high). Sprinkle each round with thyme, salt, and pepper. Coat with walnuts.

—Place the cheese in the freezer until very firm, about 20 to 30 minutes, but do not allow to freeze. Once chilled, the cheese can be kept in the refrigerator for up to 1 day.

—Combine the red wine vinegar, balsamic vinegar, and mustard in a small bowl, whisking to blend. Gradually whisk in the vegetable oil until the vinaigrette is completely emulsified. Season to taste with salt and pepper.

—Arrange the bread slices on a baking sheet. Use 7 tablespoons of the olive oil to drizzle on both sides of the bread. Sprinkle with the minced parsley. Bake until crisp and golden brown, about 12 to 15 minutes. Maintain oven temperature.

—Lightly oil another small baking sheet. In a sauté pan, heat the remaining 1 tablespoon of olive oil over medium heat. Sauté the rounds of goat cheese until the nuts are browned, about 1 to 2 minutes. Transfer the rounds to the prepared baking sheet. Bake until the cheese is warmed through, about 5 minutes.

—Toss the greens with about half the vinaigrette. Season with additional salt, pepper, and more vinaigrette as needed. In another bowl, toss the tomatoes with the remaining vinaigrette.

—Divide the greens among six serving plates. Arrange the toasted bread over greens. Top with warm goat cheese. Garnish with the tomatoes and fresh herbs; serve immediately.

Serves 6

SECRETS OF SUCCESS:

Fresh thyme. Coating the cheese first in the fresh herbs adds a clean herbal flavor to the mild goat cheese.

Chilling the cheese. The cold cheese will retain its shape while the nuts brown. The insides become warm and creamy when gently heated in the oven.

TONGUE SALAD WITH MÂCHE AND BABY BEETS

It was only a few years ago that Traci Des Jardins won the James Beard Award as a rising star while cooking at Rubicon. ❊ Her star has definitely ascended at Jardinière, the Civic Center–area restaurant she opened with designer Pat Kuleto. With a domed ceiling that's lit to look like Champagne bubbles and martini-glass cutouts on the door, this impressive restaurant creates a celebratory mood for Des Jardins's French-inspired food. ❊ In lesser hands a tongue salad would have little future on an upscale menu, but this young chef knows how to make it right. She poaches the tongue in seasoned broth, a technique that adds flavor and juiciness. Beets, mâche, and an apple cider–honey vinaigrette, capped with a drizzle of Horseradish Crème Fraîche, complete the salad and bring out the best in the meat. ❊ Obviously, this is not a simple salad, but Des Jardins is a master at balance. While the recipe calls for veal or lamb tongue, which can be hard to find, you can substitute beef tongue following the same directions.

Tongue
2 gallons water
4 carrots, sliced
3 celery stalks, chopped
2 onions, chopped
1 leek, sliced
1 head garlic, split
2 bay leaves
1 tablespoon whole black peppercorns
½ bunch fresh thyme
Salt
½ cup white wine vinegar
6 veal or lamb tongues (or 1 beef tongue), rinsed

Salad
10 medium-size beets, trimmed
Olive oil
Salt and pepper
1 cup water
Apple Cider–Honey Vinaigrette (recipe follows)
Horseradish Crème Fraîche (recipe follows)

2 bunches mâche, trimmed
3 tablespoons finely diced shallots for garnishing
2 tablespoons minced fresh chives for garnishing

Apple Cider–Honey Vinaigrette
3 tablespoons apple cider vinegar
2 tablespoons red wine vinegar
2 tablespoons honey
Salt and pepper
1 cup extra-virgin olive oil

Horseradish Crème Fraîche
1 cup crème fraîche
1 teaspoon white wine vinegar or fresh lemon juice
1 teaspoon (or more) prepared horseradish
Salt and pepper

—*To make the tongue:* Combine the water, carrots, celery, onions, and leek in a large stockpot. Place the garlic, bay leaves, peppercorns, and thyme in a piece of cheesecloth; tie into a bundle with a piece of string and add to the stockpot. Season with salt. Bring to a boil. Cook until the vegetables are tender, about 20 minutes. Strain, reserving the cheesecloth bundle. Return liquid and cheesecloth to the pot. Add the vinegar and more salt to taste.

—Add the tongue to the pot. Bring to a boil, then reduce to a simmer. Cook until the tongue is tender when pierced with a fork, about 2 to 3 hours for beef, 1½ to 2 hours for veal, or 1 hour for lamb. Cool the tongue in the cooking liquid.

—*To make the salad:* Preheat the oven to 350 degrees. Place the beets in an ovenproof container. Rub the beets with oil. Season with salt and pepper. Add the water and cover with aluminum foil. Roast until the beets can be easily pierced with a knife, about 1½ hours. Remove the foil and cool. When cool enough to handle, peel and cut the beets into wedges.

—Remove the tongue from the cooking liquid. Peel off the skin. Cut the meat into ¼-inch-thick slices.

—To serve, dress the beets and the tongue separately with the Apple Cider–Honey Vinaigrette, to prevent the beets from leaking their color onto the tongue. Place some of the Horseradish Crème Fraîche in the center of a serving plate, followed by the tongue and then the beets.

—Toss the mâche with some of the dressing and scatter on top of and around the beets. Garnish with shallots and chives.
Serves 6

—*To make the vinaigrette:* In a bowl, combine the cider vinegar, red wine vinegar, and honey and whisk to blend. Season to taste with salt and pepper. Gradually whisk in the olive oil until the mixture is completely emulsified.

—*To make the Horseradish Crème Fraîche:* Whisk the crème fraîche, vinegar or lemon juice, and horseradish to taste in a small bowl until smooth and thick. Season to taste with salt and pepper. Add more horseradish, if desired. Refrigerate until ready to use.

SECRETS OF SUCCESS:

Poaching the tongue. The tongue acts like a sponge and picks up loads of flavor from the cooking liquid.

The vinaigrette. Adding the honey to the vinegars creates a smooth, slightly sweet dressing that plays off the Horseradish Crème Fraîche, the mâche, and the earthy beets.

MEATS AND POULTRY

MOROCCAN GAME HENS WITH PRESERVED LEMONS AND OLIVES

Cornish game hens, preserved lemons, and tangy olives are an unbeatable combination. This type of gutsy dish has become the backbone of Kasbah, a beautiful restaurant in San Rafael. ❋ Chef/owner Mourad Lahlou opened the restaurant with his brother, Khalib, because they became homesick for their native cuisine while attending the University of California, San Francisco. They decided they wanted to stay here, but they still longed for the flavors of home. ❋ The restaurant they created is like no other, from the tented ceiling and Oriental rugs that line the walls, to the food. Mourad realized right away that his customers wanted fresher-tasting dishes, so he adapted his style by cooking the vegetables less and using stock instead of water to give the couscous more flavor. ❋ The Moroccan Game Hens with Preserved Lemons and Olives is one example of this fresher approach. Making this dish come to life takes time, but the results are spectacular. ❋ If you don't have a month or so to make your own preserved lemons, we have a quick method so they're ready in a week.

4 Cornish game hens
2 tablespoons fresh lemon juice
1 teaspoon kosher salt
2 tablespoons chopped garlic
3 tablespoons olive oil
2 quarts homemade chicken stock, canned low-sodium chicken broth, or water
8 large shallots, peeled and chopped
1 ½ teaspoons ground ginger
1 ½ teaspoons ground coriander
½ teaspoon freshly ground black pepper
¼ teaspoon ground turmeric
2 Preserved Lemons, rinsed and cut into thin strips (recipe follows)
24 large Moroccan pink olives or kalamata olives
2 tablespoons chopped fresh parsley
1 ½ tablespoons chopped fresh cilantro

Preserved Lemons
Lemons
Kosher salt

—Rinse the hens under cold running water; discard the giblets. Pat dry.

—Cut each hen in half (remove the backbones using poultry shears, if desired). Cut off any excess skin. Rub the hens with the lemon juice, salt, and chopped garlic, rubbing some of the mixture between the skin and the breast meat. Refrigerate for 1 hour.

—Preheat the oven to 375 degrees.

—Heat 2 tablespoons of the olive oil in a heavy large skillet over medium-high heat. Add the hens and sauté until browned on both sides. Transfer the hens to a platter. Discard the excess oil in the pan.

—Add 1 cup of the stock to the pan. Bring to a boil, scraping up any browned bits. Add the shallots and cook until translucent, about 5 minutes. Stir in the ginger, coriander, pepper, and turmeric.

—Return the hens to the pan and cook for 5 minutes, turning frequently and stirring so the spices don't burn on the bottom of the pan. Heat the remaining stock in a large stockpot. Transfer everything in the skillet to the pot. Add the remaining 1 tablespoon olive oil. The hens should be covered, or almost covered, with liquid. Bring to a boil.

—Place the pot in the oven and cook until the hens are tender but not falling apart, about 45 minutes. Transfer the hens to a clean platter.

—Tent the hens loosely with foil to keep warm, or place in a 200-degree oven.

—Transfer the cooking liquid to a wide, heavy sauté pan. Add the preserved lemons and olives. Boil over high heat until the liquid has reduced to 2 or 3 cups, about 30 minutes. Pour the sauce over the Cornish hens. Garnish with the parsley and cliantro.
Serves 4

—*To prepare quick preserved lemons:* Cut each lemon into quarters, lengthwise. Freeze for 8 hours in a glass or stainless steel bowl. Sprinkle on 1 tablespoon kosher salt for each lemon used. Stir lightly to distribute salt. Cover and let stand at room temperature for 6 days, stirring once a day. At the end of the week, refrigerate. The lemons will keep for several months.

> **SECRETS OF SUCCESS:**
>
> *The lemons.* Preserving lemons can be time consuming and take a month. By freezing them and adding salt, they are ready in a week.

TEQUILA-MARINATED CORNISH HENS

Cornish hens are great for a dinner party, but let's face it, they can be pretty boring. Not, however, in the case of this impressive dish from Las Camelias in San Rafael. ❋ Gabriel Fregoso has adapted his family recipes for the restaurant, and the hens are one of my favorites. They get an explosion of flavor from marinating 24 hours in a mixture of water, ginger, onions, garlic, and tequila. You can actually taste the warming effects of the alcohol, even after roasting. ❋ What makes this dish special is the fact that the hens are allowed to rest for 30 minutes after baking; then they're sautéed to add even more complex flavors. The sauce, made from tomatoes, mushrooms, cilantro, pickled jalapeños, and the strained liquid, completes the dish. It simmers for 30 minutes, producing a thin but intensely flavored broth. ❋ This and other dishes such as the Fish Tacos (see page 195) are served up in a charming restaurant that feels a bit like a hacienda.

3 cups water

½ cup tequila

20 garlic cloves, minced

2 ounces fresh ginger, grated

1 medium onion, chopped

1½ teaspoons kosher salt, plus additional to taste

¼ teaspoon ground black pepper, plus additional to taste

4 Cornish hens, about 18 ounces each

1 tablespoon butter

4 ounces mushrooms, thinly sliced

1 pound fresh tomatoes, peeled, seeded, and diced (see page 363)

⅓ cup coarsely chopped fresh cilantro

2 pickled jalapeños from a jar, seeded and thinly sliced

2 tablespoons olive oil

—Combine the water, tequila, garlic, ginger, onion, 1½ teaspoons
  salt, and ¼ teaspoon pepper in a bowl large enough to hold all the
  Cornish hens. Add the hens to the marinade. Make sure to get
  some of the onions and ginger inside each cavity. Cover and
  refrigerate at least 8 hours and up to 24 hours.
—Preheat the oven to 400 degrees. Remove the hens from the marinade, scraping off the onion mixture. Strain the marinade and
  reserve for sauce.
—Generously season the hens with additional salt and pepper.
  Arrange the hens on a rack in a low-sided baking pan or roasting
  pan and roast until cooked through, about 45 minutes.
—Transfer the hens to a platter; allow to stand 30 minutes. Reserve
  any juices that have collected in the pan for the sauce.
—Melt the butter in a large saucepan over medium-high heat. Add
  the mushrooms and sauté 3 to 4 minutes until soft but not
  browned. Add the tomatoes and simmer 6 to 8 minutes until the
  mixture is slightly thickened. Add the cilantro and jalapeños and
  stir for 1 minute.
—Add the reserved marinade, increase the heat to high, and bring to
  a boil. Reduce the heat and simmer until the sauce has reduced
  and thickened slightly, about 30 minutes. Add the reserved pan
  juices and continue to reduce to a broth-like consistency. Season
  to taste with salt. Remove from the heat.
—Heat the olive oil in a large sauté pan over high heat. Cut the
  Cornish hens in half and put in the pan cut side up to sear. Turn
  the hens several times to evenly brown and crispen the skin, about
  5 minutes in all. Transfer the hens to a platter. Spoon sauce over.

Serves 4

> **SECRETS OF SUCCESS:**
>
> *Marinating the hens.* Tequila and other ingredients infuse the birds with robust flavor and keep them plump and moist during roasting.
>
> *Roasting and sautéing.* The technique of roasting the birds, letting them rest, and then sautéing them over high heat produces a seductively crisp and juicy bird.

THAI-STYLE FRIED QUAIL

It seems every time a restaurant goes under, a Thai restaurant rises up in its spot. The vibrant flavors and fresh ingredients have made this style of food just about as popular as Chinese. ❋ One thing that makes Thai food so irresistible is the complex balance of ingredients—like the mix that flavors the Thai-Style Fried Quail from Thep Phanom. The restaurant opened in 1986 and still maintains its position as the best Thai restaurant in the Bay Area. ❋ The birds are rubbed with lemongrass, garlic, cilantro, and fish sauce and marinated overnight, then fried to a crisp turn and served with a dipping sauce made with fish sauce, fresh lime, chile powder, and cilantro. ❋ Chef/owner Pathama Parikanont is a self-taught cook, learning at her father's side in Thailand. He would tell her what he wanted, and she would choose the vegetables from the garden and run to the nearby rivers to catch fish and shrimp for his creations. ❋ She started with many of his recipes and has since made them her own, creating dishes that combine her Thai background and California sensibilities. ❋ The restaurant, located in a Victorian on Waller and Fillmore, feels like a turn-of-the-century parlor. It's warm and inviting and filled with Thai artwork that the owner has collected through the years.

4 quail
4 garlic cloves, minced
1 tablespoon minced lemongrass (white part only)
Stems from 1 bunch fresh cilantro, minced
1 teaspoon ground white pepper
½ teaspoon salt
2 teaspoons fresh ground black pepper
1 teaspoon Golden Mountain Sauce (or other Thai soy sauce)
1 teaspoon Tipparos Fish Sauce (or other fish sauce)
1 tablespoon vegetable oil, plus additional for frying
6 cilantro leaves for garnish
Thai-Style Spicy Sauce (recipe follows)

Thai-Style Spicy Sauce
2 tablespoons Tipparos Fish Sauce (or other fish sauce)
1 tablespoon fresh lemon juice
½ teaspoon dried chili powder
½ teaspoon minced fresh cilantro
¼ teaspoon rice powder or potato starch

—*To cook the quail:* Prepare the quail by cutting along both sides of the backbone with kitchen scissors. Place your index finger into the neck cavity and gently pull down on the backbone, removing it and the ribs. (You may need to use a boning knife to cut away ribs.) Find the hip bone and cut around it, taking care not to cut off the legs. Rinse the quail thoroughly. Dry with paper towels.

—Combine the garlic, lemongrass, cilantro stems, white pepper, and salt with a mortar and pestle and crush to form a paste. Transfer to a bowl. Add the black pepper, soy sauce, fish sauce, and 1 tablespoon oil.

—Rub each quail thoroughly with the paste. Stack the quail atop one another in a plastic bag. Squeeze out all the air and seal the bag. Refrigerate overnight.

—Remove the quail from the marinade; discard the marinade.

—Pour enough oil into a large saucepan to reach a depth of 2 inches. Heat to 375 degrees. Carefully slip 2 quail into the oil and fry about 3 minutes on each side. Remove the quails and drain on paper towels. Using tongs, repeat with the remaining 2 quail.

—Transfer to individual plates and garnish with cilantro leaves. Serve with Thai-Style Spicy Sauce.

Serves 4

—*To make the sauce:* Make this sauce the night before so the flavors have time to blend.

—Combine all the ingredients in a small bowl. Stir to blend. Cover and refrigerate overnight.

SECRETS OF SUCCESS:

The spicy paste. Rubbing the quail with a marinade of garlic, lemon grass, cilantro, fish sauce, and other ingredients and marinating overnight adds a great flavor.

Frying the quail. Cook only two quail at a time; trying to crowd more in will lower the temperature of the oil, and the skin won't be crisp.

The dipping sauce. Made a day ahead, the sauce gives an extra zip to the hot, fried quail.

ROASTED DUCK LEGS WITH PRUNES

We might as well face the fact: prunes are not glamorous. But you'd be amazed at how marvelous they taste with duck legs. The intense flavor of dried plums— a more palatable name for prunes—and the robust meat form a perfect marriage. ❋ Lucas Gasco serves this dish at his popular Spanish tapas restaurant, Zarzuela, located on the streetcar line at Hyde and Union. With stucco walls, tile floor, and crowded tables, the place has a comfortable Spanish feel. ❋ The Roasted Duck Legs with Prunes, while not difficult, requires about five hours from start to finish. However, all but the final step of warming and crisping the skin of the duck can be done ahead. Then all you need to do is to reheat the sauce.

12 Muscovy duck legs
2 medium carrots, cut into ¾-inch pieces
1 medium yellow onion, cut into large dice
18 pitted prunes
6 garlic cloves, peeled
4 whole cloves
1 small cinnamon stick, broken up
2 teaspoons salt, plus additional to taste
1 teaspoon coarsely ground pepper
3 fresh rosemary sprigs, plus additional for
    garnishing
2 small bay leaves
½ cup dry white wine
Juice of 1 orange
¼ cup extra-virgin olive oil, plus additional for
    oiling
2 tablespoons sherry vinegar
1 tablespoon brandy
1 tablespoon dry sherry
1 cup Spanish Rioja or other dry red wine
4 cups chicken stock
2 small slices of French bread, brushed with olive
    oil and toasted
1 tablespoon toasted pine nuts

—Preheat the oven to 425 degrees.

—Remove the thighbones from the duck legs (or have the butcher do it). Trim away and reserve excess fat. Cut off the bony end of the drumsticks. Place the bones and the reserved duck fat in a large roasting pan. Arrange the legs on top and add the carrots, onion, prunes, garlic, cloves, cinnamon stick, 2 teaspoons salt, pepper, 3 rosemary sprigs, and bay leaves. Pour the white wine, orange juice, ¼ cup oil, vinegar, and brandy over. Bake in the oven until the duck is tender, about 2 hours and 15 minutes.

—Uncover the pan, sprinkle the sherry over the contents, and return to the oven for 2 more minutes.

—Transfer the duck legs and prunes to a platter and set aside. Skim off the fat from the cooking liquid (there will be a considerable amount). Reserve the cooking liquid.

—Place the roasting pan over medium-low heat, add the red wine, and reduce the contents by a quarter, about 15 minutes. Add the chicken stock to the roasting pan and raise the heat to medium-high. Reduce by half, about 20 minutes. Strain the sauce and discard the bones and vegetables.

—Place the strained sauce in a blender along with the reserved cooking liquid, 6 of the prunes, the toasted bread, and pine nuts. Blend until smooth and pour the mixture into a clean saucepan. Bring to a boil, skim the fat again, and strain the sauce through a sieve. Transfer the sauce to a clean saucepan. Season to taste with salt.

—Just before serving, preheat the oven to 500 degrees. Oil a large baking pan. Place the duck legs, skin side up, on the prepared pan and bake until they become hot and crisp, about 12 minutes.

—Add the remaining prunes to the sauce. Bring to a simmer.

—To serve, place 2 duck legs on each of 6 plates. Spoon the sauce and prunes over. Garnish with rosemary. (To serve as a tapa, divide the duck and sauce among 12 plates.)

Serves 6 as an entree or 12 for tapas

SECRETS OF SUCCESS:

The prunes. Not a glamorous ingredient, but they bring an intriguing, earthy flavor to the duck.

Double cooking. The duck is first steamed on top of the vegetables and seasonings where it becomes tender and picks up the flavor of the other ingredients. Then before serving, the legs are roasted in a very hot oven, which makes them crispy on the outside and creamy inside.

Thickening the sauce. Slices of toasted bread and pine nuts are blended with the liquid ingredients to thicken and add texture to the finished sauce.

Roast Rabbit WITH WHOLE-GRAIN MUSTARD SAUCE

Roast Rabbit with Whole-Grain Mustard Sauce is a rustic dish created by Donia Bijan, the chef/owner of L'Amie Donia in Palo Alto. Few cooks have such a deft hand with such hearth-warming dishes. ❖ Bijan refers to her style as "à la bonne femme," which consists of warm, nurturing combinations such as that found in this dish. The generous use of mustard and rosemary certainly isn't subtle, but adds a burst of flavor that's just right on cool, damp nights. ❖ The dish is served with pasta so that none of the delicious mustard and rosemary sauce will go to waste. As you'll discover, Bijan cooks the type of food you just can't quit eating, but if you can, it also warms up well for leftovers. When you taste the dish you'll understand why she's considered by many to be the best chef on the Peninsula.

2 rabbits, approximately 3 pounds each, cut into
    serving pieces
Salt and freshly ground pepper
2 tablespoons butter
½ cup olive oil
2 rabbit livers (optional), cut into ¼-inch pieces
2 cups whole-grain mustard
4 tablespoons minced fresh rosemary
2 cups dry white wine
2 cups heavy cream
5 roasted garlic cloves (see Note)
1½ pounds pasta of choice, such as fettuccine

—Preheat the oven to 350 degrees.
—Season the rabbit pieces with salt and pepper. In a large skillet, melt the butter with the oil over high heat. Working in batches, add the rabbit to the skillet and cook until browned on all sides. Transfer the rabbit to a roasting pan.
—In the same skillet, sauté the livers, if desired, until browned, about 3 to 5 minutes. Transfer the livers to a plate and set aside.
—Completely coat the rabbit pieces with 1 cup of the mustard. Sprinkle with 2 tablespoons of the rosemary. Gently pour the wine around the rabbit and bake uncovered until the rabbit is tender, about 45 minutes.
—Transfer the rabbit to a platter. Tent with foil to keep warm. Pour the pan juices into a large saucepan.
—Over high heat, reduce the pan juices by half, about 15 minutes. Whisk in the cream, the roasted garlic, the remaining 1 cup of mustard, and the remaining 2 tablespoons rosemary. Stir in the reserved rabbit liver if using.
—Reduce the heat and simmer until the sauce coats the back of a spoon, about 5 minutes. Season to taste with salt and pepper. Remove from the heat.
—Cook the pasta in a large pot of boiling salted water until tender but still firm to the bite. Drain. Add the pasta to the pan with the mustard sauce. Toss to coat.
—Transfer the pasta to a large platter, top with the rabbit, and serve.

Serves 6

Note: *To roast garlic, peel the cloves and place them in a small piece of foil. Drizzle with a little olive oil. Gather the foil loosely around the garlic and roast in a 350 degree oven until the garlic is soft, about 30 minutes.*

SECRETS OF SUCCESS:

The mustard and rosemary. Some cooks might be tempted to skimp on these two very assertive ingredients, but that would be a mistake. When smoothed with cream and combined with the rabbit and pasta, the flavors mellow.

The liver. While it's optional, this addition adds a rich earthiness to the dish.

The reduction. Reducing the pan juices with cream, mustard, roasted garlic, and rosemary creates an intense, tangy sauce.

Garlic Chicken

The stir-fried Garlic Chicken served at Osaka Grill may seem pretty straightforward at first glance, but it's an innovative dish for a Japanese restaurant. ✳ For one, the recipe uses butter, rosemary, and a hefty dose of garlic—ingredients not routinely found in the Japanese kitchen. While this dish has the traditional subtle balance of flavors, the combination isn't nearly as subtle as you find in most Japanese food. ✳ But then chef/owner Noel Mok isn't an ordinary cook. He's a teppanyaki chef with a 200-year-old tradition behind him. Many people are familiar with this form of cooking at Benihana, where Mok worked for several years after studying with master chef Fukumoto Sen. The tradition blends theatrical knife skills, balance, and presentation, but Mok utilizes more subtle techniques and more innovative approaches to blending flavors. ✳ These are showcased at his handsome and moderately priced Sutter Street restaurant that has a beautiful open feel with pine and bamboo floors, a high ceiling, and beautiful art work. The Teppan tables used for both cooking and eating are set at an angle, adding visual impact and allowing more space between tables. ✳ At the restaurant Mok prepares the Garlic Chicken on a large flat griddle, but the same results can be approximated at home with a frying pan. The chicken makes an ideal week-night meal because it can be tossed together and cooked in about 30 minutes.

Chicken

4 tablespoons vegetable oil
4 boneless chicken breast halves, about 6 ounces each, cut into ¾-inch cubes
4 garlic cloves, sliced
1 sprig fresh rosemary, stem removed and discarded
12 button mushrooms, sliced
¼ cup Garlic Butter (recipe follows)
Salt and pepper
2 tablespoons chopped fresh parsley

Garlic Butter

The leftovers of this delicious mixture can be used to finish many sauces or for topping grilled chicken or steak.

6 tablespoons (¾ stick) butter at room temperature
6 tablespoons (¾ stick) margarine at room temperature
1 tablespoon plain yogurt
6 garlic cloves, finely chopped

—*To cook the chicken:* Heat 3 tablespoons of the oil in a large pan over medium-high heat. Add the chicken, garlic, and rosemary. Sauté until golden brown, about 5 minutes, stirring occasionally. Transfer to a plate. Heat the remaining 1 tablespoon of oil in the same pan over medium-high heat. Add the mushrooms and sauté until tender and their liquid is released, about 2 to 3 minutes. Return the chicken to the pan and stir to combine.

—Remove from the heat. Add the Garlic Butter and stir until melted. Season to taste with salt and pepper. Sprinkle with the parsley and serve.

Serves 4

—*To make the garlic butter:* Stir all the ingredients in a small bowl until well blended. Cover and refrigerate until ready to use. The garlic butter will keep up to 6 weeks in the refrigerator.

SECRETS OF SUCCESS:

The butter mixture. The combination of butter, margarine, and yogurt adds a velvety coating to the chicken and mushrooms.

BUTTER CHICKEN

Those who claim that all Indian food tastes alike—and in many restaurants that's a legitimate complaint—need only to taste the Butter Chicken at Amber India in Mountain View. ❋ Little wonder it's the best-selling dish at the restaurant. The sauce is an amazing amalgamation of tastes and textures. Lemon, garlic, ginger, coriander, and cumin mixed with sweet spices add to the flavor, while the tomatoes, balanced with butter, cream, and brown sugar, smoothe it all out. ❋ Marinating the chicken in yogurt and spices before cooking adds flavor and tenderizes the meat. The chicken is then roasted on the bone. Once the chicken has been cooled, the meat is removed from the bone and simmered with the sauce. The finished dish is best accompanied by steamed rice to sop up all the aromatic juices. ❋ While many Indian dishes are spicy and aromatic, the key to this dish is its delicacy and balance. The recipe has been perfected by Vijay Bist, who graduated from a culinary institute in New Delhi before going into hotel management in India, Switzerland, and France. When he came to San Francisco he completed an MBA at San Francisco State University. ❋ Bist's passion for Indian cooking led him to opening the restaurant in 1995, featuring recipes mainly from North India. ❋ Located in a strip shopping center, the restaurant looks plain from the outside, but once inside you're surrounded by the flavors of India, from the seductive smells floating from the kitchen to the authentic art work on the walls.

Chicken

3 pounds chicken pieces (2 breasts, 2 thighs, 2 legs), skinned

Juice of 1 lemon

1 tablespoon dried red pepper flakes

2½ teaspoons salt

1½ cups plain yogurt

2 tablespoons heavy cream

1½ teaspoons garlic paste (see Note)

1½ teaspoons ginger paste (see Note)

½ teaspoon ground coriander

½ teaspoon ground cumin

½ teaspoon garam masala (see Note)

Sauce

1 teaspoon ground ginger

½ teaspoon red chile powder

Pinch of garam masala

Pinch of ground mace

Pinch of ground nutmeg

½ teaspoon ground white pepper

2 teaspoons brown sugar

¼ cup (½ stick) butter

2 cups canned chopped tomatoes with juices

1 tablespoon tomato paste

2 cups (or more) water

2 tablespoons heavy cream

2 teaspoons ground fenugreek (see Note)

Salt

—*To make the chicken:* Make three parallel cuts on top of each piece of chicken. In a resealable heavy-duty plastic bag, combine the lemon juice, red pepper flakes, and 2 teaspoons salt. Add the chicken, coating well with the marinade. Seal the bag and refrigerate for 30 minutes.

—In a bowl, stir together the yogurt and cream. Add the garlic paste, ginger paste, coriander, cumin, garam masala, and the remaining ½ teaspoon salt. Blend thoroughly. When the chicken has marinated 30 minutes, add the yogurt mixture to the plastic bag. Reseal the bag. Refrigerate overnight.

—*To make the sauce:* Preheat the oven to 450 degrees. In a small bowl, combine the ground ginger, chile powder, garam masala, mace, nutmeg, white pepper, and brown sugar.

—Melt the butter in a large skillet over medium-high heat. Add the tomatoes with juices, tomato paste, water, and spice mixture. Let simmer, stirring frequently, for 20 minutes or until slightly thickened, adding more water if needed. Remove the sauce from the heat.

—Remove the chicken from the marinade; discard the marinade. Place chicken in a baking pan large enough to hold all the pieces in a single layer. Bake until cooked through, about 30 minutes. When cool enough to handle, remove the meat from the bones and cut into bite-sized pieces. Discard the bones.

—Add the chicken, cream, and fenugreek to the sauce. Simmer over medium heat until slightly thickened, about 10 minutes, stirring frequently to prevent burning. Season to taste with salt.

Serves 4

Note: *Jars of garlic paste and ginger paste are available at Asian stores or some large supermarkets. Garam masala and ground fenugreek are available at specialty food stores or Indian markets.*

SECRETS OF SUCCESS:

Marinating. A two-step marinating process adds complex flavor to the chicken. First, the chicken is marinated in seasoned lemon juice for 30 minutes to add fresh notes to the meat. Then the yogurt mixture is added and the chicken marinates overnight.

Roasting: The chicken is roasted on the bone, which also adds flavor. The meat is then cooled, boned, and added to the sauce.

The sauce. The combination of ingredients, smoothed with just a touch of cream, creates a very buttery-silken sauce.

COQ AU VIN

If you've forgotten why coq au vin became a cult classic in the 1960s, then reacquaint yourself with this recipe from Philippe Jeanty at Bistro Jeanty in Yountville. ✱ It's probably the best version I've found. The chicken is first marinated in red wine for 24 to 48 hours, which turns it purple and gives it a wonderful mahogany hue when browned. The marinade is then cooked with the browned chicken and reduced to intensify the already wonderful flavors. The addition of bacon, pearl onions, and mushrooms adds another complex flavor component. ✱ While Jeanty's recipe doesn't call for it, his Coq au Vin would be wonderful served over wide noodles, particularly if there are any leftovers. ✱ Jeanty was the chef of the pioneering Domaine Chandon in Yountville for more than twenty years before he left in 1998 to open his own place, which was nominated as one of the five "Best New Restaurants" by the James Beard Foundation. ✱ Here, in charming bistro surroundings with flower boxes at the window, Jeanty redefines the French classics. Clearly he's one of the best French cooks in the United States. Try the Coq au Vin and you'll no doubt agree.

2 large yellow onions, diced

3 shallots, diced

8 cloves garlic, roughly chopped

3 fresh parsley sprigs

5 fresh thyme sprigs

2 bay leaves

2 large chickens (3 ½–4 pounds each), cut into pieces

1½ bottles (750 ml each) good-quality Merlot or Zinfandel

Salt and pepper

½ cup olive oil

2 tablespoons all-purpose flour

½ cup Cognac

2 cups chicken stock or canned broth

1 ½ tablespoons unsweetened cocoa powder

6 ounces thick-sliced applewood smoked bacon, diced

1 basket pearl onions, blanched and peeled

1 pound button mushrooms, quartered

2 tablespoons chopped fresh parsley for garnishing

—Place the onions, shallots, garlic, parsley, thyme, and bay leaves in a large bowl. Add the chicken and wine and stir to mix well. Cover with plastic wrap and refrigerate for 24 to 48 hours.

—Remove the chicken from the marinade, reserving the marinade. Dry the chicken pieces with paper towels. Season generously with salt and pepper.

—Heat the oil in a large heavy casserole over high heat. Working in batches, add the chicken. Brown well on all sides and transfer to a platter.

—Add the flour to the casserole and cook, stirring constantly, for 2 minutes. Return the chicken to the casserole and add the Cognac. Remove from the heat. Using a long match, carefully ignite the Cognac and let the flames burn out. Add the marinade to the casserole and bring to a boil over high heat, scraping up all the browned bits from the bottom of the pan. Add the chicken stock. Reduce the heat to low, cover, and simmer until the chicken is tender, about 1 to 1 ½ hours.

—Remove the chicken from the casserole and transfer to a clean platter. Strain the sauce through a sieve. Discard the solids and return the sauce to the casserole. Put the cocoa in a small bowl and whisk in about ½ cup of sauce until smooth. Stir the cocoa mixture into the sauce in the casserole. Increase the heat to high and boil the sauce until it is reduced to about 4 cups, about 15 minutes. Season to taste with salt and pepper.

—Lower the heat to medium low and return the chicken to the casserole. Heat through.

—Meanwhile, sauté the bacon in a large skillet. As it begins to brown, add the pearl onions and the mushrooms. Cook until lightly colored, about 10 minutes. Using a slotted spoon, transfer the bacon, onions, and mushrooms to the casserole, leaving the bacon grease in the skillet. Stir the casserole to combine. Sprinkle with the chopped parsley.

Serves 8

> **SECRETS OF SUCCESS:**
>
> *The red wine marinade.* Marinating the chicken for at least 24 hours in red wine not only adds flavor but also makes the exterior look deliciously brown.
>
> *Unsweetened cocoa powder.* Stirred in as you begin to reduce the sauce, the cocoa powder lends a deep flavor to the dish.

CHICKEN CUTLET WITH COUNTRY GRAVY

At first I wanted the recipe for fried chicken from Casa Orinda in Orinda, but when I found that the secret was the pressure fryer, I knew it couldn't be reproduced at home. ❋ However, the breaded chicken cutlet, coated in fresh crumbs and sautéed in butter, is just as good and much easier for the home cook. At the restaurant, it's served with vegetables, mashed potatoes, and country gravy. For a lighter supper, replace the gravy with lemon wedges. ❋ These types of homey main courses are the backbone of the offerings at Casa Orinda, which has been in business since the 1930s and is owned by John Goyak. While you'll find some of these American specialties, the menu is also a storehouse for classic Cal-Ital cooking. ❋ The interior is kind of like Cowboy Bob meets Chez Panisse, with wagon wheel lamps, branded tabletops, western art, and a profusion of fresh flowers. It sounds kitschy, but it's actually well done and fits the neighborly mood of the restaurant.

Serve with mashed potatoes and fresh vegetables. Asparagus makes a good match for the chicken. Lemon wedges can be substituted for the gravy.

½ cup (1 stick) butter or ½ cup rendered chicken fat
6 tablespoons all-purpose flour
1 cup chicken stock
½ cup heavy cream
Salt and ground white pepper
2 whole boneless chicken breasts, halved
2 eggs
½ loaf Acme sweet batard French bread (or other sweet white bread), crusts removed, processed to coarse crumbs
½ cup (1 stick) butter, clarified (see Note)

—In a large, heavy-bottomed saucepan, melt the butter or chicken fat over medium heat. Add 3 tablespoons of the flour and stir until cooked but not brown, about 2 to 3 minutes. Add the chicken stock and cream. Simmer to desired thickness, stirring constantly. Season to taste with salt and white pepper. Keep warm.

—Put each chicken breast half between 2 sheets of plastic wrap and pound lightly with the flat side of a cleaver or a heavy mallet to a thickness of ⅜ inch, taking care to not hit the flesh so hard that it tears.

—Beat the eggs in a shallow dish to blend. Put the remaining 3 tablespoons flour on a plate, and the bread crumbs on another plate.

—Remove the chicken from between the sheets of plastic. Coat the breasts in flour, shaking off any excess. Dip into the beaten egg mixture, then into the bread crumbs, coating completely.

—Heat the clarified butter in a heavy-bottomed skillet over medium-high heat. When the butter is almost at the smoking point, add the chicken. Cook until golden brown, about 3½ minutes. Turn and cook on the second side until golden brown and cooked through, about 2 or 3 minutes. Transfer the chicken to paper towels and drain.

—Spoon gravy onto warm plates, and put the chicken on top of the gravy.

Serves 4

Note: *To clarify butter, melt it in a small saucepan over medium heat. Remove from heat and let stand for 30 minutes. Using a spoon, skim off the foamy film from the top. Spoon the clarified butter into a jar, leaving the white whey at the bottom.*

SECRETS OF SUCCESS:

Fresh bread crumbs. These are lighter and absorb the butter, creating a marvelous rich and crispy crust.

Clarified butter. The clarified butter has a higher smoking point than regular melted butter and it lends richness to the dish.

CHICKEN CACCIATORE

Chicken Cacciatore is a classic recipe that's been gently updated by May Ditano at Columbus Restaurant in the Marina. Instead of cooking everything together, each item is cooked separately and then combined, making a vibrantly fresh dish. ❋ The chicken can be served immediately, but it's great made ahead, refrigerated, and rewarmed the next day. Surprisingly, it retains its fresh character, even after reheating. ❋ Ditano's food is probably the closest thing to Italian home cooking you'll find at the restaurant. For twenty-five years she presided over a sliver of a restaurant on Broadway between North Beach and Chinatown. With a ten-seat counter and only five tables, she cooked before customers' eyes and waited tables, with only the help of a combination dishwasher/bus boy. ❋

She practically became a legend for both her strong personality and her great cooking. If she liked you, cloth napkins would replace the paper ones, and you'd likely get a special pastry at dessert. If you offended her, she would register her displeasure with an arched eyebrow and silence—if you were lucky. ❋ Once when a customer asked, "What's good?" she shot back, "Why do I have to sell my food? It's so good I shouldn't have to sell it." ❋ Several years ago she moved into a grander space that once housed Cafe Adriano. Now she has waiters and help in the kitchen, but she still cooks one of the best cacciatores around.

This dish can be made a day ahead and reheated the next day.

5 tablespoons olive oil
1 chicken, cut into 8 to 10 pieces
1 teaspoon dried Italian seasoning
2 garlic cloves, smashed
1 fresh rosemary sprig
1 yellow bell pepper, halved, each half sliced into quarters
1 red bell pepper, halved, each half sliced into quarters
1 medium yellow onion, thinly sliced lengthwise
4 ripe tomatoes, quartered
1 cup sliced button mushrooms
1 cup black or green olives with pits
1 cup dry red wine
Salt and pepper

—Preheat the oven to 400 degrees.

—In a heavy large sauté pan, heat 2 tablespoons of the oil over medium-high heat and add the chicken, Italian seasoning, garlic, and rosemary. Cook until the chicken is golden brown on all sides, about 10 minutes. Remove from the heat.

—Meanwhile, in another sauté pan, heat 1 tablespoon of oil. Add the yellow and red peppers and sauté until soft, about 5 to 7 minutes. Using a slotted spoon, transfer the peppers to a plate.

—Using the same pan, add another tablespoon of oil and heat over medium-high heat. Add the onion and sauté until golden, about 5 to 10 minutes. Using a slotted spoon, transfer the onion to another plate.

—Add the remaining 1 tablespoon of oil to the same pan over medium-high heat. Add the tomatoes and mushrooms and sauté until the mushrooms are tender, about 5 minutes.

—In a large casserole, arrange the browned chicken. Top with the peppers, onion, tomatoes, mushrooms, and olives. Pour the wine over. Sprinkle with salt and pepper.

—Place uncovered in the oven and roast until the top browns and the chicken is cooked through, about 20 to 30 minutes.

Serves 4

SECRETS OF SUCCESS:

Cooking everything separately. When combined and heated together, the ingredients still retain their individual character, making the dish taste lighter and fresher.

Preparing ahead. We like it even better the next day. The flavors meld without destroying their individual character.

GAI KRAPROW (MINCED CHICKEN WITH BASIL)

Gai kraprow, or minced chicken with basil, is a staple at just about every Thai restaurant. The version at Little Thai on Polk and Broadway is exceptional for its simplicity and clean flavors. ❋ The coarse-ground chicken, a mix of white and dark meat, is the star. The meat is moistened with a judicious amount of wine, pepper, sesame oil, garlic, jalapeño, and fresh basil, which is added at the last minute. The glistening stir-fry emerges with just enough moisture to coat the meat and just enough spice to perk up the palate. ❋ Chicken with basil makes a splendid main course served with steamed rice. It can also be an impressive appetizer when the mixture is spooned into crisp iceberg lettuce leaves and eaten like a taco. ❋ The chicken is versatile for weeknight meals. Consider doubling the batch and using the leftovers through the week: it can be served in tacos, as a main ingredient in chicken noodle soup, or much like a Bolognese sauce with pasta. ❋ Little Thai, which moved into expanded quarters at its Russian Hill address in 1998, is one of the city's best bargains considering the quality of the food. Portions are large, and flavors are clean and bold.

3 pounds coarsely ground or minced white and dark chicken meat

2½ tablespoons dry white wine

3 pinches ground black pepper

2 tablespoons Asian sesame oil

1½ tablespoons salt

2 tablespoons cornstarch

1 tablespoon garlic powder

½ tablespoon vegetable oil

2 jalapeños, sliced

½ cup thinly sliced fresh basil

—In a large bowl, stir together all the ingredients except the vegetable oil, jalapeños, and basil.

—Heat a wok or large frying pan over high heat and add the oil. Add
the chicken mixture and stir-fry until the chicken is cooked, about
5 minutes. Stir in the jalapeños and basil and serve.

Serves 6 to 8

SECRETS OF SUCCESS:

Simplicity of ingredients. There are no
heavy sauces or bottled condiments to
mask the poultry.

The texture of the chicken. It's important to
mince or coarsely grind the white and
dark meats so they absorb the flavor but
retain a slightly chewy texture.

CHICKEN IN CARAMEL SAUCE

Many experts from coast to coast claim that the Slanted Door serves the best Vietnamese food in the United States. That's quite an accolade for Charles Phan, who was in architecture and computer graphics before he followed his passion to open a restaurant with his family. ✷ At first he wanted to open a small stand serving street food, but then he found the space in the Mission and the project grew into a full-fledged restaurant. He did much of the design work himself to come up with the sleek, simple look with an open kitchen carved out of the back corner. ✷ His mother, who worked in a French household in Vietnam, picked up many cross-cultural techniques that she passed along to her son—such as mayonnaise in spring rolls. In addition, Phan searched out great food from stands all over Vietnam, which he used as inspiration for many of the dishes on the menu. ✷ One of those is the Chicken in Caramel Sauce, which is an unlikely blend of pungent fish sauce, dark brown sugar, and chicken. It may sound strange but these two radically different elements are balanced by rice wine vinegar, ginger, and chiles. It's a really simple dish to prepare, but the results are wonderful.

½ cup (packed) dark brown sugar
¼ cup water
¼ cup fish sauce (see Note)
3 tablespoons rice vinegar
1 teaspoon minced garlic
1 teaspoon dark or regular soy sauce
1 teaspoon slivered ginger
1 teaspoon ground black pepper
2 small Thai chiles (fresh or dried), broken in
   half
1 tablespoon canola oil
1 shallot, sliced
1¾ pounds skinless boneless dark-meat
   chicken, cut into bite-sized pieces
¼ pound skinless boneless white-meat chicken,
   cut into bite-sized pieces
Steamed white rice
1 fresh cilantro sprig for garnishing

—Combine the brown sugar, water, fish sauce, vinegar, garlic, soy sauce, ginger, pepper, and chiles in a small bowl. Mix well. Set the sauce mixture aside.

—Heat the oil in a large pot over high heat. Add the shallot and sauté until brown, about 5 minutes. Add the chicken and sauté until slightly browned, about 5 minutes. Add the sauce mixture and bring to a boil. Turn the heat down to medium. Cook until the liquid is reduced by half, about 12 minutes, stirring occasionally.

—Place the rice in a serving bowl. Spoon the chicken over. Garnish with cilantro.

Serves 4 to 6

Note: *Fish sauce is available in Asian markets and upscale supermarkets.*

SECRETS OF SUCCESS:

The balance of ingredients. The play between the fish sauce and brown sugar creates a complex, alluring dish.

White and dark meat. The use of both kinds of meat gives a more interesting texture to the finished dish.

PORK BRAISED IN MILK AND HERBS

One of the most charming places in North Beach is a restaurant that doesn't have a stove. Sounds strange, but owners Wally Tettamanti and Susanna Borgatti have been clever to produce a simple Italian menu where everything is baked: pasta, gratins, pizza, exceptional focaccia, and pork braised in milk. ✳ This classic Italian preparation is easy for the home cook. The pork is slow-cooked in a casserole, simmering in milk and fresh herbs—rosemary, oregano, and tarragon. After cooking for about 90 minutes, the pot is uncovered and the milk begins to reduce as the sauce turns a golden brown. The coagulated lumps, spooned over the meat, are part of the prize.

—Preheat the oven to 400 degrees.

—Place the pork in a casserole that is at least 6 inches deep and cover with all of the remaining ingredients, adding enough milk to come halfway up the sides of the meat. Cover and roast for 1½ hours or until the pork is tender, turning the pork every 30 minutes and adding more milk if the pan becomes dry.

—If after 1½ hours the meat is pale and there is a lot of milk in the pan, uncover the pot and continue to cook until the milk solids form little clusters. Roast until the pork is golden brown.

—Transfer the pork to a cutting board and let rest 10 minutes. Cut into ¼- to ½-inch slices. Arrange on plates and spoon sauce over the meat.

Serves 6

2½ pounds pork loin, tied
3 tablespoons olive oil
1 tablespoon salt
Freshly ground pepper
1 tablespoon chopped fresh rosemary
1 tablespoon chopped fresh oregano
1 tablespoon tarragon
2¼ cups (or more) whole milk

SECRETS OF SUCCESS:

The milk. Braising the pork in milk gives the meat a creamy, tender texture. The milk also doubles as a sauce for the finished dish.

ASIAN-INSPIRED COQ AU VIN

In the hands of Chris Yeo, coq au vin, the French chicken stew, takes a turn toward Asia. ❊ Yeo, the chef/owner of Straits Cafe in San Francisco, opened a second location in Palo Alto in 1998. ❊ He still serves many of his favorite Singapore-inspired dishes, such as the Long Bean and Okra Sambal (see page 264), but he's branched out with even more creative combinations at the new larger location. ❊ The Asian-Inspired Coq au Vin follows the same eclectic pattern to produce a clever and innovative dish. Instead of rosemary, thyme, and other Provençal herbs, Yeo uses star anise, and he replaces some of the wine with soy sauce. Still, the recipe is straightforward and easy. It's great for a party because it cooks slowly over two hours, and can be made ahead and reheated.

½ cup dried shiitake mushrooms
1 cup boiling water
4 tablespoons vegetable oil
5 whole garlic cloves
2 star anise pieces
1 whole chicken (about 3½ pounds), cut into 4 or 8 pieces
¼ cup dark soy sauce
3 cups dry red wine
1 tablespoon sugar
½ cup shelled fresh or canned chestnuts
3 carrots, cut into 1-inch pieces
1 basket pearl onions, peeled
Salt and pepper

—Place the mushrooms in a medium bowl. Pour the boiling water over. Let stand until the mushrooms are tender, about 30 minutes. Drain.

—Heat 2 tablespoons of the oil over medium heat. Add the garlic and star anise and stir until fragrant, about 1 minute. Add the chicken pieces and soy sauce. Cook until the chicken is browned on all sides, about 8 minutes. Add the wine, sugar, chestnuts, carrots, onions, remaining 2 tablespoons of oil, and the rehydrated mushrooms. Reduce the heat to low. Cover the pan and simmer until the chicken is tender, stirring occasionally, about 1½ to 2 hours. Season to taste with salt and pepper.

Serves 4 to 6

SECRETS OF SUCCESS:

Asian flavors with French technique. The star anise, soy sauce, dried shiitake mushrooms, and chestnuts add a whole new twist to the traditional slow-cooked classic.

A slow braise. The chicken is simmered in the sauce for up to 2 hours until the chicken is tender.

Brine for Pork, Chicken, and Turkey

Leave it to Alice Waters and her crew at Chez Panisse to come up with a recipe that's so simple and so brilliant it brings out the best in chicken, pork, or turkey. They've created a brine with sugar, salt, and just a few seasonings that infuse loads of flavor into the meats. In fact, she used this brine on her Thanksgiving turkey and reports that it was marvelous. ❊ To test how well the brine worked, I cooked two chickens side by side. One had been soaked in the brine for 24 hours, the other was simply roasted. Both cavities were filled with Italian parsley, preserved lemons, and onions, and cooked in a 400-degree oven. ❊ The difference was remarkable. While the regular roasted chicken had a deeper, richer skin color, the brined chicken was plump and juicy, albeit a little anemic in color. But the flavor was amazing and it was the moistest chicken I can ever remember eating. ❊ The next day I warmed the leftovers and the regular chicken was even drier and had that typical day-old taste, but the brined chicken still tasted moist and fresh. ❊ To achieve the browned skin you'll have to leave the chicken in the oven a little longer, but the meat will still be moist. ❊ We also tried a pork roast, brined for three days, and it came out fabulous, too. The leftovers were particularly good for sandwiches the next day.

The recipe makes enough brine for a large turkey. If brining only one chicken or a pork roast, cut the recipe in half.

2½ gallons cold water
2 cups kosher salt
1 cup sugar
2 bay leaves, torn into pieces
1 bunch fresh thyme, or 4 tablespoons dried
1 whole head of garlic, peeled
5 whole allspice berries, crushed
4 juniper berries, crushed

—Place the water in a large pot that can easily hold the liquid and the meat you intend to brine.

—Add all the ingredients and stir for a minute or so until the sugar and salt dissolve.

—Refrigerate poultry in the brine for 24 hours; pork for 3 days. If the meat floats to the top, use a plate or other weight to keep it completely submerged in the brine.

—*To cook chicken:* Stuff the cavity with onions, lemon wedges, and herbs such as thyme, parsley, and rosemary. Rub the skin with oil to help browning. Sprinkle with fresh ground pepper. (Salt isn't needed because of the brine.) Cook uncovered in a 400-degree oven until done, about 1 hour and 15 minutes for a 3 ½- to 4-pound chicken.

—*To cook turkey:* Stuff the cavity with lemons, herbs, and onions, if desired. Rub the skin with oil and sprinkle with fresh ground pepper. Cook uncovered in a 400-degree oven for 12 to 15 minutes per pound until the internal temperature at the thickest part of the thigh registers at least 165 degrees.

—*To cook a boneless pork roast:* Sprinkle the roast with pepper and herbs such as sage, thyme, or tarragon, if desired. Roast uncovered in a 400-degree oven for about 12 to 15 minutes per pound or until the internal temperature reaches 150 to 160 degrees.

> **SECRETS OF SUCCESS:**
>
> *The brine.* The brine infuses flavor into pork, chicken, and turkey and makes the meat tender and succulent.

PORK CUTLETS STUFFED WITH BRAISED SAUERKRAUT

This recipe from Bruno Viscovi of Albona is inspired by the cooking of Istria, which shares influences from Austria and Hungary. Sauerkraut is an integral part of the combination, and the leftovers make a wonderful second-day meal with sausage or even grilled chicken. ✽ The jarred sauerkraut is embellished with prosciutto, onion, apple, and all kinds of seasonings. During cooking, the apples, prunes, white wine, and butter work to glaze the meat and form a sauce.

Sauerkraut
One 32-ounce jar sauerkraut, rinsed and drained
3 ounces prosciutto fat, diced
3 tablespoons peanut oil
1 tablespoon unsalted butter
1 medium onion, finely chopped
1 Pippin apple, peeled and grated
One 2-ounce slice of prosciutto, finely diced
2 bay leaves
6 whole cloves
Pinch of dried red pepper flakes
¾ cup (or more) beer
2 tablespoons chopped fresh Italian parsley

Apples and Prunes
3 Granny Smith apples
3 tablespoons fresh lemon juice
1 tablespoon unsalted butter
16 pitted prunes
1 teaspoon brown sugar
¼ teaspoon ground cinnamon
¼ teaspoon grated lemon zest
Pinch of freshly grated nutmeg

Pork
8 boneless pork cutlets, ½-inch thick
6 pitted prunes, coarsely chopped
All-purpose flour
Salt and pepper
3 tablespoons peanut oil
1½ tablespoons unsalted butter
3 fresh sage leaves
3 fresh thyme sprigs
¼ cup dry white wine
⅓ cup chicken stock, warmed
1 tablespoon finely chopped Italian parsley

—*To make the sauerkraut:* Squeeze out as much liquid as possible from the sauerkraut. Set aside.

—In a large heavy-bottomed ovenproof skillet over low heat, combine the prosciutto fat and oil and render the fat, being careful not to let the fat scorch. Discard the brown bits. Add the butter and increase the heat to medium. When the butter is melted, add the onion and sauté until golden brown, about 15 minutes. Add the apple and sauté for 2 minutes. Add the diced prosciutto, bay leaves, cloves, and red pepper flakes. Stir for 2 more minutes. Increase the heat to high. Add the sauerkraut, a little at a time, stirring constantly until all the liquid has evaporated.

—Add 5 tablespoons of beer. Cover the skillet and reduce the heat to low. Braise for about 30 minutes, adding more beer as needed to prevent scorching.

—Preheat the oven to 300 degrees.

—Uncover the skillet and discard the bay leaves and the cloves. Transfer the uncovered skillet to the oven. Bake the sauerkraut for 15 minutes to intensify flavors. Remove from the oven and stir in the parsley.

—*To make the apples and prunes:* Peel and core the apples. Slice into 24 equal wedges and immediately coat them with the lemon juice. Drain the apples and pat them dry with paper towels. Melt the butter in a large nonstick pan over medium heat. Add the apples, prunes, brown sugar, cinnamon, lemon zest, and nutmeg. Sauté until the apple slices are tender, about 5 minutes. Remove the pan from the heat. Keep in a warm place.

—*To make the pork:* Place each pork cutlet between 2 layers of plastic wrap. Pound the cutlets to ¼-inch thickness. Place 3 tablespoons of sauerkraut along the center of each cutlet. (Reserve the leftover sauerkraut for other uses.) Place the chopped prunes on top of the sauerkraut. Roll the meat, tucking in the open ends of the cutlets to seal in the stuffing. Use kitchen string to tie them so they don't unravel.

—Season the flour with salt and pepper and dredge the pork rolls in the flour mixture. Heat the oil in a large frying pan over medium-high heat. Add the pork to the skillet and brown on all sides.

—Discard the oil. Reduce the heat to low. Add 1 tablespoon of butter and the herbs. Continue to cook the pork, turning occasionally, until the internal temperature is 140 degrees, about 10 minutes.

—Transfer the meat to a platter and tent with foil. Remove the herbs from the skillet. Add the wine, and increase the heat to high. Boil until reduced by half. Add the warmed stock a little at a time.

Whisk in the remaining ½ tablespoon butter. Simmer the sauce until it's reduced slightly and takes on a velvety texture, about 3 minutes.

—Transfer the pork to warm serving plates. Pour the sauce over the top and garnish with the apples and prunes. Sprinkle with parsley.

Serves 4

SECRETS OF SUCCESS:

Pounding the pork. The cutlets should be thin enough to easily roll around the sauerkraut.

The prunes and apples. These add a sweet component to balance the sauerkraut and round out the dish.

GRILLED PORK MEDALLIONS WITH BLUE CHEESE AND POLENTA

Most people think of fruit when they think of pork. This recipe is different because it relies on savory ingredients to bring out the subtle, sweet richness of the pork tenderloin. The sauce is made with tangy Gorgonzola, creating an enticing counterpoint to the sweet meat. ❈ The first time I ran across this dish was at Antica, the charming neighborhood Italian restaurant at the corner of Polk and Union. Chef Ruggero Gadaldi has created a menu that reads like the offerings of most other Italian restaurants, but tastes worlds apart. ❈ While the restaurant is small, it's developed a Bay Area following thanks to the cooking, first-rate service, and charming interior filled with warm wood accents and an ebony-stained floor.

Pork

1 quart water

½ cup brown sugar

¼ cup pickling spices

¼ cup cider vinegar

1 carrot, coarsely chopped

1 celery stalk, coarsely chopped

½ onion, chopped

1 teaspoon kosher salt

3 whole pork tenderloins, about 1 pound each

6 bamboo skewers

Polenta

6 cups water

1 ½ teaspoons salt

1 ½ cups instant cornmeal

2 tablespoons butter

2 tablespoons grated Parmesan cheese

Garnish

1 teaspoon butter

4 ounces thinly sliced pancetta, cut into small pieces

Sauce

½ cup heavy cream

3 ounces Blue Castello or Italian Dolcelatte Gorgonzola, crumbled

Salt and pepper

Olive oil

—*To make the pork:* Bring the water to boil in a large nonreactive saucepan. Add the brown sugar, pickling spices, vinegar, carrot, celery, onion, and salt. Simmer 20 minutes. Remove from the heat and cool to room temperature.

—When the marinade is cool, cut each tenderloin into 10 medallions. Thread 5 medallions on each skewer. Place the skewers in a nonreactive container and pour on the cooled marinade. Cover and refrigerate at least 4 hours or overnight.

—*To make the polenta:* Bring the water to a boil in a large pot and stir in the salt. Add the cornmeal in a slow stream, whisking constantly. When the water returns to a boil, reduce the heat and cook until thick, about 5 to 10 minutes, stirring frequently. Stir in the butter and Parmesan. Remove from the heat. Cover to keep warm.

—*To make the garnish:* In a small pan, melt the butter over low heat. Add the pancetta and sauté until golden brown. Drain the pancetta on a paper towel.

—*To make the sauce:* Pour the cream into a small saucepan. Simmer over medium heat until slightly thickened, about 5 to 10 minutes. Add the blue cheese to the cream and stir until the cheese melts. Strain, if desired.

—Prepare a grill (medium-high heat) or preheat the broiler. Remove the skewers of pork from the marinade and pat dry. Season with salt and pepper and brush with olive oil. Grill or broil the pork to medium doneness, about 5 minutes on each side.

—*To assemble:* For each serving, place a large spoonful of polenta on the side of a heated dinner plate. Ladle some of the sauce on the other half of the plate. Remove the pork medallions from one skewer and arrange over the sauce. Sprinkle the pancetta over the pork and the polenta.

Serves 6

SECRETS OF SUCCESS:

The marinade. Allowing the pork tenderloin to steep in the slightly sweet marinade intensifies the flavor of the meat, creating a more dramatic contrast to the tangy blue cheese sauce.

The blue cheese sauce. While most chefs add fruit to pork, this sauce sets up an electrifying contrast to the sweet marinated meat.

PORK TENDERLOIN CONFIT

Confit is popular all around Gascony and the Basque region in France, where Gerald Hirigoyen grew up. But this technique of cooking and preserving food in fat was always used on duck—a relatively rich fowl—and on fatty cuts of meat. ❖ When Hirigoyen moved to California and learned a lighter style of cooking, he came up with the clever idea of making confit with a lean cut of meat—pork tenderloin. Only a little of the fat is absorbed, and the payoff is a succulent, richly textured piece of meat bursting with flavor. ❖ The tenderloin is marinated for 24 hours in garlic and herbs before it is gently cooked in lard. After cooking, it is refrigerated in the lard for up to a week before being reheated and served. ❖ The meat must be prepared ahead, but the process itself is easy. The tenderloins are perfect for a dinner party because they need only to be reheated for 10 minutes before serving. ❖ Pork Tenderloin Confit has been a specialty of Fringale since it opened to rave reviews more than seven years ago. At the restaurant, Hirigoyen serves it on braised cabbage and tops it with an onion marmalade. Preparing it at home, I've found that it's equally good served with sautéed apples. ❖ At a time when most people thought French food was on the wane, Hirigoyen created a moderately priced and exceptionally pretty brasserie the South of Market area. The modern interior, with long windows overlooking the street, helps to create a marvelous urban synergy with the chef's stylish combinations that blend French technique with his childhood traditions and his well-honed California sensibilities.

The pork is particularly good served with sautéed apples. Lard can be found in the refrigerator cases at many grocery stores. Begin this recipe at least 2 days before serving.

2 pork tenderloins (about ¾ pound each)
1 tablespoon kosher salt
1 tablespoon whole black peppercorns, crushed
4 garlic cloves, thickly sliced
2 fresh thyme sprigs
2 bay leaves
2 pounds lard
1 teaspoon minced fresh parsley for garnishing

—Place each tenderloin on a length of plastic wrap. Season with the salt, pepper, and garlic, pressing the garlic cloves onto the surface of the meat. Place a sprig of thyme and a bay leaf on top of each. Wrap each tenderloin in the plastic wrap and refrigerate for 24 hours.

—Melt the lard in a large sauté pan over medium-high heat. When the lard is very hot, add the tenderloins. Reduce heat, cover, and gently simmer until the pork is tender, about 30 to 40 minutes. Check the meat regularly; it should remain soft and white while cooking. If it begins to brown, reduce the heat.

—Transfer the tenderloins to a storage container and pour in enough fat to completely cover. Cool. Cover and refrigerate for at least 24 hours or up to 1 week.

—To serve, preheat the oven to 450 degrees.

—Bring the tenderloins to room temperature. Remove the pork from the container and scrape off the lard. Place the tenderloins in a baking dish and roast until warmed through, about 10 minutes.

—Carve the confit into ½-inch-thick slices and garnish with parsley.

Serves 4 or 5

SECRETS OF SUCCESS:

Marinating. To add an extra jolt of flavor, the meat is marinated in garlic and herbs for 24 hours before cooking.

Lard. The tenderloins are gently cooked in lard and refrigerated in the fat for up to a week before serving. The longer they sit, the better they'll be.

PORK CHOPS WITH CHERRY PEPPER RAGOUT AND GREEN OLIVE TAPENADE

Why is it that just about everybody pairs pork with fruit? At times it works, but often it feels like dessert came early. ✱ That's why the Pork Chops with Cherry Pepper Ragout and Green Olive Tapenade at Globe is so refreshingly different. After all, pork is a sweet meat, so why not pair it with something spicy? ✱ At Globe, the pork chops are browned, then baked quickly in a hot oven with the cherry peppers, so the meat picks up a dash of spiciness. Then to accentuate the positive, chef/owner Joseph Manzare tops it with a green olive tapenade. It's a wonderful interplay of tastes that, contrary to conventional wisdom, brings out the best in the meat. ✱ Manzare and partner Mary Klingbeil know how to satisfy customers. He was a chef at Spago in Los Angeles, where they met. He also won acclaim as the chef of the Royalton in New York. Little wonder that with the late night hours—the restaurant stays open until 1 A.M.—Globe attracts the after-hours chef crowd. ✱ And the ambiance is just as good. It feels kind of like a crowded speakeasy, tucked away in a 1911-era building that began life as a blacksmith shop.

Pork Chops
5 tablespoons olive oil
4 garlic cloves, smashed
1 medium white onion, diced
1 medium red onion, diced
1 red bell pepper, diced
1 green bell pepper, diced
1 yellow bell pepper, diced
12 ounces sweet cherry peppers from a jar, 1 cup liquid reserved
4 ounces sliced spicy cherry peppers from a jar, ½ cup liquid reserved
2 cups chicken stock
1 fresh thyme sprig
Four 10- to 12-ounce pork chops
Salt and pepper
Green Olive Tapenade (recipe follows)

Green Olive Tapenade
1 canned anchovy fillet, drained well
1 garlic clove
Zest of 1 lemon
4 ounces pitted green olives, pureed
½ cup olive oil
Juice of 1 lemon
Freshly ground black pepper

—*To make the pork chops:* Preheat the oven to 475 degrees.

—In a large ovenproof sauté pan, heat 4 tablespoons of the olive oil over medium-high heat. Add the garlic and cook until golden brown, about 3 minutes. Add the white and red onions and red, green, and yellow bell peppers and sauté until the onions become translucent, about 5 minutes. Add both the sweet and spicy cherry peppers and cook for another 5 minutes. Add the reserved liquid from the sweet and spicy cherry peppers along with the chicken stock and thyme. Bring to a boil, reduce the heat, and simmer until slightly reduced, about 10 minutes.

—In another large sauté pan, heat the remaining 1 tablespoon of oil over medium-high heat. Sprinkle the pork chops with salt and pepper. Add the chops to the pan and brown, about 5 minutes on each side. Place the pork atop the pepper mixture and roast in the oven until the internal temperature of the pork reaches at least 130 degrees, about 15 minutes.

—Place the pork chops on individual serving plates. Spoon pepper mixture around the chop and spoon the Green Olive Tapenade over.

Serves 4

—*To make the tapenade:* With a mortar and pestle, mash the anchovy, garlic, and lemon zest until it reaches a paste-like consistency. Stir in the olive puree, then the olive oil and lemon juice. Season to taste with black pepper.

SECRETS OF SUCCESS:

The spicing. The cherry peppers and the tapenade bring out the natural sweetness in the pork.

Searing, then roasting. The chops are first seared on top of the stove, then cooked atop the peppers in the oven to marry the flavors.

BABY BACK RIBS WITH GINGER-SOY GLAZE

For whatever reason, ribs have become one of the ultimate comfort foods. They show up at both down-home and elegant restaurants. Few rib recipes, however, pack as much flavor as Ginger Island's Baby Back Ribs with Ginger-Soy Glaze. They remind me of a day in the tropics—warming breezes, cool water, and fragrant orchids. ❋ Located in the ever-expanding Fourth Street shopping area in Berkeley, Ginger Island even has a tropic flair in the dining room decor with a retractable roof. ❋ While several chefs have come and gone at this popular restaurant, the ribs are a signature dish, and they're always great no matter who cooks them. ❋ To achieve the succulent tenderness, they're cooked three times. First they're rubbed with a five-spice mix and steamed, a technique used to produce the ribs in many Chinese restaurants. During the steaming phase the meat is brushed with a mushroom-soy glaze. Then the ribs are covered with orange juice and rice wine vinegar and baked. Finally they're put on the grill to char the outside and add a bit of smokiness. If you like, you can complete the first two steps earlier in the day, and grill them later. ❋ While still hot from the grill, the ribs are tossed with a ginger-soy glaze. They're now ready to eat: gooey, exotically flavored, and tender to the bone.

Ribs

2 racks pork baby back ribs (about 3 ½ pounds total)
3 tablespoons Five-Spice Mix (recipe follows)
Mushroom soy sauce (or dark soy sauce)
¼ cup orange juice
¼ cup rice wine vinegar
Ginger-Soy Glaze (recipe follows)

Five-Spice Mix

1 cinnamon stick (about 3 inches long)
4 pieces star anise
1 teaspoon whole cloves
1 tablespoon fennel seeds
1 tablespoon whole black peppercorns

Ginger-Soy Glaze

1 cup dark corn syrup
½ cup honey
¼ cup sugar
¼ cup fresh lemon juice
¼ cup soy sauce
2 tablespoons mushroom soy sauce or dark soy sauce
¼ cup julienned ginger
1 julienned red bell pepper

—*To cook the ribs:* Rub the ribs with the Five-Spice Mix and brush
   lightly with the mushroom soy sauce or dark soy sauce. Place the
   ribs on a rack over boiling water in a large pot. Cover and steam
   for 40 minutes, brushing occasionally with the soy sauce.
—Preheat the oven to 350 degrees.
—Transfer the ribs to a baking dish and pour on the orange juice
   and vinegar. Cover with foil and bake until the ribs are tender,
   about 35 minutes.
—Prepare a grill (medium-high heat) or preheat the broiler. Grill or
   broil the ribs until lightly charred, about 5 to 7 minutes.
—Cut between each rib and toss with the Ginger-Soy Glaze.
   Serves 4

—*To make the spice mix:* Dry toast all the ingredients in a sauté pan
   over medium heat until fragrant, about 2 minutes. Let cool slightly. Grind in a spice grinder to a medium-fine consistency.

—*To make the glaze:* Combine the corn syrup, honey, sugar, lemon
   juice, soy sauce, and mushroom soy sauce in a medium pot over
   medium-high heat. Bring to a boil, stirring until the sugar dissolves. Reduce the heat. Simmer to reduce to a thick glaze, about
   15 minutes. Remove from the heat and stir in the ginger and the
   bell pepper. Cool.

SECRETS OF SUCCESS:

The cooking method. Cooking the ribs
three times—steaming, baking, and then
grilling—imparts an incredible amount
of flavor and makes them extra tender
and juicy.

The seasonings. The five-spice powder,
mushroom soy sauce, ginger, and orange
juice give the ribs a unique character.

TAMARIND-GUAVA BARBECUED SPARERIBS

Stephen Ganner has developed one of the most interesting rib recipes I've run across, and when you see the list of ingredients, you'll know why. ✢ The ribs are first marinated overnight in Guinness stout before being baked in the marinade. Then there's the barbecue sauce that gets a unique flavor from guava jelly, tamarind, and red wine. Chipotle chiles add a smoky note. The ribs are then served with an explosive Spicy Pickled Cabbage Slaw (see page 268). ✢ Part of the reason for the far-away feel of the recipe is Ganner's background. He was born and trained in Scotland and then cooked on a cruise ship in the Caribbean before moving to Miami Beach. ✢ He hooked up with The Rooster a few years ago and found that his background was a great match for the world-inspired cuisine served at this Mission-area restaurant. ✢ The interior has a cave-like feel and the chandeliers are made from recycled and found objects such as silverware, making a cozy but very urban feeling restaurant with a clientele as eclectic as the menu.

3 pounds baby back ribs, cut into 4 equal portions
1 pint Guinness stout
Salt and pepper
2 teaspoons olive oil
2 shallots, sliced
½ cup dry red wine
1 cup guava jelly
2 cups beef or chicken stock
5 large chopped tomatoes, fresh or canned
6 fresh tamarind pods, or 4 ounces tamarind pulp
1 dried or canned chipotle chile
1 cinnamon stick
2 tablespoons apple cider vinegar

—Place the ribs in a large shallow baking pan that holds them in a single layer. Pour the Guinness over. Cover and refrigerate for at least 4 hours or preferably overnight.

—Preheat the oven to 250 degrees. Season the ribs with salt and pepper. Cover the pan tightly with foil. Bake until the meat is almost falling from the bone, about 2 hours, turning the ribs once. Remove the ribs from the pan and cool.

—Meanwhile, heat the olive oil in a large saucepan over medium heat. Add the shallots and sauté until golden brown, about 10 minutes. Add the red wine and reduce until a tablespoon of liquid remains, about 5 minutes. Stir in the guava jelly, stock, tomatoes, tamarind, chipotle, and cinnamon stick. Bring the mixture to a boil, stirring until the jelly melts.

—Reduce the heat to low and simmer 1 hour to blend flavors and thicken. Strain the sauce through a fine sieve. Stir in the vinegar. Season to taste with salt and pepper.

—Prepare the grill (medium-high heat). Brush the ribs liberally with the barbecue sauce. Either grill or alternately cook in a sauté pan until warm, turning frequently and basting occasionally with the sauce, about 6 minutes.

—Transfer the ribs to a platter and serve.

Serves 4

Note: *The tamarind pods, chipotle chile, and guava jelly can be found at most Latin and some specialty food markets.*

SECRETS OF SUCCESS:

The Guinness. Marinating the ribs in the dark beer helps to tenderize and add flavor to the meat.

Double cooking. After the ribs are slow-cooked in a 250-degree oven with beer, they're covered with the sauce and grilled.

The sweet and acidic balance. The apple cider vinegar stirred into the sauce at the end of cooking adds a tangy element to balance the sweet guava jelly and to soften the smokiness of the chipotle.

TIBETAN LAMB STEW WITH DAIKON

Tibetan Lamb Stew with Daikon is a fine introduction to Lhasa Moon, the Bay Area's only Tibetan restaurant. Versions of this dish are popular all over that arid, mountainous country. In fact many travelers carry this stew with them on their long arduous journeys. ✳ But this version, interpreted by owner Tsering Wangmo, should be reserved for a special dinner at home because the preparation is more complicated. ✳ The stew is given an earthy zest with daikon, a giant radish, which takes on a soft juicy quality when cooked. The main flavorings come from ginger, caramelized onions, garlic, and Sichuan-style pepper. ✳ If you like, you can enjoy the dish as a simple stew, which gets even better after a night in the refrigerator. For company fare, the daikon and lamb are removed from the broth and sautéed with additional onion and tomatoes. Then just enough broth is added back to cover. The sauce is reduced and greens such as spinach are added to the mix. ✳ The service can be slow at Lhasa Moon, but the attitude is warm and caring. The interior is simple and comfortable with a leaf-patterned carpet, dark green tablecloths, and windows overlooking Lombard Street. It adds up to a pleasant environment for exploring this rustic cuisine.

1 pound lamb shank

2 pounds daikon, cut into 2-inch-thick slices

1 large onion, quartered

3 inches fresh ginger, crushed

5 garlic cloves, peeled

¼ teaspoon ground emma or Sichuan pepper

Salt

1 tablespoon oil

1 onion, finely chopped

½ teaspoon paprika

1 medium tomato, chopped

½ to 1 bunch spinach fresh leaves, chopped

—Place the lamb in a large casserole pan. Add the daikon, quartered
onion, ginger, garlic, and emma. Add enough cold water to cover.
Bring to a boil. Reduce the heat to low and simmer until the
daikon is soft and translucent, about 1½ hours. Season to taste
with salt. Remove the lamb and the daikon from the liquid, reserving the liquid. Remove the lamb meat from the bone. Cut the
lamb into 1-inch cubes. Cut daikon into 1-inch cubes. Set aside.
—In a large saucepan, heat the oil over high heat. Add the chopped
onion and sauté until golden brown, about 5 minutes. Add the
paprika and stir to mix, about 30 seconds. Add the tomato. Add
the reserved lamb and daikon, and enough cooking liquid to cover.
Bring to a boil and reduce the broth slightly, about 10 to 15 minutes. Reduce the heat and add the spinach. Cover and steam until
the greens are just wilted, about 2 to 3 minutes.
—Serve immediately.

Serves 4

SECRETS OF SUCCESS:

The daikon. This peppery radish retains
its shape and texture, adding a refreshing juiciness to the stew.

A second cooking. After being stewed, the
lamb and daikon are sautéed with an
additional onion to intensify the blend.

SLOW-ROASTED LAMB SHANKS WITH ROASTED ROOT VEGETABLES

Lamb shanks are one of the most popular dishes in Bay Area restaurants these days, but none are better than those produced by David Kinch at Sent Sovi Restaurant in Saratoga. ❊ They come out of the kitchen with a wonderful luster that resembles polished mahogany. The moist, rich meat is infused with flavor and literally falls off the bone. The shanks are served with a melange of roasted root vegetables—carrots, potatoes, parsnips, and turnips—making this an ideal cool-weather combination. This dish is also great for company because the meat can be prepared ahead and gently reheated just before serving. ❊ While the dish is earthy and delicious, Kinch is a refined, sophisticated cook. The chef's charming, unpretentious restaurant seats only forty people and has a homey, French country feel. He opened Sent Sovi with partner Aimee Hebert in 1995 after stints as executive chef at Silks and Ernie's. ❊ Clearly, Kinch is one of the best chefs in the Bay Area. If you don't believe it, try the lamb shanks.

Lamb

6 lamb shanks, about 14 ounces each
Salt and pepper
¼ cup olive oil
2 celery ribs, thinly sliced
1 onion, cut into large dice
1 large turnip, cut into large dice
1 carrot
1 whole head of garlic, halved horizontally
1 bunch fresh thyme
1 fresh rosemary sprig
1 teaspoon fennel seeds
1 teaspoon coriander seeds
1 tablespoon whole black peppercorns
1 bay leaf
3 fresh parsley sprigs
1 bottle (750 ml) dry white wine
1 quart (or more) water, chicken broth, or lamb stock
Roasted Root Vegetables (recipe follows)
Chopped fresh parsley for garnishing (optional)

Roasted Root Vegetables

1 large celery root, peeled and cut into bite-sized pieces
6 small turnips, peeled and cut into bite-sized pieces
6 medium parsnips, peeled and cut into bite-sized pieces
6 baby carrots
6 fingerling potatoes
2 tablespoons olive oil
1 teaspoon chopped fresh thyme leaves
Sea salt or kosher salt
Splash of water

—*To cook the lamb:* Preheat the oven to 475 degrees.

—Rub the shanks with salt and pepper and place them meaty side up in a roasting pan. Roast for 25 minutes, or until nicely browned. Remove from the oven.

—Reduce the oven temperature to 250 degrees.

—Heat the olive oil in a large sauté pan over medium-high heat. Add the celery, onion, turnip, carrot, and garlic and sauté, stirring occasionally, until the vegetables soften and caramelize, about 15 minutes.

—Stir in the thyme, rosemary, fennel seeds, coriander seeds, peppercorns, bay leaf, and parsley sprigs. Increase the heat to high, add the wine, and deglaze the pan, scraping up all the browned bits from the bottom of the pan. Boil until the liquid has reduced by a third, about 10 to 15 minutes.

—Pour the mixture over the lamb in the roasting pan, spreading the vegetables on top, but not completely covering the shanks. Add enough water, chicken broth, or lamb stock to almost cover the meat. Cover the pan with aluminum foil and roast until the lamb is almost fork tender, about 6½ hours, basting with the pan juices every hour and adding more water or stock if needed.

—Remove the foil and continue to roast until the lamb is falling off the bone, about 30 minutes. Transfer the shanks to a platter and cool to room temperature. Strain the braising liquid and skim off the fat.

—When ready to serve, slowly reheat the shanks in the braising liquid.

—Portion the Roasted Root Vegetables onto six plates, center a lamb shank on each portion, and spoon a little of the braising liquid over the top. Garnish with chopped parsley, if desired.
Serves 6

—*To cook the vegetables:* Preheat the oven to 375 degrees.

—Place the vegetables in a large roasting pan. Add the olive oil; toss until the vegetables are coated. Sprinkle with the thyme and salt; toss again. Splash with water. Cover with foil and roast 30 minutes.

—Uncover and roast until the potatoes are tender and the vegetables begin to brown slightly, about 30 minutes.
Serves 6

> **SECRETS OF SUCCESS:**
>
> *Long, slow cooking.* The lamb shanks come out richly flavored and fork-tender because of the long braising time (7 hours) in a low-temperature oven (250 degrees).
>
> *Making ahead.* The lamb is an ideal dish for entertaining because it's best when made the day before and reheated slowly in the braising juices.

LAMB SKEWERS WITH SPICY YOGURT DRESSING

Sometimes the best recipes also have the most interesting stories. The Lamb Skewers with Spicy Yogurt Dressing from Oberon are based on a family recipe given to owner and host Zoran Matulic by his mother, who lives in the coastal town of Split in what is now Croatia. ❖ This recipe has it all: The lamb skewers are easy to assemble ahead and are perfect for outdoor grilling. The ground lamb mixture is stirred together the day before and allowed to rest. The chile-mint yogurt sauce can also be made ahead to blend the flavors, or it can be made at the last minute, depending on the cook's schedule. ❖ When it's time to serve, the host only needs to form the meat into logs, thread the skewers, and quickly cook the meat. The combination of sweet onions, scallions, and garlic bring out a sweet intensity in the lamb. ❖ This is one of the best dishes served at Oberon, which has accents of Middle Eastern, French, and Italian cooking. Matulic had been the "front man" at many of the city's best restaurants before going out on his own at Oberon. He's a consummate host, and the restaurant has become popular for those who want to have dinner in a comfortable, pampering place suitable for quiet conversation. And prices are moderate, which makes it a prime neighborhood destination.

Lamb

1 tablespoon olive oil

2 medium yellow onions, finely diced (about 1 ½ cups)

1 pound ground lamb

2 scallions (white part only), minced

2 garlic cloves, minced

1 tablespoon minced fresh mint

1 ½ teaspoons salt

½ teaspoon ground pepper

16 six-inch wooden skewers

1 cup Spicy Yogurt Dressing (recipe follows)

Spicy Yogurt Dressing

2 cups plain yogurt

½ teaspoon cayenne pepper

1 tablespoon finely chopped fresh mint

Salt and pepper

—*To cook the lamb:* The day before serving, heat the olive oil in a sauté pan over low heat. Add the onions and cook slowly until translucent, about 30 minutes. Drain any excess oil.

—Break the ground lamb up into a bowl. Add the onions, scallions, garlic, mint, salt, and pepper. Mix well. Cover and refrigerate overnight.

—When ready to serve, soak 16 six-inch wooden skewers in water for 30 minutes. (This helps prevent the skewers from burning on the grill.) Preheat a grill (high heat).

—Divide the lamb mixture into 16 equal pieces. Shape each piece into a 1-inch diameter log, approximately 3-inches long. Thread each piece lengthwise onto a skewer.

—Grill lamb to medium rare, turning once, about 5 minutes. Serve with Spicy Yogurt Dressing.

Serves 4

—*To make the dressing:* Mix the yogurt, cayenne, and mint in a small bowl. Season to taste with salt and pepper. Serve at room temperature with the lamb skewers.

SECRETS OF SUCCESS:

Sweating the onions. Cooking the onions slowly over low heat produces a rounded sweetness.

Overnight marinating. Letting the ground lamb and onion mixture rest overnight infuses flavor throughout the meat.

Fire and ice. The combination of hot cayenne and cooling mint lends a dramatic note to the yogurt dipping sauce.

LAMB CHOPS MILANESE

If you want the most authentic Italian food, you don't need to go to Italy. Instead go to Oakland, where Paul Bertolli, who was the chef at Chez Panisse for more than a decade, has transformed Oliveto into one of the best Italian restaurants in the United States. ✶ The Lamb Chops Milanese is an interpretation of a dish normally made with veal. The double chop is pounded and then breaded in egg, flour, and bread crumbs before being quickly fried in olive oil to a crisp crunch. ✶ Few dishes are quite as simple or as delicious. Bertolli is so pure in his views on food that he makes most of his own products, including prosciutto, sausage, pasta, and even balsamic vinegar. His meats are equally without pretense, cooked on a spit and simply served with natural juices. ✶ Oliveto is a modern restaurant, with the feel of a loft, recently updated to better suit his lusty cuisine.

8 double lamb chops (about 4 ounces each)
Salt and freshly ground pepper
2 eggs, beaten to blend
¼ cup all-purpose flour
1 cup coarse, fresh sourdough bread crumbs with crusts
Olive oil for cooking
8 anchovy fillets, packed in oil, drained and halved lengthwise
Lemon wedges for garnishing

—Remove one of the bones from each chop and all surrounding silver tendon. Place a piece of plastic wrap over each chop. Using a meat mallet, gently pound the chops, keeping the remaining bone intact, to a thickness of about ¼-inch. Salt and pepper both sides of the lamb and let stand 10 minutes.

—Dip each chop into the eggs, then lightly in the flour, and then into the bread crumbs, coating the meat well on all sides.

—Pour olive oil to a depth of ¼ inch up the sides of a large heavy skillet. Heat over high heat. Toss a few bread crumbs into the oil. If it's hot enough they will sizzle and brown. Working in batches, add the chops and fry to a deep crusty brown on both sides and medium-rare in the middle, about 5 to 7 minutes.

—Transfer cooked chops to paper towels to drain and then to a warm oven until all are cooked.

—Place 2 chops on each of four dinner plates. Top each with an anchovy piece and serve with lemon wedges.

Serves 4

> **SECRETS OF SUCCESS:**
>
> *The breading.* The progression of dipping the lamb first into the beaten egg, then into flour and bread crumbs results in a very crisp crust that seals in the juices.
>
> *The lemon.* Never under estimate the power of this ingredient in adding a finishing touch to the lamb.

Minute Steak

After more than fifty years in the same location on Broadway, Alfred's moved to a new Financial District location that once housed the equally famous Blue Fox. ❊ While it got a new upscale décor—deep-red accents and crystal chandeliers—the food has remained much the same. The restaurant still serves one of the best steaks in the city. ❊ Alfred's uses a mesquite grill for its signature cuts, but one of my favorite dishes is the minute steak, which is quickly pan-grilled. It can be done in only a few minutes on a home stove by pounding the tenderloin to about a 3⁄8-inch thickness. ❊ Of course, the name is a bit of a misnomer, at least for the at-home cook. It really needs about a minute on each side. I guess we could call it the two-minute steak, but it doesn't quite have the same cachet, does it? ❊ Still, it's one of those last-minute dishes that can be prepared in a flash. You can marinate the steak in the olive oil, salt, and pepper while you change clothes or open a bottle of wine. ❊ The most time-consuming chore is heating up the cast-iron grill pan, which will take a good ten minutes to get as hot as possible. After a minute on each side, the steak comes out with perfect crusty grill marks outside and a succulent pink interior. ❊ It's so effortless that it's perfect for a special dinner for two. Just add some roasted potatoes and a steamed vegetable, and you can clink your wineglass over one of the best meals around.

2 filet mignons, 8 ounces each
3 tablespoons olive oil
2 garlic cloves, minced
½ teaspoon freshly ground black pepper
Salt

—Pound the filets to about ⅜-inch thickness.

—Combine the olive oil, garlic, and pepper in a shallow container large enough to hold the meat in a single layer. Place the meat in the container and turn to coat with the marinade. Let marinate until ready to cook, from 10 minutes up to several hours.

—Heat a cast-iron grill pan over high heat until very hot. This will take about 10 minutes. Place the meat in the hot pan and generously salt the top. Grill for 1 minute, turn the meat over, and season the other side with salt. Cook 1 minute longer. The meat will still be bright pink in the center.

—If grilling one filet at a time, place the finished steak in a warm oven while cooking the second.

Serves 2

SECRETS OF SUCCESS:

Pounding the meat. This increases the grill surface so the meat cooks quicker and has a more concentrated, caramelized flavor.

Coating with oil. Marinating the meat with oil and garlic adds flavor and allows for more uniform browning without burning.

TERRORIZED STEAK

Reed Hearon, chef/owner of Rose Pistola, isn't joking when he uses the term "terrorized" to describe his steak. ❉ The marinade is loaded with seasonings that, on first glance, seem excessive: ⅓ cup dried red chile flakes, ¼ cup black pepper, and a whole cup of rosemary. But this form of excess produces an amazing flavor. ❉ It's "terrorized" a second time by using high heat to produce a smoky char. Then when nearly done, Hearon removes the steak from the heat for 10 minutes or so before returning it to the grill for the final cooking. That too makes a big difference because it allows the heat to distribute evenly throughout the steak, creating a uniformly pink center. ❉ The steak emerges from the fire crusty outside and juicy inside. It's then topped with a compound butter and served with a refreshing watercress salad. ❉ Hearon has many tricks up his sleeve, which is why Rose Pistola is one of the best Italian restaurants in the Bay Area for both food and ambiance. The open kitchen is equipped with four fireplaces for grilling, roasting, and braising dishes. The tile floor, stylish lights, and black-and-white photographs on the walls makes this a grand stage for the Ligurian-inspired Italian food.

Steaks

1 cup fresh rosemary leaves, chopped
½ cup chopped fresh marjoram
½ cup garlic cloves, finely chopped
⅓ cup dried red pepper flakes
¼ cup salt
¼ cup ground black pepper, plus additional for seasoning
1½ cups olive oil
6 New York steaks
6 tablespoons Compound Butter (recipe follows)

Salad

1½ teaspoons fresh lemon juice
Pinch salt
¼ cup extra-virgin olive oil
1 to 2 bunches watercress (enough for 6 small salads)

6 lemon wedges for garnishing

Compound butter

Leftover butter can be stored in the freezer and tossed in hot noodles as a side dish, used as a topping on grilled or sautéed meats, or spread on bread before cooking or grilling.

3 canned anchovy fillets, drained
2 small garlic cloves
Zest of 1 lemon
½ teaspoon salt
½ teaspoon ground black pepper
½ cup (1 stick) unsalted butter at room temperature
½ bunch chives, minced

—*To make the steaks:* Combine the rosemary, marjoram, garlic, dried red pepper, salt, and ¼ cup pepper in a medium bowl. Stir in the olive oil.

—Place the steaks in a pan large enough to hold them in a single layer and pour the marinade over, turning several times so the steaks are well covered. Marinate for at least 2 hours or overnight.

—Preheat the grill (high heat). Rub off the excess marinade from the steaks. Season lightly with fresh pepper. Cook until almost cooked to the desired doneness, about 4 minutes per side for medium-rare. Transfer the steaks to a platter and let stand for 10 to 20 minutes. Return to the hot grill and finish cooking, about 1 to 2 minutes more.

—(Alternatively, the steaks can be cooked indoors on a grill pan, in a skillet, or in a broiler using the same resting time.)

—Transfer the steaks to individual plates, and top each steak with a pat of the Compound Butter.
Serves 6

—*To make the salad:* Whisk the lemon juice and salt together in a small bowl to dissolve. Gradually whisk in the olive oil. Set aside.

—Drizzle the dressing over the watercress; toss to coat. Place alongside the steaks. Serve with lemon wedges.
Serves 6

—*To make the compound butter:* Use a mortar and pestle to pound together the anchovies, garlic, lemon zest, salt, and pepper. When smooth, transfer to a small bowl and stir in the softened butter and chives. Form into a log and refrigerate or freeze until firm.

SECRETS OF SUCCESS:

Lots of spice. The marinade seems excessive but it imparts a powerful jolt to the meat.

Resting the steak. The beef is cooked almost until done and then removed from the heat, which allows the juices to redistribute. Then it's returned to the grill, which produces a crusty exterior and an evenly pink and moist interior.

The compound butter. The melting butter softens and finishes the dish.

S E A R E D   B L A C K   P E P P E R – L A V E N D E R   F I L E T   O F   B E E F

It's a marvelous triad—beef, lavender, and black pepper. But it took John McReynolds at Cafe La Haye to bring it to everyone's attention. Most people might not even recognize the taste of lavender when it's pressed into a filet mignon and seared, but it brings out a hidden sweetness in this lean, tender cut. ❋ This charming restaurant is one of the most exciting to open in Sonoma in the last several years. That says a lot considering that this thirty-two-seat cafe, located just off the square, is so small and unassuming. ❋ From the beginning courses—organic greens with blue cheese, beets, and spiced walnuts, and house-smoked salmon on warm potato cakes—to the Meyer lemon cheesecake for dessert, the American-inspired food is enticing. ❋ The open kitchen is about the size of a postage stamp, carved out of one corner of the two-tiered interior. ❋ McReynolds and partner Saul Gropman, who handles the front of the house, make a great team. Not only is the food excellent, but the service is smooth and seamless, and the prices are moderate.

Filet of Beef

6 filet mignon steaks, each 1½ inches thick and 8
    ounces
Salt
1 tablespoon whole dried lavender blossoms
1 tablespoon coarsely ground fresh black pepper
    (preferably black telicherry)
1 tablespoon unsalted butter
3 tablespoons olive oil
Red wine butter (recipe follows)
Gorgonzola-Potato Gratin (see page 254)

Red Wine Butter

The recipe can be halved if desired. Leftover butter can be frozen and used to sauce pasta, season vegetables, or melt atop grilled or sautéed meats.

1 tablespoon olive oil
1 pound chuck or stewing beef, cut into cubes
Salt and pepper
1 yellow onion, chopped
1 carrot, chopped
1 celery stalk, chopped
1 garlic clove, smashed
1 fresh thyme sprig
1 bay leaf
1 tablespoon tomato paste
1 bottle (750 ml) dry red wine
1 cup (2 sticks) butter at room temperature

—*To cook the beef:* Preheat the oven to 400 degrees.

—Season both sides of each steak with salt. Mix together the lavender and pepper and press the mixture into both sides of the steaks.

—Melt the butter with the oil in a large cast-iron frying pan over high heat. Add the steaks and fry about 2 minutes on each side. Transfer the pan to the oven and roast to desired doneness, about 5 minutes for medium rare. Transfer the steaks to a heated plate and let rest 2 to 3 minutes.

—Top each portion with a pat of Red Wine Butter. Serve with Gorgonzola-Potato Gratin.

Serves 6

—*To make the red wine butter:* Heat the oil in a large heavy-bottomed pan over medium heat. Working in batches, season the meat with salt and pepper and add to the pan. Brown well on all sides. Transfer the meat to a plate when done with each batch. Add the onion, carrot, and celery and cook until just beginning to caramelize, about 10 minutes. Add the garlic, thyme, bay leaf, tomato paste, and wine. Return the meat to the pan and cook over medium heat until the liquid is reduced by three-quarters, about 1 hour.

—Pass the mixture through a food mill. Mix in the butter by hand or in a food processor. Shape into logs and chill or freeze until ready to use.

Makes about 2 cups

SECRETS OF SUCCESS:

Lavender and black pepper crust. The spiciness of the pepper and the herbal qualities of the lavender bring out a rich sweetness in the filet mignon.

The red wine butter. Through intense reduction, the butter is packed with flavor and tames any rough edges of the bold seasonings.

FLATIRON POT ROAST WITH A STEW OF VEGETABLES

Universal Cafe is known as a trendy, industrial-chic restaurant for the oh-so-cool set. Interestingly, one of the most popular items on the menu is the pot roast. It seems that as people turn away from cooking at home they crave comfort food in restaurants. ✳ Julia McClaskey, the chef who created the dish but has since left the restaurant, updated this classic by using flatiron steak and a red wine sauce, but the flavors are as homey as a Midwestern Sunday supper. ✳ When the meat is almost done, the chef tosses in parboiled carrots, parsnips, and fava beans and cooks them until they're just tender. ✳ In the restaurant, the dish is served with mashed potatoes flavored with chives, but at home you can save time by adding partly cooked potatoes with the other vegetables for a sat-

isfying one-pot meal. ✳ Flatiron steak is a lean cut that's not always available in the self-service case at most grocery stores. However, you can call ahead and have the butcher set one aside for you. ✳ If you're preparing the roast for a dinner party, the meat can be cooked ahead, sliced, and gently re-warmed in the juices.

Salt and freshly ground black pepper
2 flatiron steaks, about 2½ pounds each
2 tablespoons olive oil
2 carrots, coarsely chopped
2 celery stalks, coarsely chopped
2 leeks, washed and coarsely chopped (white and
   tender part of green only)
1 yellow onion, coarsely chopped
4 garlic cloves, minced
1½ cups dry white wine
4 cups (or more) unsalted chicken stock, preferably homemade
1 can (14 ½ ounces) chopped tomatoes, drained
1 bunch fresh thyme
2 tablespoons whole black peppercorns
2 cups 4 x ½-inch carrot sticks
2 cups peeled, chopped parsnips
2 cups peeled pearl onions
1 cup fresh fava beans, skins removed

—Preheat the oven to 350 degrees. Generously salt and pepper the entire surface of the steaks. Heat the oil over high heat in a Dutch oven or deep ovenproof skillet just large enough to hold the meat in a single layer. When the oil is very hot but not smoking, add the meat and sear on all sides to form a crust. Transfer the meat to a platter, leaving the juices in the pan.

—Reduce the heat to medium-high and add the chopped carrots, celery, leeks, onion, and garlic. Cook until the vegetables look slightly dry and are browned but not scorched, about 8 minutes. Add the wine and simmer 2 minutes. Add 4 cups of stock, the canned tomatoes, thyme, and peppercorns. Bring to a boil, then carefully return the meat to the pot.

—Bring to a boil again, making sure there is enough liquid to completely submerge the meat; if not, add more chicken stock to cover. When the liquid boils, cover the pot and place it in the oven. Bake until the meat is fork tender but not falling apart, about 2 to 3 hours.

—Meanwhile bring a large pot of salted water to a boil. Add the carrot sticks and cook until almost tender. Using a slotted spoon, transfer the carrots to a colander. Rinse under cold water to stop the cooking and set the color. Repeat with the parsnips, pearl onions, and fava beans, cooking each separately. Drain the vegetables well. Set aside.

—Transfer the meat to a platter; tent with foil to keep warm. Strain the cooking juices into a large saucepan and skim the fat from the surface of the juices, if desired. Adjust the seasonings with additional salt and pepper, if necessary.

—Add the parboiled vegetables to the juices and simmer over medium heat until tender, about 10 to 15 minutes. Carve the meat into long ½-inch-thick slices.

—Arrange on a platter and spoon the vegetables around the meat. Spoon some of the pan juices over the top.

Serves 8

> **SECRETS OF SUCCESS:**
>
> *The cut.* The flatiron steak is leaner and easier to handle than more traditional cuts used for pot roasts.
>
> *Browning the meat.* Searing the meat in a hot skillet not only produces a crusty caramelized exterior, but it helps to seal in the juices.
>
> *Adding the vegetables.* Finishing the parsnips, fava beans, and carrots in the rich wine broth flavors both the natural juices and vegetables.

SPANISH-STYLE SHORT RIBS

With chocolate, orange, and sherry you might think that Heidi Krahling was making dessert rather than a main course. But when the meaty short ribs come out of the oven after three hours, they're rich, juicy, and absolutely delicious. ✳ Krahling, who owns Insalata's restaurant in San Anselmo, has a homey rustic style that draws inspiration from Spain, France, the Mediterranean, and the Middle East. ✳ The ribs have lineage to the Catalan region in Spain. The meat is browned in oil and removed from the pan, being replaced by onions, carrots, celery, and garlic. After the vegetables are well caramelized, red wine is added and reduced over high heat. Finally the ribs are returned to the pan and baked in a 300-degree oven for three hours or more. ✳ By that point the wine sauce is already bursting with flavor. But even more character is added with chocolate, sherry, fresh herbs, and the zest of two oranges. These additions create a wonderful, aromatic sauce that coats the meat. ✳ Although the recipe calls for homemade beef stock, there's so much going on that if you cheat and use the canned variety, I'm not sure even Krahling would know the difference. ✳ The restaurant, which also has a carry-out counter where you can pick up some of the popular dishes to take home, has become one of the best places for a great meal in Marin County. The expansive space, dominated by the open kitchen, has an upscale but relaxed ambiance.

The ribs are terrific with mashed potatoes, potato gratins, or simple roasted red-skinned potatoes.

3 tablespoons olive oil
Salt and pepper
5 to 5 ½ pounds short ribs of beef (2½ inches wide)
2 medium yellow onions, quartered, each quarter halved
1 celery rib, cut into 1-inch pieces
1 carrot, cut into 1-inch pieces
2 garlic cloves, smashed
2 cups dry red wine
One 14½ ounce can whole plum tomatoes with juices, chopped
½ cup tomato paste
1 fresh thyme sprig
12 cups beef stock
2 cups dry sherry
3 tablespoons chopped unsweetened chocolate
1 tablespoon chopped fresh thyme
1½ teaspoons chopped fresh marjoram
Zest of 2 oranges
2 tablespoons butter

—Preheat the oven to 300 degrees.

—In a heavy-bottomed casserole, heat the olive oil over medium-high heat. Generously salt and pepper the ribs. Add the ribs to the casserole and cook until brown on all sides, about 10 minutes.

—Transfer the ribs to a platter. Add the onions, celery, carrot, and garlic to the casserole and sauté until caramelized, about 5 minutes. Add the red wine. Increase the heat to high and boil until the liquid is reduced by half. Add the tomatoes with juices, tomato paste, and thyme sprig. Stir to combine. Return the ribs to the pan. Add the stock. Bring to a boil. Cover and bake in the oven until the meat pulls easily away from the bone, about 3 hours.

—Transfer the ribs to a clean platter. Strain the pan juices. Return the juices to the casserole. Add the sherry and simmer over medium-high heat until reduced by a third, about 15 minutes. Stir in the chocolate, chopped thyme, marjoram, orange zest, and butter. Season to taste with salt and pepper.

—Return the ribs to the pan and simmer 2 minutes to rewarm.

Serves 6

SECRETS OF SUCCESS:

The sauce. Most recipes would consider the red wine sauce used for cooking the ribs as good enough, but in this recipe the sauce is further enlivened with the addition of unsweetened chocolate, orange zest, and sherry.

Oven baking. Cooking the ribs slowly for three hours infuses them with flavor and makes them exceptionally tender.

Braised Short Ribs with Pureed Potatoes and Madeira Truffle Sauce

I first encountered the braised short ribs with truffles and Madeira sauce at Campton Place, the restaurant that launched the careers of Bradley Ogden, Jan Birnbaum, and now Todd Humphries. ❊ Humphries left in 1999 to become executive chef of the floundering Wine Spectator Greystone Restaurant in St. Helena. He also took his signature recipe with him. No matter where it goes, it's a must-order item. ❊ The Madeira gives fork-tender ribs a hint of sweetness balanced by the earthiness of truffles. Since truffles are expensive and not readily available to the home cook, you can leave them out or substitute 3 or 4 finely diced shiitake mushrooms, or a spoonful of white truffle oil at the last minute. ❊ The rich, aromatic dish is served with creamy mashed potatoes whipped with lots of butter and cream. If you're like me, you won't be able to stop eating them. ❊ The delicious short ribs fit nicely into the menu at this impressive, casual restaurant that's run by the Culinary Institute of America in the historic stone building. With an open kitchen in the middle and an expansive loft-like feel, the restaurant is a popular stop for people visiting Napa Valley. Since it's located on a hill, the terrace in front offers a sweeping view of the valley.

Short Ribs

¼ cup vegetable oil
12 beef short ribs, bone in
Salt and pepper
1 onion, chopped
1 celery stalk, roughly chopped
1 carrot, roughly chopped
1 bottle (750 ml) ruby port
1½ quarts veal stock
Potato Puree (recipe follows)
Madeira Truffle Sauce (recipe follows)
Fresh chervil sprigs for garnishing

Madeira Truffle Sauce

This sauce takes a while to reduce in stages, but it can be made a day ahead and reheated.

2 tablespoons butter
1 shallot, minced
1 winter truffle, fresh or frozen, finely chopped, or 3 or 4 finely chopped fresh shiitake mushrooms, or 1 teaspoon truffle oil
Salt and pepper
2 cups Madeira
2 cups chicken stock
2 cups veal stock

Potato Puree

3 medium-sized russet potatoes, peeled
¾ cup heavy cream
½ cup (1 stick) butter, cut into small pieces
Salt and ground white pepper

—*To cook the ribs:* Preheat the oven to 350 degrees. In a large Dutch oven, heat the oil over medium-high heat. Season the short ribs with salt and pepper. Add to the pan and brown on all sides, about 10 minutes. Transfer the ribs to a platter. Add the onion, celery, and carrot to the pan over medium-high heat and sauté until slightly brown, about 8 minutes.

—Drain excess fat from the pan. Add the port and bring to a boil. Reduce the port by three-quarters, about 30 minutes. Return the ribs to the pan and add the veal stock. Add water if needed to completely cover the ribs.

—Bring to a boil. Cover and bake in the oven until the ribs are tender, about 2 to 2½ hours.

—Cool to room temperature. Refrigerate the ribs in the braising liquid overnight in the refrigerator.

—Preheat the oven to 350 degrees.

—Place the pan with the chilled ribs on top of the stove over high heat. Bring to a boil. Cover and place in the oven for 10 minutes more to warm through. Transfer the ribs to a platter, tent with foil, and keep warm.

—Place the pan on top of the stove over high heat. Bring to a boil and reduce the juices to a glaze consistency, about 30 minutes.

—Place a spoonful of the Potato Puree in the center of each of 6 dinner plates. Make a well in the center of the potatoes. Place 2 short ribs in the well. Pour Madeira Truffle Sauce on the short ribs and garnish with chervil.

Serves 6

—*To make the sauce:* Melt the butter in a medium saucepan over medium-high heat for 2 minutes. Add the shallot and chopped truffles or shiitake mushrooms. Season with salt and pepper. Add the Madeira. Bring to a boil and reduce until almost all the liquid has evaporated, about 15 to 20 minutes. Add the chicken stock and boil until the sauce is reduced to a syrupy consistency, about 15 to 20 minutes. Add the veal stock and reduce the sauce by half, about 10 to 15 minutes. (If using truffle oil instead of the truffle or mushrooms, add it here.) Season to taste with salt and pepper.

—*To make the puree:* Cook the potatoes in a large pot of boiling salted water until tender, about 45 minutes. Drain. Cut the potatoes into eighths and run through a food mill. Transfer the potatoes to a medium saucepan.

—Bring the cream just to a simmer in a small saucepan. Add the warm cream and the butter to the potatoes. Mix well and season to taste with salt and pepper.

SECRETS OF SUCCESS:

An overnight rest. The meat acts like a sponge and soaks up the aromatic braising juices when allowed to sit overnight in the refrigerator.

Reduce. Reduce. Reduce. Reducing first the Madeira, then the chicken stock, and finally the veal stock is a way to add complexity and intensity to the sauce.

Glazing the meat. The cooking liquid is used as a glaze for the meat, adding even more punch to the ribs.

THE BEST HAMBURGER

In the race for best hamburger there's really no competition—Zuni always comes out on top. For one it's served on focaccia with pickled zucchini, red onions, and aioli. But in reality what makes it so great is the meat. I've never tasted a burger that has a better consistency or better flavor. And yes, there's a secret that's so simple but so important in making the burger: Salt. ❋ Chef/owner Judy Rodgers is an amazing cook, which is why this restaurant is a perennial favorite with locals. Other chefs would love to have her complaint: that most customers come again and again for the hamburger and never bother with her specials. ❋ The look of Zuni can't be replicated, it just happened. As the restaurant expanded and took over adjoining storefronts, it created a warren of dining rooms, a strange configuration that works beautifully. ❋ There's something about the food and the mood set here that makes you want to come back. It also attracts the most eclectic crowd: Politicians, celebrities, drag queens, and everything in between.

One 2½ pound piece of chuck, well marbled with fat
½ tablespoon fine sea salt

—Trim the meat of any discoloration, but do not trim any fat. Cut the meat into long thick pieces (or "ropes"). Place the meat in a large bowl and toss it with the sea salt. Cover and refrigerate overnight.

—Up to 5 or 6 hours before cooking, set up a meat grinder with $^3/_{16}$-inch holes. Grind the meat twice. Shape the ground meat into thick, ½-pound patties, taking care not to warm the meat in your hands. Refrigerate until ready to cook.

—Cook on top of the stove, or grill over medium-high heat to medium rare.

Serves 5

SECRETS OF SUCCESS:

Choosing the meat. Use only chuck, which has a good proportion of lean to fat. You want about 18 percent fat.

Salting the meat. After cutting the meat into strips, it's salted and allowed to sit overnight. The meat comes out moist and delicious, disproving the adage that salting before cooking makes meat dry.

Grinding the meat. It's coarse ground twice so that the texture is tender and the salt is distributed throughout the patty, not just sprinkled on top.

CALF'S LIVER WITH CARAMELIZED APPLES AND ONIONS

Just about anyone would love liver with all the bells and whistles Cindy Pawlcyn adds to it: tart sliced apples, crisp bits of pancetta, pearl onions, butter, and Calvados or apple brandy. ❄ It was a decade ago when I first had this dish at Mustards in Napa Valley and I remember it even today. There's a lot about Pawlcyn's food that evokes those memories. Although she's gone on to be involved in many restaurants—Buckeye Roadhouse and Fog City Diner included—Mustards still holds a special place in her heart. You'll find her behind the line cooking on many days. ❄ This low-slung roadhouse with a whimsical fountain in front made onion rings and house-made ketchup a national passion. Even today as the competition has intensified, the restaurant remains in top form. ❄ As for the liver, it can either be grilled or sautéed in equal amounts of butter and oil. The onions and apples are caramelized, and then a sauce is made with veal stock and apple brandy, with a last minute flourish of crisp pancetta.

The liver is great served with mashed potatoes, polenta, or risotto.

2 tablespoons butter
1 pound cipolline or pearl onions, blanched and peeled
4 large, sweet-tart apples (such as Fuji or Granny Smith), cored and cut into ½-inch-thick wedges
¼ cup Calvados
1 cup veal stock
Salt and pepper
1 tablespoon olive oil
6 slices calf's liver (about 6 ounces each), cleaned
4 ounces pancetta, cut into matchsticks and cooked until crisp, or 4 strips of chopped crisp-cooked bacon

—Melt 1 tablespoon of the butter in a large sauté pan over high heat. Add the onions and apples and sauté until golden brown, about 8 to 10 minutes. Add the Calvados and bring to a boil. Using a long-handled match, carefully light the Calvados. When the flames die out, stir to scrape up any brown bits from the bottom of the pan.

—Add the veal stock and bring to a boil. Cook until the sauce coats the apple-onion mixture, about 3 minutes. Season the sauce to taste with salt and pepper. Set aside.

—Melt the remaining 1 tablespoon of butter with the oil in another large sauté pan. Season the liver with salt and pepper. Working in batches, add the liver to the pan and cook until golden on both sides and slightly creamy in the center, about 4 to 5 minutes. Transfer the liver to a platter. (Alternately, the liver can be grilled. Be sure to oil the grill rack before adding the liver.)

—If you are using pancetta, add it to the sauce and pour the sauce over the cooked liver. If you are using bacon, pour the sauce over the liver and sprinkle the crisply cooked bacon over the top.

Serves 6

SECRETS OF SUCCESS:

Caramelizing the apples and onions. This concentrates the sugars and works to soften the gamy edges of the liver.

The Calvados. The brandy also helps to smooth out the sauce.

Cooking the liver. You want a little pink in the center or the liver can become dry and leathery.

FISH AND SEAFOOD

GRILLED FILLET OF PACIFIC SALMON WITH THAI RED CURRY SAUCE

Terra, one of the top restaurants in the Napa Valley, feels like a Tuscan villa, so it's surprising to find dishes such as Grilled Fillet of Pacific Salmon with Thai Red Curry Sauce on the same menu as French and Italian specialties. ✳ But few cooks have the talent of Hiro Sone, who owns the restaurant along with his wife, Lissa Doumani. They met while he was a chef at Spago in Los Angeles and she was working in the pastry kitchen. Now he's in charge of the kitchen and she oversees the dining room at this fresh and exciting St. Helena restaurant. ✳ This recipe has a lot of ingredients and steps, but it's really not difficult, and the results are well worth the effort. First you make the spicy curry sauce, then prepare the purple cabbage with a soy-rice wine vinegar dressing. Near serving time, make the basmati rice, then grill or sauté the salmon. It's a combination that works all the senses, the hallmark of any great dish.

Rice

2¼ cups water

1½ cups Basmati rice

3 tablespoons unsalted butter

Pinch of salt

Sauce

4½ teaspoons peanut oil

2¼ teaspoons garlic

2¼ teaspoons peeled and minced fresh ginger

1 tablespoon curry powder

1 tablespoon Thai Red Curry Paste (see Note)

1 tablespoon paprika

1½ teaspoons coriander seeds, crushed

1 teaspoon ground cumin

2½ cups canned unsweetened coconut milk

5 tablespoons plus 1 teaspoon canned tomato puree

4½ teaspoons soy sauce

3 tablespoons brown sugar

Cabbage Salad

4 cups loosely packed julienned cabbage

⅔ cup julienned cucumber

⅓ cup fresh cilantro leaves

⅓ cup fresh mint leaves

1 teaspoon soy sauce

1 tablespoon rice wine vinegar

Salmon

6 six-ounce salmon fillets, about ¾-inch thick

1 tablespoon olive oil

Salt and pepper

½ cup coarsely chopped peanuts

—*To make the rice:* Preheat the oven to 350 degrees. In a small oven-proof saucepan over medium-high, combine the water, rice, butter, and salt. Bring to a boil. Cover with a tightfitting lid. Cook in the oven until the rice is tender and the liquid has been absorbed, about 12 minutes. Fluff with a fork. Set aside and keep warm.

—*To make the sauce:* Heat the oil in a medium saucepan over medium heat. Add the garlic and ginger and sauté until light brown, about 5 minutes. Add the curry powder, curry paste, paprika, coriander seeds, and cumin. Reduce the heat to low and sauté until fragrant, about 2 minutes. Add the coconut milk, tomato puree, soy sauce, and brown sugar. Bring to a simmer and remove from heat. Do not let the sauce boil. Keep warm or reheat gently before serving.

—*To make the cabbage salad:* Combine the cabbage, cucumber, cilantro, and mint in a medium bowl. Add the soy sauce and vinegar and toss to coat.

—*To make the salmon:* Prepare the grill (medium-high heat). Alternately, heat a sauté pan over high heat. Brush the salmon with the olive oil and season with salt and pepper. Grill or sauté the salmon to desired doneness, about 2½ minutes per side for medium-rare.

—*To serve:* Place about ½ cup of the basmati rice in the center of each of 6 plates, then place the salmon on top. Pour about ½ cup of the sauce around the outside edge. Place a small pile of the cabbage salad on top of the salmon. Try to get as much elevation on the salad as possible. Sprinkle the sauce with the peanuts.

Serves 6

Note: *Red Curry Paste is available in the Asian foods section of some supermarkets or at Asian markets.*

> **SECRETS OF SUCCESS:**
>
> *Thai Red Curry Sauce.* The combination of ingredients is what makes this sauce special.
>
> *Cabbage salad.* The cabbage, cucumbers, and mint help to cool the fire of the curry, setting up the palate for the next bite.

SALMON CURRY

Many people aren't familiar with Burmese food, but their curiosity will be piqued once they try Philip Chu's Salmon Curry. Of course, he takes some creative license, as all California-based chefs do. He admits there is no salmon in Burma, but the sauce is part of his heritage. ❈ Chu, who brought Burmese food to the Bay Area in 1983, has a background in architecture, but his first love was cooking. He opened a tiny restaurant in Oakland's Chinatown, where he mixed in a few Burmese dishes with the more familiar Chinese selections. As the popularity of the restaurant grew, he moved to Rockridge in 1992, where he was able to expand the menu and to have more inviting surroundings. ❈ Burmese curry is similar to what you might find in Thai restaurants, but instead of being fiery hot,

the dish relies on a careful balance of spicy, sweet, and sour, which comes from tamarind powder, found in some specialty groceries and in Asian markets. ❈ The flavors are vibrant thanks to a blend of tomatoes, onions, lemongrass, ginger, and a bit of turmeric, which adds a yellow hue. The salmon steaks are cooked on top of this spicy blend, forming a sauce to flavor the fish. ❈ If you were going to eat this dish at the restaurant, I'd recommend starting with the ginger salad made with sixteen different ingredients, including peanuts, crunchy yellow lentils, shrimp powder, fried garlic, and cabbage. At home I'd start with an arugula salad with toasted nuts. To accompany the salmon, consider spinach or other leafy cooked vegetables and of course steamed rice to soak up all to the wonderful juices.

½ cup vegetable oil
1 large yellow onion, finely chopped
1 lemongrass stalk (white part only), smashed
2 ripe tomatoes, cut into wedges
1 ounce fresh ginger, smashed
6 cups water
8 fresh cilantro sprigs
3 garlic cloves, minced
1 tablespoon tamarind powder or 4 tablespoons of rice wine vinegar
1 tablespoon fish sauce
1 teaspoon ground turmeric
¾ tablespoon salt
½ teaspoon paprika
½ teaspoon ground white pepper
1 serrano chile, sliced
2 tablespoons sugar
4 salmon steaks, each about 1-inch thick
8 kalamata olives, pitted and chopped for garnishing

—In a large deep sauté pan or wok over a medium-high burner, heat the oil to 350 degrees. Add the onion and stir-fry until lightly golden. Add the lemongrass, tomatoes, and ginger. Stir-fry for 1 minute. Add the water, 4 of the cilantro sprigs, and the garlic, tamarind powder, fish sauce, turmeric, salt, paprika, pepper, and chile. Bring to a boil. Cook for 10 minutes to blend flavors. Stir in the sugar. Add the salmon and reduce the heat to medium-low. Cook until the salmon is just cooked through, about 7 to 8 minutes.

—Gently remove the salmon from the pan and place on plates. Strain the cooked sauce and pour over the salmon. Garnish with the remaining 4 cilantro sprigs and olives.

Serves 4

SECRETS OF SUCCESS:

The curry. You'll discover an incredible balance of sweet, sour, and acid in the curry sauce.

Simmering the salmon. The raw steaks are added and allowed to simmer in the sauce, soaking up the spicy juices.

PAN-SEARED HALIBUT WITH LEEK AND PERNOD SAUCE

Distilled spirits can work wonders in cooking, and Roland Passot uses them with abandon at all his restaurants: La Folie in San Francisco and at Left Bank in Menlo Park and Larkspur, where I first tasted the Pan-Seared Halibut with Leek and Pernod Sauce. ❋ The fish is quickly seared in butter and oil with a shot of Pernod, a French liqueur with licorice overtones. Then the sauce is added. The dish is quick for the home cook because it doesn't require making stock; instead it's made with cream, butter, vermouth, and Pernod. The sauce is then processed in the blender, making it thick and silky. ❋ The dish is one of my favorites at this active Marin County brasserie. The large outdoor patio overlooking the street makes you feel like you're on a European vacation.

Sauce
3 tablespoons butter
2 shallots, chopped
2 leeks, chopped (white parts only)
1 cup dry vermouth or dry white wine
Juice of 1 lemon
½ cup heavy cream
Salt and pepper

Fish
2 ounces clarified butter (see page 362) or
    vegetable oil
4 six-ounce halibut fillets, preferably local
Salt and pepper
¼ cup Pernod

24 asparagus spears, trimmed and peeled
3 tablespoons olive oil or butter
Minced chives for garnishing

—*To make the sauce:* In a heavy-bottomed saucepan, melt 1 tablespoon of the butter over low heat. Add the shallots and leeks and
cook until soft, about 10 minutes. Add the vermouth and lemon
juice. Increase the heat to medium and simmer until the liquid is
reduced by half, about 15 minutes. Stir in the cream and continue
to simmer until the sauce thickens slightly, about 10 minutes.
—Transfer the sauce to a blender and add the remaining 2 tablespoons butter. Blend until smooth. Strain through a very fine
strainer (chinois). Season to taste with salt and pepper.

—*To make the fish:* In a large sauté pan over medium-high heat, heat
the clarified butter or oil. Season the fish with salt and pepper.
Add the fish to the pan and sauté until golden brown and just
cooked through, about 3 to 5 minutes per side. Transfer the fish to
a plate. Tent with foil to keep warm. Deglaze the pan with the
Pernod. Add the sauce and bring to a boil. Remove from heat.
—Cook the asparagus in a pot of lightly salted boiling water until
almost tender, about 5 minutes. Drain and immediately place the
asparagus in a bowl of ice water to cool. Drain. In a large pan, heat
the olive oil over medium-high heat. Add the asparagus and sauté
until tender, about 2 minutes. Season to taste with salt and
pepper.
—Arrange the asparagus in the center of each of four plates. Place
the halibut atop and drizzle with the sauce. Sprinkle with chives
and serve.

Serves 4

> **SECRETS OF SUCCESS:**
>
> *Using the blender.* This helps to emulsify
> the sauce, making it thick and creamy.
>
> *The Pernod.* This liqueur is a secret ingre-
> dient in many French-inspired fish
> recipes, because it adds a subtle back-
> ground note of licorice that enhances the
> fish.

PETRALE SOLE WITH BROWN BUTTER AND TOASTED CAPERS

Petrale sole with lemon butter is a San Francisco classic that you'll find at all the restaurants that line Fisherman's Wharf—and dozens elsewhere. ❋ With a little tweaking, former chef Michael Sabella has come up with a variation that makes this classic dish even better. Instead of regular lemon butter, he uses brown butter, which gives a nutty flavor. Then he sprinkles fried capers over the top for a briny crunch. The fish is quickly sautéed and surrounded by spinach accented with lemon and garlic. Toasted croutons add another unexpected element to the finished dish. ❋ Well-known designer Gary Hutton redecorated the interior several years ago, making it one of the prettiest dining rooms on the Wharf. Hutton retained some of the 1950s charm and updated it to a Gucci-meets-the-Jetsons look. ❋ The food is a notch above the competition, too, partly because of the more innovative preparations of seafood but also because of the live fish tanks that ensure freshness. It's one of the best places in San Francisco for fresh crab and lobster, as well as Petrale sole.

4 slices French bread, each about ⅜-inch thick, crusts removed, cut into ⅜-inch cubes

3 tablespoons plus ¼ cup olive oil

1 tablespoon plus 1 teaspoon capers, drained and patted dry

9 tablespoons butter

2 lemons, peeled and separated into segments (see page 363)

1 cup cooked, peeled bay shrimp

1 pound fresh spinach, washed and stemmed

4 garlic cloves, minced

1 teaspoon salt, plus additional to season

2 tablespoons all-purpose flour

Freshly ground black pepper

4 Petrale sole fillets, 7 to 8 ounces each

—Preheat the oven to 350 degrees.

—Toss the bread with 2 tablespoons of the olive oil in a large bowl until the cubes are evenly coated. Spread the cubes on a baking sheet and bake until crispy, about 20 minutes. Remove from the oven and set aside.

—Heat the ¼ cup oil in a small frying pan over high heat. Add the capers and fry until the buds open and the oil stops crackling, about 2 minutes. Using a slotted spoon, transfer the capers to paper towels to drain.

—Melt 8 tablespoons of the butter in a small sauté pan over medium heat. When the butter turns brown, add the lemon segments and shrimp. Reduce the heat to medium-low and cook about 1 to 2 minutes. Keep warm over very low heat.

—Melt the remaining 1 tablespoon butter in a large sauté pan over medium heat. Add the spinach, garlic, and 1 teaspoon salt. Stir until the spinach is wilted and tender, about 3 to 4 minutes. Keep warm over very low heat.

—Heat the remaining 1 tablespoon oil in a large sauté pan over medium-high heat. Season the flour generously with salt and pepper. Dust the fish fillets with the seasoned flour, shaking off excess. Add the fish to the sauté pan and sauté until browned and the flesh is no longer translucent, turning once, about 3 to 5 minutes per side.

—Portion the spinach into the center of each of 4 warmed serving plates, creating a depression in the middle for the fish. Place a fillet in the center of the spinach and spoon sauce over the top. Sprinkle with the fried capers and croutons.

Serves 4

SECRETS OF SUCCESS:

The sauce. Instead of a traditional butter sauce, the recipe uses brown butter paired with toasted capers.

The lemon. The lemon flesh melts away during cooking so you don't have to worry about the membranes between sections.

The croutons. You may be tempted to skip the croutons on top of the dish, but they add a needed crunch and textural contrast that brings all the elements together.

ROASTED SEA BASS WITH CABBAGE PURSES

Carlo Middione is a master at Southern Italian cooking, as shown in his Roasted Sea Bass with Cabbage Purses. He takes a rich moist fish and contrasts it with the tart earthiness of olives, salty capers, and piquant vinegar. It creates an unexpected synergy. ✳ In this dish, the sea bass is marinated for several hours in olive oil, then the fish is cooked in a hot oven, along with the cabbage purses. ✳ The cabbage purses are made from leaves of steamed cabbage filled with a seasoned mixture of purple cabbage. ✳ Middione, who owns Vivande, is both a great cook and an excellent teacher. He has written several popular cookbooks and starred in a national television cooking show. But his true culinary stage is his Opera Plaza restaurant where the impressive decor features whimsical murals, brightly colored lights, and an open kitchen that lets the customer feel like part of the action. ✳ This dish was made often by Middione's father, who grew up in Sicily, and it's now being kept alive by Middione.

6 six-ounce sea bass fillets, each about
    1¼-inches thick
Extra-virgin olive oil for coating
1 head purple cabbage, about 1½ pounds
Salt
4 tablespoons extra-virgin olive oil
½ cup red wine vinegar
Freshly ground black pepper
3 tablespoons drained capers
½ cup pitted black salt-dried cured olives or
    kalamata olives, coarsely chopped
Lemon wedges

—Place the sea bass in a deep dish and coat liberally with the olive oil. Cover and refrigerate at least 2 hours and up to 1 day.

—Remove 6 outer leaves from the cabbage without tearing them. Cook the leaves in a large pot of boiling salted water until tender, about 6 minutes. Drain. Rinse under cold water and drain well.

—Core and slice the remaining cabbage into ½-inch-thick pieces. Heat 2 tablespoons of the olive oil over medium heat. Add the sliced cabbage and cook about 5 minutes, stirring often. Stir in the vinegar. Season to taste with salt and pepper. Cook until the cabbage is tender, stirring occasionally, about 20 minutes.

—Crush the capers in a small bowl with the back of a spoon, making a paste. Stir the paste and olives into the cabbage. Stir in the remaining 2 tablespoons oil.

—Preheat the oven to 500 degrees. Lightly oil a baking sheet.

—Line a 6-ounce ladle with one of the whole cabbage leaves, with the excess leaf hanging over the edge. Fill with the seasoned cabbage. Fold the edges over to seal the purse. Slide the purse out and place it seam side down on the prepared baking sheet. Repeat with the remaining cabbage leaves and filling. Bake for 10 to 15 minutes. Remove from oven.

—Meanwhile, transfer the marinated sea bass to a rimmed baking sheet. Drizzle with the marinade oil. Sprinkle liberally with salt and pepper. Bake until golden brown, about 10 minutes. Return the cabbage purses to the oven to rewarm if necessary.

—Divide the cabbage purses and sea bass among 6 plates. Drizzle the fish with extra-virgin olive oil. Serve with lemon wedges.

Serves 6

SECRETS OF SUCCESS:

Using the ladle. Lining the ladle with a cabbage leaf and adding the filling for the cabbage purses makes it easy to fold.

High heat. Roasting the fish at high heat cooks it quickly and seals in the juices.

BLACK BASS WITH PINE NUT GRATINEE

When Julian Serrano left Masa's, people wondered if his replacement, Chad Callahan, could carry on the four-star tradition. ❊ After working for Serrano for eight years, Callahan had learned his lessons well, and his food is just as good. While his style is similar, he's also putting his stamp on the menu. Like Serrano, the plates may have lots of different elements, but the balance is superb. ❊ In the case of the Black Bass with Pine Nut Gratinee the elements come together miraculously. ❊ The preparation isn't complicated, although there are four steps involved: The fish is sautéed and then broiled with a toasted pine nut crust. The spinach is sautéed in brown butter with golden raisins and whole pine nuts. The sauce is made with the golden hue of saffron, and pista-chio oil and balsamic vinegar are drizzled on top at serving time. If pistachio oil isn't available, any full-flavored oil like hazelnut, walnut, or a good-quality peppery olive oil will work fine. ❊ All the components come together spectacularly, just like they do at the restaurant. Little wonder Masa's, along with Fleur de Lys, is one of the best French restaurant in the city. ❊ The restaurant features two fixed price menus with choices in each category. The extensive wine list is tailored to the food and many wines are available by the glass, including Chateau d'Yquem. ❊ The interior has a luxurious feel, with tablecloths to the floor and an impressive table setting that sparkles in the soft lighting. The deep red color scheme gives everyone a healthy glow, while the food adds the smile.

Beurre Blanc
½ cup plus 2 tablespoons dry white wine
1 shallot, chopped
1 small bay leaf
2 tablespoons heavy cream
1 cup (2 sticks) chilled unsalted butter, cut into
    pieces
½ teaspoon crushed saffron threads
2 tablespoons water

Fish
8 tablespoons unsalted butter
¼ cup toasted pine nuts
¼ cup golden raisins
½ pound fresh baby spinach, stems removed
Salt and pepper
4 black bass fillets
8 tablespoons extra-virgin olive oil
5 ounces pine nuts, toasted and finely chopped
¼ cup dry bread crumbs
2 tablespoons aged balsamic vinegar

—*To make the beurre blanc:* Place the ½ cup white wine, shallot, and bay leaf in a small saucepan over medium-high heat. Boil until almost all liquid evaporates, about 10 minutes. Stir in the cream. Remove from heat. Whisk in the butter until completely emulsified. Keep warm. Place the crushed saffron in a separate small saucepan over medium-high heat with the water and the remaining 2 tablespoons white wine. Boil until reduced by half, about 2 minutes. Pour into the beurre blanc and whisk to blend. Strain the sauce through a fine strainer (chinois). Keep warm.

—*To make the fish:* Melt 4 tablespoons of the butter in a large saucepan over medium heat. Add the ¼ cup pine nuts and the raisins and cook until the butter browns, about 5 minutes. Add the spinach and sauté until wilted, about 5 minutes. Season to taste with salt and pepper. Keep warm.

—Preheat the broiler. Season the black bass on the flesh side with salt and pepper. Heat 2 tablespoons of the oil in a nonstick skillet over medium-high heat. Add the fish, flesh side down, and cook until crisp, about 3 to 5 minutes. Turn and cook for 30 seconds more. Transfer the fish to a baking sheet, skin side up.

—In another skillet, melt the remaining 4 tablespoons butter. Add the chopped pine nuts and bread crumbs, and stir until moistened. Spoon the bread crumbs onto the fish. Put the fish under the broiler until the bread crumbs are golden brown, about 3 to 5 minutes.

—Whisk the vinegar and remaining 6 tablespoons oil in a small bowl to blend.

—Divide the spinach into equal portions in the center of 4 plates. Top with the fish. Pour saffron beurre blanc around the fish, then spoon 1 teaspoon of balsamic vinaigrette around and on the saffron sauce, and on top of the fish , if you like. (Save remaining vinaigrette for another use.)

Serves 4

> **SECRETS OF SUCCESS:**
>
> *Saffron.* This gives a rich golden color to the sauce and an herbal background that brings complexity to the butter sauce.
>
> *The topping.* The buttery mix of pine nuts and bread crumbs add a rustic note that pairs well with the bass, spinach, and raisins.

SEA BASS WITH GARLIC, CHILE ARBOL, AND LIME

It may be surprising to learn that some of the best fish in the Bay Area can be found at Cafe Marimba, a casual Mexican restaurant in the Marina. ❈ Started by Reed Hearon and Louise Clement, the restaurant specializes in the coastal cuisine of Mexico. The pairing of sea bass and smoky chiles is phenomenal in the Sea Bass with Garlic, Chile Arbol, and Lime. In preparing the dish, an arbol chile puree, a type of dried chile widely available at specialty food stores and ethnic markets, is seared into the white-fleshed fish. The fish comes out of the frying pan spicy hot. It's served with a wedge of lime, which helps to tame the fire. ❈ At Cafe Marimba, which is now owned solely by Clement, the food is as bright as the decor, awash in primary colors and Mexican folk art.

Sea Bass
6 tablespoons canola oil
Kosher salt
Freshly ground black pepper
2 pounds Chilean sea bass, cut into 6 portions
¼ cup Arbol Chile Puree (recipe follows)
6 arbol chiles for garnishing
6 fresh cilantro sprigs for garnishing
1 lime, cut into 6 wedges

Arbol Chile Puree
1 cup dry arbol chiles (see Note)
2 cups hot water
4 large garlic cloves
Kosher salt

—*To cook the fish:* Put the oil on a dinner plate with a rim and season generously with salt and pepper. Dip each piece of fish into the oil mixture and turn to liberally coat.

—Heat a large heavy-bottomed sauté pan over high heat. Working in batches, add the fish to the pan. Top each fillet with 1 teaspoon Arbol Chile Puree. Cook until golden brown, about 5 minutes. Turn the fish and spread another 1 teaspoon of the Arbol Chile Puree on the cooked side. Continue to cook until the fish just loses the translucent center, about 3 to 5 minutes.

—Transfer the fish to plates. Garnish with dried arbol chiles, cilantro, and lime.

Serves 6

Note: *Although not originally called for in the recipe, I've found that you can make a sauce from what's left over in the pan that's great with the fish or drizzled over rice. When the fish are cooked add about $^{1}/_{2}$ cup of water to the pan (use the reserved water from soaking the chiles in the Arbol Chile Puree). Bring to a boil, scraping up all the browned bits from the bottom of the pan. Reduce the liquid by half, then add another $^{1}/_{4}$ cup of water. Boil a minute more. Spoon sauce over each fillet.*

—*To make the puree:* Heat a large sauté pan over high heat. Add the chiles and toast until fragrant, about 1 to 2 minutes. Transfer the chiles to a large bowl. Pour the hot water over and soak until tender, about 1 hour. Drain, reserving the liquid. Place the chiles, garlic, and ¼ cup of reserved liquid in a blender and puree until smooth. Add more reserved liquid if necessary to create a smooth puree. Strain. Season to taste with salt.

Note: *Arbol chiles are available at specialty food stores, ethnic markets, and in some supermarkets.*

SECRETS OF SUCCESS:

Searing the fish. The spicy arbol chile puree is seared right into the fish, giving it a crusty exterior.

The lime. Don't consider this only a garnish; it helps to balance and tame the heat of the chiles.

WILD STRIPED BASS WITH MEYER LEMON, JERUSALEM ARTICHOKES, AND SALSIFY

The combination of ingredients that accompanies Aaron Peters's Wild Striped Bass is exciting: crescent potatoes, salsify, and Jerusalem artichokes. Then the plate is rounded out with a delicate parsley salad, glistening with a Meyer Lemon Vinaigrette. ❋ This is one of the staple dishes at Aram's, a Pan-Mediterranean restaurant tucked into an alleyway off Sacramento in Presidio Heights. ❋ Located in the former home of Rosmarino, the restaurant is now owned by Khajag and Hildy Sarkissian, who owned Caravansary restaurants and introduced the Aram sandwiches to the Bay Area. ❋ For his part, Peters trained in much the same manner as the best European chefs. He started working in the kitchen of Kuleto's when he was sixteen years old and then moved on to Aqua, Square One, and PlumpJack Cafe. At Aram's, which has a comfortable feel and a stylish decor that reflects the affluent neighborhood, Peters crafts some creative dishes using simple techniques and out-of-the-mainstream ingredients. However, in the case of this fish dish, both the Jerusalem artichokes, also known as sunchokes, and the salsify, sometimes called the oyster plant because of the similar flavors, are available at many upscale supermarkets. ❋ If Meyer lemons aren't available, any variety will do. And if you can't find the wild striped bass, then sea bass will work fine, too.

Vegetables

½ pound Jerusalem artichokes, peeled and cut into ¼-inch-thick slices

½ pound Ruby crescent or any red-skinned potatoes, cut into ¾-inch pieces

½ pound of salsify, peeled and cut into ¾-inch pieces

2 tablespoons olive oil

Salt and freshly ground pepper

2 cups unsalted chicken stock

1 tablespoon chopped fresh thyme

2 tablespoons butter

Meyer Lemon Vinaigrette

1 Meyer lemon or any other lemon

1 tablespoon Champagne vinegar

1 teaspoon rice wine vinegar

1 tablespoon minced shallot

2 teaspoons Dijon mustard

3 tablespoons extra-virgin olive oil

Salt and freshly ground pepper

Fish

6 wild striped bass or sea bass fillets, about 5 ounces each

Salt and freshly ground pepper

4 tablespoons olive oil

1½ cups Italian parsley leaves

—*For the vegetables:* Preheat the oven to 400 degrees. Combine the Jerusalem artichokes, potatoes, and salsify in a large ovenproof skillet. Add the oil and toss to coat. Season with salt and pepper. Roast for 15 minutes. Transfer the pan to the stove over medium heat. Add the stock and thyme. Bring to a boil, scraping up any browned bits. Continue to cook until the liquid is reduced by about 1/3 and is slightly thickened, about 10 minutes. Add the butter and stir until melted. Season with additional salt and pepper if necessary. Remove from the heat.

—*For the vinaigrette:* Zest the lemon, leaving the zest in long threads, and reserve for the salad. Squeeze the juice from the lemon into a small bowl. Add the Champagne vinegar, rice wine vinegar, shallot, and mustard. Gradually whisk in the olive oil. Season to taste with salt and pepper.

—*To make the fish:* Season the fish liberally with salt and pepper. In a large sauté pan, heat 2 tablespoons of the oil until just smoking. Gently add 3 pieces of fish, skin side down. Cook until the skin is brown and crispy, about 3 minutes. Using a spatula, carefully turn the fish over and continue cooking until the fish is just cooked through, about 3 minutes. Transfer the fish to a platter. Keep warm. Repeat the process with the remaining oil and fish.
—Combine the parsley leaves and reserved lemon zest in a small bowl. Add the vinaigrette and toss to coat. Divide the vegetables among 6 plates. Top with fish. Garnish each plate with parsley salad and drizzle with any remaining vinaigrette.

Serves 6

SECRETS OF SUCCESS:

Cooking the fish. The oil should be smoking hot before putting the fish in the pan; this creates a brown crisp exterior and a moist, flaky interior.

Using dry heat and wet heat to cook vegetables. The root vegetables are first roasted and then braised in chicken stock, a technique that enhances the taste and texture.

Parsley salad. The combination of parsley and lemon adds a striking, refreshing note.

CATFISH IN SPICY LIME SAUCE

It was in 1983 that Joanna Doung opened what is believed to be the first Cambodian restaurant in the United States. With the womb-like decor including lots of pillows on the banquettes along the wall and high-quality native art, she has created a comfortable, authentic environment for the food. ❋ In many cases the cuisine shares similarities with India, Indonesia, Vietnam, and China, but the key is the balance of flavors, as shown in the Catfish in Spicy Lime Sauce. ❋ The recipe is relatively easy to put together, but some of the ingredients—lemongrass, Kaffir lime leaves, galangal, fish sauce, and oyster sauce—may require a trip to an Asian market. ❋ The dish has a haunting flavor and requires three steps. The first is making the Cambodian five-spice paste. Second is marinating the fish in a combination of soy, oyster, and fish sauces. And the final step is making the spicy lime sauce, a simple combination of garlic, chiles, lime, fish sauce, and a little sugar for balance. ❋ When ready to serve, Doung pan-fries the fish in oil. Then she stirs in the five-spice paste and the lime sauce, which is brought to a quick boil before the fish is returned to the pan. ❋ None of the steps are difficult, and the rewards are worth it.

Catfish
1 cup Cambodian Five-Spice Paste (recipe
    follows)
2 tablespoons oyster sauce
1½ tablespoons soy sauce
½ tablespoon fish sauce
1 tablespoon sugar
4 catfish fillets, 6 to 8 ounces each
5 cups vegetable oil for frying, plus 1 tablespoon
Spicy Lime Sauce (recipe follows)
Sliced cucumbers for garnishing
Fresh cilantro sprigs for garnishing

Cambodian Five-Spice Paste
⅔ cup water
½ cup thinly sliced lemongrass
4 garlic cloves
½ teaspoon ground turmeric
4 Kaffir lime leaves (see Note)
2 slices galangal (see Note)

Spicy Lime Sauce
⅔ cup water
6 garlic cloves
1 to 3 small dried red chiles (optional)
2 tablespoons sugar
2 tablespoons fish sauce
1 tablespoon fresh lime juice

—Stir together ½ cup of the Cambodian Five-Spice Paste, the oyster sauce, soy sauce, fish sauce, and sugar in a small bowl until the sugar dissolves.

—Place the fish in a pan large enough to hold the fillets in a single layer. Add the marinade and turn the fish to coat. Cover and refrigerate for 20 minutes or up to 2 hours.

—Heat the 5 cups of oil in a deep frying pan over medium-high heat. Scrape off and discard the marinade from the fish.

—Working in batches, carefully add the fillets to the hot oil and lower the heat to medium. Fry until the fish no longer feels stiff when a fork is inserted into the thickest part, about 3 minutes per side. Transfer the fish to paper towels and drain.

—In another large skillet, heat the remaining 1 tablespoon of oil. Add the remaining ½ cup Cambodian Five-Spice Paste and stir well to blend. Stir in the Spicy Lime Sauce. Bring to a boil and reduce the heat to low. Gently lay the cooked catfish fillets in the pan and spoon the sauce over the top. Simmer until the sauce coats the fish, about 2 minutes.

—Transfer the fish to plates. Garnish with slices of cucumber on the side, and top with cilantro.

Serves 4

—*To make the paste:* Place all the ingredients in a blender. Puree until smooth, about 20 to 30 seconds.

—*To make the sauce:* Puree the water, garlic, and dried chiles in a blender until a paste forms. Pour into a bowl. Add the sugar, fish sauce, and lime juice. Stir until the sugar dissolves.

Note: *Kaffir lime leaves and galangal are available seasonally in Asian markets or in some upscale supermarkets.*

> **SECRETS OF SUCCESS:**
>
> *Marinating the fish.* This helps to remove any of the muddy flavors characteristic of catfish.
>
> *The five-spice paste.* This is an essential part of the flavoring that gives the fish an incredible balance.

PAN-ROASTED SPEARFISH WITH ROCK SHRIMP, OKRA, CORN, AND BARLEY RAGOUT

Michael Dotson has cooked all around the Bay Area. I first became aware of his talent at the PlumpJack Cafe in Lake Tahoe and caught up with him again at the Slow Club in San Francisco, where I was enamoured with his Pan-Roasted Spearfish with Rock Shrimp, Okra, Corn, and Barley Ragout. ❉ He's now moved to Heirloom in Sonoma, but fortunately he took his recipe with him and it's available there (when the ingredients are in season, of course). ❉ Spearfish is a mild, meaty firm-fleshed fish that is at its best when pan roasted and served atop the marvelous ragout. If spearfish isn't available, mahi mahi, escolar, or sea bass make good substitutes. ❉ The restaurant, which was redone in late 1998, is on the Square in Sonoma and has a charming old California-Victorian look with hardwood floors, high-back chairs, wainscoting below butter-colored walls, and Craftsman-style lights and sconces. ❉ Dotson's cooking, however, is thoroughly modern, as shown by this fish dish.

2 ears fresh sweet corn, shucked
About 1 cup milk
Salt and freshly ground pepper
8 okra pods, sliced into ¼-inch pieces
2 tablespoons olive oil
Four 5-ounce portions spearfish, mahi mahi, escolar, or sea bass
2 tablespoons butter
1 leek, diced
2 cups cooked barley
2 cups lobster or chicken stock
6 ounces rock shrimp
1 bunch fresh chervil

—Cut the kernels from the corn cob and place in a small saucepan. Add enough milk to cover. Season with salt and pepper. Bring to a simmer over medium heat. Immediately drain, discarding the liquid. Cool the corn in a single layer on a cookie sheet.

—Blanch the okra in a medium pot of boiling salted water for 30 seconds. Drain; transfer to a bowl of ice water to stop the cooking. Drain. Set aside.

—Heat the olive oil over medium-high heat in a heavy-bottomed sauté pan large enough to fit the fish in a single layer. Season the fish lightly with salt and pepper. Cook the fish in the oil until golden brown, about 3 minutes per side. Transfer the fish to a plate and cover with foil to keep warm.

—Drain any excess oil from the pan. Melt the butter in the same pan over medium-high heat. Add the leek and sauté until soft, about 3 to 5 minutes. Add the barley and stock and cook until the stock has reduced by a quarter, about 8 to 10 minutes. Add the shrimp and cook for 1 minute. Add the blanched corn and okra. Season with salt and pepper. Simmer until the shrimp are cooked through and the corn and okra are hot, about 1 minute.

—Divide the ragout between 4 soup plates, making sure there is enough broth to cover the bottom of each plate. Top each with a piece of fish and garnish with an equal portion of chervil. Serve immediately.

Serves 4

SECRETS OF SUCCESS:

The ragout. The combination of ingredients is innovative and delicious.

Blanching the okra. Slicing and cooking the okra for 30 seconds in boiling salted water, and then cooling in ice water, helps to remove some of its characteristic sliminess.

MISO-GLAZED BLACK COD

At Hawthorne Lane, David and Anne Gingrass combine Eastern and Western flavors on the same menu. You can get a Gorgonzola pizza with toasted walnuts and balsamic onions in the bar, for example, or a crispy duck spring roll in the main dining room. ✳ This is one of the few Western restaurants to feature a fish tank for live prawns, which are used in many dishes. My favorite dish is the rich, velvety-textured Miso-Glazed Black Cod. The fish marinates overnight, which imparts a distinctive flavor. Then it's simply broiled, emerging from the oven with a caramelized top and just a hint of sweetness. ✳ The fish can be served on its own or with Sesame Spinach Rolls (page 274), flavored with lime-soy vinaigrette. It's an innovative preparation you won't find anywhere else. ✳

The Gingrasses met when they were students at the Culinary Institute of America in upstate New York. In the early 1980s, they moved to California and both wound up at Spago in Beverly Hills. They married in 1985 and were tapped by Wolfgang Puck to open Postrio, his first restaurant outside Los Angeles. ✳ The duo quickly shot to the top rank of San Francisco chefs and, after working at Postrio more than five years, they left to open their own restaurant, Hawthorne Lane, in 1995. ✳ The loftlike building features an expansive interior with refined finishing elements, including a polished elliptical bar, beautiful table settings, and splashy modern artwork on the walls.

3 tablespoons warm water
3 tablespoons sugar
¼ cup (2 ounces) yellow miso paste (see Note)
2 tablespoons mirin (sweet rice wine)
2 tablespoons sake
4 black cod fillets (about 3 ounces each)
Sesame Spinach Rolls with Soy-Lime Vinaigrette
    (page 274)

—Combine the water and sugar in a small pan and bring to a boil. Remove from heat and cool to room temperature. Stir in the miso paste, mirin, and sake.

—Place the cod fillets in a small glass container that will hold them in a single layer. Pour the marinade over the fish and turn the fillets to coat both sides with the marinade. Cover and refrigerate for at least 4 hours and up to 24 hours.

—Preheat the broiler. Place the marinated cod on a baking sheet or pan. Broil until just cooked through and lightly browned, about 5 to 7 minutes.

—Serve with the Sesame Spinach Rolls with Soy-Lime Vinaigrette.

Serves 4

Note: *Yellow miso paste is available at Asian markets, specialty foods stores, or in the Asian foods section of some supermarkets.*

SECRETS OF SUCCESS:

Sugar in the sauce. Black cod is a rich, silky-textured fish that can lose much of its charm when overcooked. The trick is to get a deep mahogany color without drying out the fish. The Gingrasses solved the problem by using a bit of sugar in the sauce. It's the same technique that gives Chinese-style duck its rich color. The delicate fish browns yet remains moist.

AHI BURGERS WITH HORSERADISH–CHINESE CABBAGE SLAW

Spicy, vibrant, and delicious food is what you'll find at AsiaSF, and the ahi burger is a prime example. Chef Matthew Metcalf pairs the ground tuna with a teriyaki glaze and fresh horseradish–Chinese cabbage slaw on a scallion focaccia roll, creating one of the most unusual and delicious burgers around. ✽ The good-humored chef is fighting an uphill battle for recognition, however. He's competing with a sexy room where two of the walls glow and slowly change from red to pink to gold. And the central bar, covered in red vinyl, doubles as a stage for the entertainers, who also double as waiters. They're "gender illusionists," meaning guys who dress up and perform in a variety of outfits from outrageous to sexy. It's sophisticated and all-around good fun. ✽ And, in the end, Metcalf's food really does upstage the "girls."

Burgers
2 pounds ahi tuna (preferably grade No. 1)
1 bunch scallions, thinly sliced on the bias
2 tablespoons Worcestershire sauce
1 tablespoon chopped garlic
2 teaspoons peeled and chopped fresh ginger

Slaw
1 head napa cabbage
2 carrots
½ cup rice wine vinegar
¼ cup sugar
2 tablespoons peeled and finely grated fresh
   horseradish
2 tablespoons kosher salt

Teriyaki Glaze
1 cup soy sauce
½ cup peanut oil
¼ cup brown sugar
3 tablespoons dry sherry
2 tablespoons chopped garlic
2 tablespoons peeled, chopped fresh ginger
1 tablespoon rice wine vinegar
1 tablespoon (or more) cornstarch
1 tablespoon (or more) cold water

6 sesame rolls
Peanut oil for cooking
Salt and freshly ground pepper
Sandwich picks

—*To make the burgers:* Carefully remove all the skin and the deep red meat that runs down the side of the fish and discard.

—Cut the fish into ¾-inch cubes and place in a food processor. Pulse quickly 2 or 3 times. Scrape down the sides of the work bowl and pulse again once or twice. Do not overprocess the fish. It should still be in little chunks, but should hold together when formed into a patty. Transfer the fish to a bowl. Add the scallions, Worcestershire sauce, garlic, and ginger; mix gently by hand until incorporated.

—Form the mixture into 6 patties, place on a plate, cover with plastic wrap, and refrigerate for at least 2 and up to 8 hours.

—*To make the slaw:* Remove and discard the darker green leaves from the cabbage, then cut the head in half lengthwise. Remove the core. Place a cabbage half cut side down on a cutting board. Starting at the end opposite the core, slice the cabbage into thin ribbons. Place in a large mixing bowl. Repeat with the other half.

—Using a mandoline, cut the carrots into julienne strips, or grate on the large holes of a box grater. Add to the cabbage, along with the vinegar, sugar, horseradish, and salt; mix well.

—Let stand at room temperature for 1 hour. Adjust seasoning if necessary.

—*To make the glaze:* Combine the soy sauce, oil, brown sugar, sherry, garlic, ginger, and vinegar in a small saucepan. Bring to a boil over high heat. Reduce the heat to a simmer. Stir together the cornstarch and water in a small bowl. Slowly add to the soy sauce mixture, whisking constantly. Bring to a boil; remove from heat.

—The glaze will thicken as it cools. It should be the consistency of ketchup. If it is not thick enough, add a little more cornstarch-water mixture and bring to a boil.

—Store any leftovers in the refrigerator for up to 3 weeks.

—*To assemble the burgers:* Preheat the oven to 350 degrees. Arrange the rolls on a baking sheet. Place in the oven to warm while cooking burgers.

—Heat a nonstick sauté pan over high heat. Add just enough peanut oil to thinly coat the bottom of the pan.

—Season the ahi burgers with salt and pepper. Working in batches, add the burgers to the pan. Fry for about 45 seconds on each side for medium-rare.

—For each burger, place an ahi patty on the bottom half of a roll and spoon on 1 tablespoon of the teriyaki glaze and a half-inch layer of slaw. Replace the top half of the roll.

—Insert 4 small sandwich picks in the top of the roll, centering one in each quadrant. Cut the sandwich into quarters and arrange on a plate, cut sides facing out. Garnish with the extra slaw.

Serves 6

SECRETS OF SUCCESS:

The tuna. Use only top-grade fish. To save time, ask your fishmonger to skin the fillets and remove any dark flesh.

Grinding in the food processor. Pulse only a couple of times so the meat is in tiny chunks. It shouldn't be pureed or smooth.

Peanut oil. This oil has a higher smoking point than other oils. The burgers need the high heat to sear the outside.

The standing time. Forming the burgers several hours before cooking allows the flavors to become infused throughout. Letting the burgers stand a minute or two after cooking helps redistribute the juices.

GREEN PEPPERCORN SWORDFISH

Maurizio Bruschi is a fourth-generation Italian cook who began working with his grandmother in the family restaurant in Rome when he was only fifteen years old. ❊ Ten years later, he came to San Francisco and worked in various restaurants, but his first love has always been Roman cooking. His dishes, such as the Green Peppercorn Swordfish, have maximum flavor derived from minimum ingredients. Here the fish fillets are breaded with crumbs and fried to a golden crunch. All that's needed to complete the dish is lemon and green peppercorns. It takes just 10 minutes to prepare. ❊ Bruschi opened Ideale in North Beach in 1993. In this simple storefront restaurant that exudes casual charm, he indulges his Roman roots and produces many dishes from his homeland.

—Rinse the fish fillets and pat dry. Beat the eggs in a bowl. Place the bread crumbs in another shallow bowl. Working with one fillet at a time, dip the fillets in the egg, turning to coat, then into the bread crumbs, turning so both sides are well covered. Press the fillet with both hands to make the crumbs adhere securely.

—Heat 6 teaspoons of oil in a large frying pan over high heat. Add the fillets and sauté for 2 minutes on each side until cooked through. Sprinkle the fish with salt to taste and then transfer to paper towels to drain. Arrange the fish on a heated platter and tent with foil to keep warm.

—Combine the green peppercorns with the lime or lemon juice, parsley, scallion, and the remaining 2 teaspoons oil in a small bowl. Season to taste with salt. Pour the mixture over the hot swordfish.

Serves 4

4 swordfish fillets, about 8 ounces each
2 eggs
Bread crumbs
8 teaspoons extra-virgin olive oil
Salt
1 teaspoon green peppercorns
Juice of 4 limes or 2 lemons
2 teaspoons finely chopped fresh Italian parsley
1 teaspoon chopped scallion

SECRETS OF SUCCESS:

Pressing the crumbs. The bread crumbs need to be pressed firmly into the fish so the coating sticks. This results in a crisp, crunchy exterior.

Cooking the fish. Swordfish is a type of fish that is best when cooked through. If it's undercooked it will be gummy.

FISH TACOS

Gabriele Fregoso at Las Camelias creates great fish tacos that are bursting with flavor. It's a simple blend of snapper and fresh tomato salsa, sautéed with a little butter for added richness. ✳ The dish is also fast; it can be made in less than thirty minutes. While the fish is traditionally served with warm corn tortillas, it is also good atop crisp tortilla chips as an appetizer.

—Cut the snapper fillets lengthwise into 2 to 3 strips, then finely slice across the grain. Set aside.

—In a small bowl, combine the tomatoes, onion, and jalapeños. Set aside.

—In a large sauté pan over medium heat, melt the butter over medium-high heat. Add the fish and sauté until it turns white, about 3 minutes. Add the tomato mixture and stir for an additional 2 to 3 minutes. Stir in the lime juice and cilantro. Season to taste with salt.

—Serve with warm corn tortillas or corn chips.

Serves 4 to 6

1 pound fresh red snapper fillets
2 medium tomatoes, cut into ¼-inch dice
½ onion, cut into ¼-inch dice
1 to 3 pickled jalapeños, from a jar, drained and cut into ¼-inch dice
1 tablespoon butter
Juice of 1 lime
½ bunch fresh cilantro, coarsely chopped
Salt
Warm corn tortillas or tortilla chips

SECRETS OF SUCCESS:

Dicing the fish. Cutting the snapper into small chunks makes it cook quicker and gives more flavor when combined with the other ingredients.

A little bit of butter. This goes a long way to richen and smooth the other ingredients.

YELLOW CURRY PRAWNS

Year after year, Marnee Thai in the Sunset District is listed as one of the Bay Area's favorite restaurants. And anyone who's tasted Chai Siriyarn's Yellow Curry Prawns will know why. If you think all curries are pretty much the same, this recipe will convince you otherwise. ❊ Good curry is a blend of more than a dozen ingredients, so it's much more complicated that opening a jar of yellow powder from the grocery store. Once you taste this version, the extra effort will seem like a small price to pay. ❊ Siriyarn's curry is a blend of chiles, garlic, lemongrass, ginger, galangal, Kaffir lime, shrimp paste, coriander, cumin, and cloves. It's a haunting combination that seems to sweeten the prawns and soak into the little cubes of potatoes. ❊ The sauce is made with coconut milk, which smoothes the raw edges of the spices and makes the dish velvety in texture, with flavors that literally unfold in the mouth.

Yellow Curry Paste

6 to 8 small dried red chile peppers (2 to 3 inches long)
1 tablespoon coriander seeds
1 teaspoon fennel seeds
¼ teaspoon whole white peppercorns
3 whole cloves
1 generous tablespoon thinly sliced garlic
2 tablespoons thinly sliced shallot
1 tablespoon thinly sliced lemongrass
1 teaspoon peeled and finely chopped fresh ginger (see page 362)
1 teaspoon peeled and finely chopped galangal root (see Note)
1 teaspoon finely chopped lime peel (preferably Kaffir lime, if available)
½ teaspoon shrimp paste (see Note)
1 teaspoon salt
1 tablespoon yellow curry powder
¼ teaspoon ground turmeric

Prawns

20 medium prawns, shelled and deveined
2 cups canned unsweetened coconut milk
1 pound Yukon Gold potatoes, peeled and cut into ½-inch cubes
3 cups chicken stock
1 cup half-and-half
2 teaspoons of palm sugar or brown sugar
2 tablespoons fish sauce
Kosher salt
Freshly ground white pepper

—*To make the yellow curry paste:* Place the chiles in a small bowl. Pour enough hot water over to cover. Let stand until soft, about 15 minutes. Drain, reserving liquid. Finely slice the chiles.

—In a small skillet over medium heat, toast the coriander seeds, fennel seeds, peppercorns, and cloves until fragrant, about 3 to 5 minutes, stirring frequently to prevent burning. Transfer to a spice grinder and grind to a fine powder. Place in a blender with all of the remaining ingredients and the chiles. Puree until a fine, smooth paste forms, about 3 to 5 minutes. If necessary, add ⅓ cup of reserved chile water to facilitate blending.

—*To make the prawns:* Parboil the prawns in a large pot of boiling water for 10 to 15 seconds. Drain well.

—In a medium saucepan over medium heat, bring 1 cup coconut milk to a boil and cook, stirring often, until slightly reduced, about 5 to 7 minutes. Add the yellow curry paste and stir until almost all the liquid evaporates and the mixture becomes dry and fragrant, about 5 to 10 minutes. Transfer the mixture to a larger pot and add the remaining coconut milk, potatoes, and 2 cups of the chicken stock. Cook over medium-high heat, about 12 minutes, stirring frequently. Add the rest of the chicken stock, half-and-half, sugar, and fish sauce. Add the prawns and bring to a boil. Immediately remove from the heat. Let stand until the prawns are just cooked through, about 3 minutes. Season to taste with salt and pepper and serve.

Serves 4

Note: *Galangal is available in Asian markets or in the ethnic section of some supermarkets. Shrimp paste can be purchased in Asian markets. To make it at home, mash cooked shrimp with a little water.*

SECRETS OF SUCCESS:

The curry. Most take shortcuts, but the mix of toasted spices produces an exceptional dish.

The potatoes. Cutting the potatoes into cubes and adding them to the sauce makes a perfect foil to the intense curry.

Precooking the prawns. Parboiling the prawns for about 15 seconds before adding to the curry allows the cook to better control the cooking time. The prawns are plumper and more succulent.

TIGER PRAWNS WITH TAMARIND

Tamarind, the brown pod popular in both Asian and Mexican cooking, has an affinity for seafood. With its complex sweet and sour flavor, it's nature's perfect balance. ❄ Chef Dieu Ho at Le Colonial pairs this sauce with tiger prawns for a quick and easy sauté. Making the tamarind sauce also requires lemongrass, ginger, and fish sauce, but once made it's versatile. Ho says it's great with crab (see the recipe from the Golden Turtle on facing page) and can serve as a dipping sauce for fried dishes such as calamari. ❄ Another idea: Mix the sauce into softened butter. It makes a delicious topping for fish, especially swordfish and mahi mahi.

—*To make the sauce:* Heat the peanut oil in a small saucepan over medium heat. Add the water, tamarind, sugar, ginger, and lemongrass. Bring to a boil. Reduce the heat and simmer until thickened, about 20 minutes, stirring occasionally. Stir in the fish sauce. Pass the mixture through a sieve. Set the sauce aside.

—*To make the prawns:* In a large sauté pan or wok, heat the oil over medium heat. Add the shallots, garlic, and red and green jalapeños and sauté until soft, about 3 minutes. Add the prawns and sauté 2 minutes. Add the sauce and stir gently, cooking until sauce begins to boil and the prawns are just cooked through. Transfer to a warmed platter and serve immediately.

Serves 4

Note: *Wet tamarind is available in Asian markets or in the ethnic section of many supermarkets.*

Sauce

3 tablespoons peanut oil

3 cups water

7 ounces wet tamarind, broken into small chunks (see Note)

¾ cup sugar

1 ounce ginger, peeled and sliced (see page 362)

1 ounce fresh lemongrass, cut into 1-inch pieces and lightly crushed

1 tablespoon fish sauce

Prawns

1 teaspoon peanut oil

¼ cup sliced shallots

2 garlic cloves, crushed

1 red jalapeño, thinly sliced into rings

1 green jalapeño, thinly sliced into rings

2 pounds (about 16 to 24) black tiger prawns, peeled and deveined

SECRETS OF SUCCESS:

The sauce. The interplay between the ginger, tamarind, and jalapeños makes this special.

TAMARIND CRAB

Crab takes on an exotic dimension at the Golden Turtle where it's given a Vietnamese treatment with tamarind and soy sauce. ❈ Tamarind seems to have an affinity for crabmeat. Its sweet and sour flavor really brings out the best in the crab. It's a messy thing to eat, but as you pick the meat from the shell you can't help but get the tamarind glaze on your fingers and onto the snowy white meat. ❈ Golden Turtle, owned by Kim and Kham Tran, is located in a converted Victorian where you walk over a Koi pond at the entrance. The restaurant has a comfortable upscale feel and serves some dishes you won't find anywhere else.

—Preheat the oven to 350 degrees.

—Remove the top crab shell in one piece. Cut the crab into quarters. Place the crab quarters and shell on a baking sheet and cook in the oven for 10 minutes.

—Meanwhile, in a large skillet, heat the oil over medium-high heat. Add the onion and garlic and sauté until golden brown, about 3 to 5 minutes. Add the remaining ingredients and cook until well combined, stirring frequently, about 5 minutes. Add the baked crab pieces and shell and continue to cook until the crab is well coated, about 5 minutes.

—Remove the crab and arrange on a plate, placing the shell on top to resemble a whole crab.

Serves 2 to 4

Note: *Tamarind sauce is available at some Asian markets.*

1 fresh crab, cleaned
2 tablespoons vegetable oil
¼ yellow onion, chopped
5 garlic cloves, minced
1 tablespoon tamarind sauce (see Note)
1 tablespoon sugar
1 tablespoon soy sauce
2 tablespoons butter
1 tablespoon water

SECRETS OF SUCCESS:

The sauce. The garlic, tamarind, soy, butter, and onion add intense flavors to the crab.

Baking and sautéing the crab. Baking the crab first evenly cooks the meat inside the shell. The hot crab is then sautéed in the sauce.

CRAB CAKES

For twenty years John Drocco has garnered a loyal following with his brash brand of seafood at P.J.'s Oysterbed, where Louisiana meets California in the Sunset District. He's also taught them about seafood, and the retail case in front is always filled with the latest catch of fresh fish, waiting to be taken home and cooked. ❊ Crab cakes are a signature item; they're plump and juicy with a bold seafaring flavor and just a whisper of bell pepper. The recipe was an amalgamation of what Drocco learned from repeated trips to the Chesapeake Bay and Louisiana. He discovered the mayonnaise that lends moisture at one place; crushed cracker crumbs for texture at another; and a dash of Worcestershire sauce for complexity at still another. He also discovered the sweet allure of blue crab. However, this delicacy may be hard to find, and Dungeness works nearly as well. Be sure to include some rich claw meat in the blend for both flavor and texture. Serve with aioli or garlic mayonnaise.

1 tablespoon oil, plus more for oiling pan
½ green bell pepper, finely diced
½ red bell pepper, finely diced
1 small white onion, finely diced
3 celery stalks, finely diced
½ pound blue crab claw meat or Dungeness crab meat
½ pound blue crab lump meat or Dungeness crab meat
2 large eggs
1 teaspoon Coleman's dry mustard
¼ teaspoon cayenne pepper
¼ teaspoon ground black pepper
1 tablespoon Worcestershire sauce
1 tablespoon fresh lemon juice
1 cup mayonnaise
1½ cups saltine crackers, coarsely crushed

—In a medium saucepan, heat the oil over medium-high heat. Add the bell peppers, onion, and celery and sauté until soft, about 5 minutes. Transfer to a medium bowl. Add the remaining ingredients, except for the crackers. Gently fold in the crackers and stir gently to blend. Refrigerate 1 hour.

—Form the crab mixture into 1-inch-thick patties. Lightly oil a large sauté pan and place over medium-high heat. Working in batches, add the patties, and cook until golden brown, about 3 to 4 minutes per side. Serve immediately.

Makes 6 to 8 large crab cakes

SECRETS OF SUCCESS:

Saltine crackers. Most recipes call for bread crumbs, but the crushed crackers give a lighter texture.

Mayonnaise. This gives the crab cakes a moist, creamy consistency.

The crab meat. Using both claw and lump meat adds a variety of textures to the cake.

GLAZED OYSTERS WITH LEEKS

Gary Danko has been a traveling chef: Chateau Souverain in Geyserville, the Ritz Carlton in San Francisco, Viognier in San Mateo, and now at his own restaurant, called Gary Danko. ❋ A former James Beard winner for Best Chef in California, Danko is also considered one of the best chefs in the country. And the Glazed Oysters with Leeks is a signature dish wherever he goes. ❋ Oysters never tasted better than when treated to Danko's masterful touch. Biting into the oyster releases its briny essence, setting up a startling contrast to the luxurious sauce.

4 cups water
½ cup diced leeks, white part only
30 fresh oysters in the shell
½ cup dry white wine
½ cup bottled clam juice
½ cup fish fumet or stock
2 small shallots, minced
1 tablespoon Cognac or Armagnac
1 fresh thyme sprig
1 bay leaf
¼ cup heavy cream
6 tablespoons unsalted butter, cut into small cubes
2 zucchini
2 tablespoons chopped fresh chives
2 tablespoons chervil fresh leaves

—In a medium pot, bring the water to a boil. Blanch the leeks in the water for 5 minutes. Drain, reserving ¼ cup of the cooking liquid. In a small sauté pan, combine the leeks and reserved cooking liquid over very low heat. Cover and cook until tender, about 5 minutes. Do not salt; the oysters' juices salt the dish. Remove from the heat.

—Shuck the oysters, reserving ½ cup of the juices. Combine the wine and clam juice in a small stainless steel or non-reactive sauce pan. Add the oysters and swirl to rinse. Using a slotted spoon, transfer the oysters to a bowl. Add the fumet, reserved oyster juice, shallots, Cognac, thyme, and bay leaf to the rinsing liquid. Heat and simmer until reduced by two-thirds, about 15 minutes. Stir in the cream. Bring to a boil. Reduce heat. Add the butter and whisk until emulsified and the sauce coats the back of a spoon. Strain through a fine strainer, pushing on the solids to extract all the liquid. Keep the sauce warm.

—Using a very small melon baller, carve out pea-sized balls from the zucchini, allowing about 6 to 8 per person. Cook 1 minute in a small pot of boiling water. Drain. Set aside.

—Combine the sauce and the leeks in a medium saucepan over medium heat. Bring to a boil. Add the oysters and zucchini balls and swirl until the oysters are just cooked, about 45 seconds. Spoon onto individual plates and garnish with chives and chervil. Serve immediately.

Serves 6

SECRETS OF SUCCESS:

Poaching the oysters. The sauce becomes the poaching medium for the oysters, which take only about 45 seconds to cook.

Oyster juice. The juice from the oysters is incorporated back into the sauce.

The leeks. Cooking the leeks in water, instead of oil or butter, gives them a milder, more subtle flavor.

Unusual garnish. The tiny zucchini balls add a whimsical touch and texture.

BAKED MUSSELS

Few dishes are better—and easier to prepare—than mussels. In most cases, they are steamed, but Aperto bakes them, which produces a vibrantly flavored dish that looks as good as it tastes. ❋ The seafood is flavored with fennel, bright dots of cherry tomatoes, and arugula. The wine and butter that are used as a sauce become even better when mingled with the natural juices from the mussels and vegetables. ❋ At Aperto, the mussels are cooked in the oven and transferred to the stove top to reduce the juices and concentrate the flavors. These make an impressive starter to any meal, or for an informal get-together they can become the main course. ❋ It's this casual type of dish, crafted by Chris Shepherd, that has made Aperto on Potrero Hill a popular hangout. The storefront space, with an open kitchen carved out of one corner, is always crowded and has a comfortable homelike quality reflected in the California/Italian food.

¼ cup olive oil

1 fennel bulb, thinly sliced

2 pounds Prince Edward Island black mussels, scrubbed and debearded (see page 362)

1 cup cherry tomatoes, halved

¼ dry white wine

6 ounces arugula (about 2 cups loosely packed)

½ cup (1 stick) unsalted butter, cut into small cubes

Salt and pepper

—Preheat the oven to 450 degrees.

—Heat the oil in a large, oven-proof sauté pan over medium-high heat. Add the fennel and sauté until it begins to caramelize, about 8 to 10 minutes. Add the mussels, cherry tomatoes, and wine; bring to a boil. Remove from the heat. Spread the arugula over the mussels, dot with butter, and season with salt and pepper.

—Place the pan in the oven and bake until the mussels open, about 5 to 7 minutes. Remove the pan from the oven and place over medium heat. Boil until the liquid has reduced slightly, about 2 minutes. Discard any mussels that have not opened.

—Arrange mussels in circles in each of 4 serving bowls and pour the arugula-tomato mixture into the center.

Serves 4

SECRETS OF SUCCESS:

Roasting the mussels. This no-fuss method is actually easier than cooking on the stove top and creates a more intense flavor.

The arugula. The arugula roasted on top of the mussels adds a distinctive peppery aroma to the mussel and keeps them moist.

IRON SKILLET ROASTED MUSSELS

When people think of LuLu, one dish comes to mind: the Iron Skillet Roasted Mussels. This was the first place in the Bay Area to do them. ✳ It's a simple idea, as most innovations are: The seafood is roasted with dry heat, which makes the shells brittle and gives the mussels a firmer texture and more concentrated flavor. ✳ At LuLu, the mussels are roasted in a wood-fired oven, which imparts a smoky quality. At home, they can be cooked in a dry cast-iron skillet on top of the stove. You won't get the smokiness, but they're still delicious. And it only takes a few minutes for them to open. ✳ The mussels are served with a clarified butter sauce redolent of garlic, thyme, and pepper, making a truly wonderful dish. ✳ This type of lusty dish is the hallmark of LuLu, which was started by Reed Hearon but is now operated by Jody Denton. This South of Market restaurant also pioneered the use of microphone headphones à la Madonna. The cooks in the front kitchen can communicate with the cooks in back without shouting. ✳ Little wonder this was necessary, because this loft-like restaurant can be very noisy, though the crowds don't seem to mind. It just gives them an excuse to savor the food without having to have a dinner conversation.

1 cup (2 sticks) butter
2 garlic cloves, lightly crushed
2 teaspoons cracked black pepper
1 fresh thyme sprig
1 bay leaf
2 pounds Prince Edward Island black mussels, scrubbed and debearded (see page 362)
Salt and freshly ground pepper
Juice of 1 Meyer lemon or other lemon
Lemon wedges

—Place the butter, garlic, pepper, thyme, and bay leaf in the top of a double boiler. Cook about 1 hour until the butter has separated from the milk solids and the flavors have blended. Skim off the milk solids from the top of the butter. Strain out the herbs and spices. Set the clarified butter aside.

—Heat a large cast-iron skillet over medium heat until hot, about 2 to 3 minutes. Spread the mussels evenly over the surface of the skillet and increase the heat to high. Cook until the mussels open, about 3 to 4 minutes. Discard any that do not open. Sprinkle salt and pepper liberally over the mussels. Remove from the heat.

—Stir the lemon juice into the clarified butter. Serve the mussels immediately in the cast-iron skillet with the clarified herb butter and lemon wedges.

Serves 4 to 6

SECRETS OF SUCCESS:

Dry heat. Roasting the mussels without any liquid concentrates the flavor and firms the texture.

The drawn butter. The garlic/herb dipping sauce provides a rich moistness for the mussels.

Mussels with curry sauce

If I had to name the top-selling shellfish served in Bay Area restaurants, it would be mussels. It doesn't matter whether the cuisine is Chinese, Thai, Italian, or French, you'll find them on just about every menu. ❉ One of the best and most unusual preparations is at Plouf, developed by former chef Scott Barton. Several things set it apart: the addition of curry powder balanced by apple and celery; smoothing the sauce with crème fraîche (or cream) and coconut milk; and finally, adding Champagne vinegar infused with chiles for a sizzling kick. It adds up to a marvelous dish that's easy to prepare at home. Be sure to leave enough time to make the habañero vinegar, which is best if made one day ahead. ❉ Plouf, a French-inspired seafood restaurant, has a way with mussels. No other restaurant in the Bay Area has a bigger selection. In all, there are eight preparations on the menu. ❉ Tucked away on Belden Lane—a block-long alley in the Financial District—Plouf feels like a find. The fireplace in the corner is great on cool evenings, and a wall of windows in front can be thrown open in warm weather to bring the outside in. With all the tables out front the area has become a popular after-work hang out.

Mussels

3 tablespoons unsalted butter
2 large yellow onions, diced
3 celery ribs, diced
1 tablespoon Madras curry powder
Pinch of saffron threads
2 Granny Smith apples, peeled and diced
1½ teaspoons (or more) salt
½ teaspoon (or more) ground white pepper
1½ cups dry white wine
⅓ cup crème fraîche or heavy cream
⅓ cup plain nonfat yogurt
⅓ cup canned unsweetened coconut milk (preferably Chaokoh brand)
1 tablespoon (or more) Habañero Vinegar (recipe follows)
3 pounds Prince Edward Island black mussels, scrubbed and debearded
2 tablespoons minced fresh chives for garnishing

Habañero Vinegar

½ habañero or jalapeño chile, seeded and chopped
2 tablespoons Champagne vinegar

—*To cook the mussels:* In a heavy-bottomed pot large enough to hold all the mussels, melt the butter over medium heat. Add the onions, celery, curry powder, and saffron. Sauté until tender and translucent, about 7 to 10 minutes. Add the apples and sauté until soft, about 5 minutes. Stir in 1½ teaspoons salt and ½ teaspoon white pepper.

—Stir in the wine, crème fraîche, yogurt, coconut milk, and 1 tablespoon Habañero Vinegar. Bring to a simmer. Add the mussels, cover the pan, and cook until the mussels open, about 6 minutes.

—Remove the pan from the heat and discard any unopened mussels. Add additional salt, pepper, or Habañero Vinegar, if desired.

—Ladle the mussels and sauce into serving bowls. Garnish with chopped chives.

Serves 6

—*To make the vinegar:* For best results, prepare the vinegar at least 1 day before serving. You can make the vinegar the same day, but allow it to steep at least 1 hour before adding to the recipe.

—Combine the chile and vinegar in a small bowl. Let stand at room temperature at least 1 hour and up to 24 hours. Strain. Refrigerate until ready to use.

> **SECRETS OF SUCCESS:**
>
> *The sauce.* Crème fraîche, yogurt, and coconut milk, paired with a fiery chile vinegar and curry powder, works wonders on the mussels.
>
> *The apples.* The crisp Granny Smiths offer a clean contrast to the rest of the dish.

BOUILLABAISSE WITH FENNEL

Fabrice Canelle, who was the chef at Brasserie Savoy before he took off for the Russian Tea Room in New York, made the best bouillabaisse I've ever tasted. The seafood stew was so basic to him that he forgot the defining ingredient when he sent in the recipe: the half bulb of fennel anchored on the bottom of the soup plate. ✤ "Oh, you're right," he said when I called. "I didn't realize it was that distinctive." But it was. The fennel turns what is a delicious but ordinary stew into an extraordinary melange. Not only is the seared-then-baked fennel the focal point of the dish, but the licorice flavor is incorporated in the stock. Aside from the fennel, the recipe calls for carrots, potatoes, and all kinds of seafood. ✤ Making the bouillabaisse is labor intensive, but it makes a great one-dish meal for a casual dinner party. First you need to make a fish *fume*, or stock, then prepare the vegetables and seafood. To complete the dish, you also need a *rouille*, a mayonnaise with a spicy kick, which is slathered on toast and served with the stew.

Stock
1½ cups extra-virgin olive oil
¼ garlic head, unpeeled
¼ cup diced onion
10 saffron threads
½ cup diced carrot
½ cup diced leek
½ cup diced fennel
½ cup peeled and diced potato
Kosher salt and ground black pepper
2 cups diced ripe tomato
Zest from ¼ of an orange
½ teaspoon fennel seeds
6 fresh basil leaves
1 fresh rosemary sprig
2 cups dry white wine
3 tablespoons Pernod
4 cups fish stock or 2 cups bottled clam juice
    and 2 cups water

Rouille
¼ red bell pepper
½ cup crushed garlic

3 egg yolks
Juice of 1 lemon
Pinch of cayenne pepper
2½ cups extra-virgin olive oil
Salt and pepper

Fennel garnish
2 tablespoons olive oil
3 fennel bulbs, halved
3 tablespoons Pernod
1 star anise piece

Bouillabaisse
18 Manila clams, scrubbed
18 Prince Edward Island black mussels, scrubbed
    and debearded (see page 362)
6 medium shrimp
1½ pound Petrale sole, cut into 1-inch pieces
¾ pound red snapper, cut into 1-inch pieces
½ pound lingcod, cut into 1-inch pieces
Salt and pepper
12 to 18 baguette slices, toasted

—*To make the stock:* In a large sauté pan, heat the olive oil over medium-high heat. Add the garlic, onion, and saffron. Stir until the saffron releases its color, about 1 to 2 minutes. Add the carrot, leek, fennel, and potato. Sauté for 5 minutes, stirring frequently. Season with salt and pepper. Add the tomatoes, zest, fennel seeds, basil leaves, and rosemary and stir for a few more minutes. Stir in the white wine and Pernod. Simmer for 5 minutes. Add the stock, cover the pan, and slowly simmer for 20 minutes to blend flavors. Remove from the heat. Reserve 2 cups for the fennel.

—*To make the rouille:* Combine the red pepper, garlic, egg yolks, lemon juice, cayenne, and ½ cup of the olive oil in a processor and process to blend. Gradually add the remaining olive oil and process until the mixture is slightly thick and golden yellow in color. Season to taste with salt and pepper. Set aside.

—*To prepare the fennel:* Heat the oil over high heat in a large sauté pan. Add the fennel and cook until brown, about 3 to 5 minutes. Add the reserved 2 cups stock, Pernod, and star anise. Reduce heat to low. Cover the pan and simmer until the fennel is tender, about 20 minutes. Set aside.

—*To make the bouillabaisse:* Heat the stock to a simmer. Add the clams and cook about 7 to 10 minutes. Add the mussels and cook for 1 minute. Add the shrimp, sole, snapper, and lingcod and cook just until the shrimp turn pink, about 3 minutes. Remove from the heat. Discard any clams or mussels that do not open. Season to taste with salt and pepper.

—Place half a fennel bulb in the bottom of each of 6 bowls. Ladle the bouillabaisse over the fennel. Spread the baguette slices generously with rouille. Garnish the bowls with baguette slices.

Serves 6

> **SECRETS OF SUCCESS:**
>
> *Echoes of licorice.* This distinctive flavor is repeated in the fennel, Pernod, and in the dried fennel seeds.
>
> *Hidden orange.* Although the zest of ¼ orange doesn't seem like much it has a magical effect on the seafood, adding a fresh lively note.

PASTA, GRAINS, AND MEATLESS COURSES

VEGETABLE BROCHETTES WITH MARINATED TOFU

The tofu brochettes have been on the menu at Greens since it opened more than twenty years ago. This preparation transforms tofu into something truly special. ❋ In this dish, bland is banned, as cubes of the white soy protein are marinated in a vibrant vinaigrette and threaded on skewers with a garden of vegetables. Smoky nuances of wood and charcoal are picked up during grilling, and more flavor is added by brushing on a marinade, creating an explosion of flavors that will make avowed carnivores take notice. ❋ What's on the brochettes aside from the tofu changes with the season: Sweet corn, zucchini, and new potatoes in summer; winter squash, slices of sweet potato, and fennel in winter. ❋ This recipe begs for variation, and it's always changing in the restaurant. Chef Annie Somerville may marinate the tofu in Indian spices and serve it with cashew basmati rice, cucumber raita, and mango-papaya chutney. Other times she might give the marinade an Asian accent and serve the brochettes with peanut-jasmine rice. For a Southwest flair, she suggests a chipotle-lime vinaigrette. Then brush on chipotle butter during grilling. At lunch the most popular way to serve them is by brushing on a piquant mustard butter. ❋ It is dishes like this that have made Greens the premier vegetarian restaurant in the country. When it was opened as part of the Zen Center, it garnered immediate publicity not only for the food, but also for the innovative wine list and the views of the Golden Gate Bridge and the Marin Headlands.

10 small new potatoes or other potatoes, cut into 1-inch cubes
1 ear of corn, cut into ½-inch-thick rounds
16 medium mushrooms, stemmed
1 bell pepper (any color), cut into squares
8 cherry tomatoes
16 boiling onions, parboiled and peeled
2 or 3 zucchini, cut into rounds
16 to 24 ounces Marinated Tofu (recipe follows), cut into 1-inch cubes
8 bay leaves
Brochette Marinade (recipe follows)
Salt and pepper

Brochette Marinade
2 tablespoons red wine vinegar or sherry vinegar
1 tablespoon Dijon mustard
1 tablespoon finely chopped fresh herbs such as parsley, thyme, and marjoram
1 garlic clove, finely chopped
¾ cup olive oil
Salt and pepper

Marinated Tofu
16 to 24 ounces firm tofu, cut into 1-inch-thick slices
1 cup water
½ ounce dried porcini or shiitake mushrooms

2 teaspoons dried oregano or marjoram
½ cup olive oil
½ cup sherry vinegar or red wine vinegar
½ cup dry red wine
½ cup tamari soy sauce
4 whole cloves
2 garlic cloves, sliced
½ teaspoon salt
Three grinds of fresh black pepper

—Prepare the grill (medium-high heat) and position the rack 6 to 8 inches above the grill. Parboil the potatoes until almost tender, about 10 to 12 minutes. Parboil the corn until almost tender, about 2 to 3 minutes.

—Starting and ending with mushrooms, skewer the vegetables, Marinated Tofu, and bay leaves.

—In a pan or baking sheet large enough to hold all the brochettes, brush them generously with the Brochette Marinade, making sure all sides are coated.

—Grill the vegetable skewers until hot and brown, brushing occasionally with Brochette Marinade and turning frequently, about 5 to 10 minutes. Transfer the skewers to a serving platter. Brush with remaining marinade. Season to taste with salt and pepper and serve.

Makes 8 skewers

—*To make the brochette marinade:* Mix the vinegar with the mustard, herbs, and garlic. Whisk in the oil and season with salt and pepper.

—*To make the tofu:* Place the tofu slices on the back of a baking sheet. Drain the water from the tofu into the sink by lifting one edge of the sheet. Cover the tofu with another tray. Set a weight of roughly 3 pounds atop the second tray. Let the tofu drain for about 30 minutes.

—Bring the water to a simmer in a medium saucepan. Add the mushrooms and simmer until tender, about 15 minutes. Remove from heat. Toast the oregano or marjoram in a small skillet over low heat until fragrant, about 3 to 5 minutes. Add to the mushrooms. Add the olive oil, vinegar, wine, soy sauce, cloves, garlic, salt, and pepper to the mushrooms and water. Bring to a boil. Simmer slowly until flavors blend, about 5 minutes.

—Arrange the tofu in a single layer in a non-corrosive pan. Strain the marinade through a coffee filter or paper towel. Pour the marinade over the tofu. Cover. Refrigerate at least 1 day and up to 5 days.

SECRETS OF SUCCESS:

Marinating the tofu. Buy firm, Chinese-style tofu and allow it to soak in the vinaigrette for at least 24 hours; it's best after 2 or 3 days.

Brushing on the marinade. Keeping the vegetables glazed with a vinaigrette or flavored butter adds additional flavor and keeps everything moist.

Vegetable Milhojas with Basil, Tomato, and Goat Cheese

Spanish cuisine isn't necessarily known for its vegetarian specialties, but any successful restaurant in San Francisco—especially one that attracts a young crowd—has to offer more than your basic plate of grilled vegetables. ❊ So chef Bernat Dones uses his imagination. He's created one of the most enticing vegetable main courses I remember eating. It's made of paper-thin layers of celery root, squash, eggplant, and zucchini. The vegetables are moistened with a drizzling of basil oil and topped with tomatoes and a creamy crumble of goat cheese. ❊ It's a perfect dish for this trendy Mission urban-chic restaurant which incorporates new and old elements: modern blue and yellow glass pendant lights hang over the tiled bar and kitchen, and rustic pine floors provide a visual contrast to the sleek molded wood chairs and the cool blue and yellow color scheme. ❊ With its sophisticated interior and innovative recipes, Pintxos (pronounced PEEN-chos) does for Spanish/Basque food what the groundbreaking Slanted Door did for Vietnamese.

Milhojas

1 tablespoon olive oil
½ pound tomatoes, peeled, seeded, and diced (see page 363)
6 garlic cloves, smashed
5 fresh basil leaves
Salt and pepper
½ pound eggplant
½ pound zucchini
½ pound kabocha or other autumn squash, peeled
½ pound celery root, peeled
About 4 tablespoons Basil Oil (recipe follows)
½ pound soft, fresh goat cheese (such as Montrachet), crumbled

Basil Oil

Any remaining basil oil can be refrigerated for up to a month to be used in salads or as a flavoring for meats.

½ bunch fresh basil (about 70 leaves)
½ cup olive oil
Salt and pepper

—*To make the milhojas:* Heat the olive oil in a large skillet over medium-high heat. Add the tomatoes, garlic, and basil leaves. Season to taste with salt and pepper. Sauté for 1 minute. Remove the garlic and basil. Refrigerate the tomato sauce for at least 1 hour.

—Preheat the oven to 450 degrees.

—Using a mandoline, cut the eggplant into thin circles about ⅛-inch thick. Cut the zucchini into long strips, about ⅛-inch thick. Cut the squash and celery root into ¹/₁₆-inch-thick slices.

—Heat a large non-stick skillet over medium-high heat. Do not add any oil. Sprinkle the zucchini with salt and pepper. Add to the skillet and sauté until just soft, about 2 minutes per side. Transfer to a platter.

—Repeat the seasoning and sautéing about 2 minutes per side with the eggplant. Transfer the eggplant to the platter. Sprinkle the celery root with salt and pepper. Add to the skillet and sauté until barely soft, about 3 minutes per side. Transfer to the platter. Repeat the seasoning and sautéing 3 minutes per side with the squash. Transfer to the platter.

—Using an 8x8-inch oven-proof glass pan, layer the vegetables, beginning with enough of the celery root to cover the bottom of the pan, followed by some of the eggplant, squash, and zucchini. Drizzle with 1 tablespoon of basil oil and repeat the layering process until all the vegetables are used, using 1 tablespoon Basil Oil between each complete set of vegetables.

—Pour the tomato sauce over the vegetables. Sprinkle the goat cheese on top. Bake until the cheese starts to brown, about 6 minutes. Drizzle with the remaining 1 tablespoon of Basil Oil and serve.

Serves 4

—*To make the basil oil:* Drop the basil leaves into a medium pot of boiling water and drain immediately. Then plunge the leaves into a bowl of ice water. Remove the leaves. Pat dry. Put the leaves in the bowl of a food processor. Pulse to chop. Slowly add the oil. Season to taste with salt and pepper.

Makes about ½ cup

> **SECRETS OF SUCCESS:**
>
> *Slicing the vegetables:* It's important to cut them as thin as possible, so the ingredients meld.
>
> *Dry sautéing the vegetables.* The paper-thin vegetables are first cooked in a dry skillet to soften, brown, and intensify the flavors.
>
> *A turn in the oven:* After layering the sautéed vegetables, the casserole is baked, which further helps to unify the dish.

VEGETABLE LASAGNA

At La Villa Poppi you'll find one of the best vegetable lasagnas around, produced by chef/owner Greg Sweeting. The wide tender noodles are layered with thinly sliced eggplant and zucchini, lightly coated in a mildly spicy marinara sauce and rich béchamel. ❋ The tiny store-front restaurant in the Mission has only seven tables, all set with mismatched chairs. Obviously people come here for the food, not the decor. ❋ Sweeting cooks everything, with no help from a sous chef or prep cook. His cooking inspiration—and the name of the restaurant—came from the Italian village where Sweeting trained. In San Francisco he's also worked at Mecca and La Folie. ❋ Sweeting limits the frequently changing menu, but the lasagna is a staple.

Marinara Sauce
¼ cup olive oil
1 garlic clove, thinly sliced
1 teaspoon dried red pepper flakes
3 bay leaves
Two 28-ounce cans crushed Italian tomatoes,
    drained
½ cup (or more) water
8 fresh basil leaves
1 teaspoon sugar
Salt

Vegetables
Salt
1 to 2 large Italian eggplants, cut lengthwise into
    ⅛-inch slices
Olive oil for greasing
3 to 4 medium zucchini, cut lengthwise into
    ⅛-inch slices

Béchamel Sauce
1 cup (2 sticks) unsalted butter
1 cup all purpose flour
1 quart whole milk
Salt
Pinch of freshly ground nutmeg

Olive oil
1 pound lasagna noodles
½ to 1 cup freshly grated Parmesan cheese

—*To make the marinara sauce:* Heat the oil in a large saucepan over low heat. Add the garlic, red pepper flakes, and bay leaves and stir until fragrant, about 3 to 5 minutes. Add the tomatoes and ½ cup water. Simmer uncovered until sauce thickens slightly, stirring occasionally, about 30 minutes. Stir in the basil and sugar. Season to taste with salt. Add more water if you want a thinner sauce. Puree sauce in blender, if desired.

—*To make the vegetables:* Lightly salt both sides of the sliced eggplant and place them between layers of paper towels. Put a flat, heavy object (such as a baking pan with a brick) on top to gently extract the bitter moisture. Let the eggplant "dry" like this for at least 20 minutes or up to 2 hours.

—Prepare a lightly oiled grill (medium heat) or heat a lightly oiled sauté pan over medium heat. Grill or sauté the eggplant until tender, about 3 or 4 minutes per side. Set aside.

—Blanch the zucchini in a large pot of boiling water for 1 minute. Drain. Place the zucchini in a large bowl of ice water to stop the cooking and to retain the bright green color. Drain. Set aside.

—*To make the béchamel sauce:* In a saucepan, melt the butter over low heat. Whisk in the flour until thoroughly combined. Stir until flour is cooked but not browned, about 5 minutes. Warm the milk in a small saucepan over low heat. Slowly whisk the milk into the flour mixture until the sauce is silky and smooth. Continue to cook over very low heat until thick, about 30 minutes, stirring frequently to prevent the sauce from scalding on the bottom. Season to taste with salt and nutmeg. Remove from heat, cover, and keep warm until ready to use.

—Preheat the oven to 375 degrees. Lightly oil a 9x13 casserole dish.

—Cook the lasagna noodles in a large pot of boiling salted water until tender but still firm to bite. Drain. Place the noodles in a bowl of cold water to stop the cooking. Drain. Place the noodles in a large container and coat with enough olive oil to prevent them from sticking together.

—Place a layer of noodles in the prepared casserole dish. If necessary, cut the noodles to fit the casserole so there are no gaps between the noodles and the pan. Spread the noodles with a thin layer of béchamel sauce, then a thin layer of marinara sauce, to completely cover the noodles. Place a layer of eggplant on top of the sauce, then zucchini. (The vegetables do not need to be placed as close together as the noodles.) Sprinkle lightly with the Parmesan cheese. Repeat the steps, using all of the noodles, sauce, vegetables, and cheese, making about 5 layers, ending with cheese.

—Cover the dish with aluminum foil and bake until browned and bubbling, about 45 minutes. Cut into squares and serve.

Serves 6

> ### SECRETS OF SUCCESS:
>
> *Two sauces.* The tomato sauce adds flavor and acidity, and béchamel adds a rich creaminess.

QUAIL EGG RAVIOLI

Of all the stuffed pastas in the city, the most novel and impressive is the egg ravioli at Postrio. When you cut into the toothsome pasta, yolk oozes out and flavors whatever is below. At Postrio it's a brown butter sauce and grilled quail. The quail is the star ingredient, but in my mind the pasta always upstages it. (At home the quail can be sautéed in olive oil or cooked on a hot grill, then placed atop the ravioli.) ❖ Since opening more than a decade ago Wolfgang Puck's first San Francisco restaurant has been one of the most popular in the city, sporting one of the most impressive decors, too. The grand staircase leading down to the main dining room would make Dolly Levi proud. Everyone has his or her fifteen seconds of fame descending the wide staircase. ❖ And the food, crafted by brothers Mitchell and Steven Rosenthal, mixes France, the Mediterranean, Asia, and a little bit of San Francisco into a menu that remains on the cutting edge of culinary trends.

Ravioli

2 tablespoons olive oil

2 pounds fresh spinach, washed and stemmed

1 garlic clove, chopped

2 ounces mascarpone cheese

2 ounces plus ⅓ cup grated Parmesan cheese

Freshly ground nutmeg

Salt and pepper

16 quail eggs (see Note)

2 sheets Saffron Pasta, 19x10 inches and ¹/₁₆-inch thick (recipe follows)

6 tablespoons (¾ stick) butter

1½ tablespoons fresh chopped thyme

4 fresh Italian parsley sprigs for garnishing

Saffron Pasta

Alternatively, fresh pasta sheets can be purchased in some ethnic markets or upscale super markets.

Pinch of saffron threads

3 tablespoons warm water

½ pound all-purpose flour

⅔ pound semolina flour

Pinch of salt

2 eggs, beaten to blend

3 tablespoons (or more) olive oil

—*To make the ravioli:* In a large sauté pan, heat the olive oil over medium heat. Add the spinach and garlic and cook until the spinach wilts, about 5 minutes. Transfer to a colander to drain and cool. Place the spinach in a cheesecloth and squeeze until dry. Finely chop the spinach. Place in a medium bowl. Add the mascarpone cheese and 2 ounces of Parmesan. Season to taste with nutmeg, salt, and pepper. Divide the mixture into 16 balls.

—Lay out one pasta sheet. Arrange the spinach balls down the center of the pasta, with enough room in between so the finished ravioli can be cut with a 3-inch round pasta cutter. Make a well in the middle of each spinach ball to hold the quail egg.

—Separate the quail eggs one at a time; discard whites or save for another use. Place one yolk in each spinach well. With a pastry brush, lightly brush water around the 16 spinach wells to seal the ravioli. Place the other sheet of pasta over the spinach. Using your fingers, press around each spinach ball to seal the ravioli. Using a 3-inch round serrated pasta cutter, cut out the ravioli. Lightly press the edges of the ravioli to ensure they are sealed.

—Cook the ravioli in a large pot of simmering salted water until tender but still firm to bite, about 3 to 5 minutes.

—Meanwhile, cook the butter in a medium sauté pan over medium heat until brown, about 5 minutes. Drain the ravioli well and place 4 in the center of each of 4 serving plates, slightly overlapping. Sprinkle with the remaining ⅓ cup Parmesan cheese and chopped thyme. Spoon the hot brown butter over. Garnish with parsley. Serve immediately.

Serves 4

Note: *Quail eggs are available at specialty food markets and Asian markets.*

—*To make the saffron pasta:* Put the saffron in a small cup with the warm water and set aside for 5 minutes.

—On a clean cutting board or countertop, combine the flour, semolina, and salt. Make a well in the center and add the eggs, 3 tablespoons of olive oil, and 1 tablespoon of the saffron water to the well. Using your hands, start working the dough from the outside in, folding and kneading. If the mixture seems dry, add more of the saffron water or oil and continue kneading until the dough is smooth, about 5 minutes. Form the dough into a ball and cover with a damp towel. Allow to rest at room temperature for about 30 minutes. Roll out the dough to desired thickness.

SECRETS OF SUCCESS:

The quail egg. The raw quail egg comes only to the soft-boiled stage, so when pierced the bright yellow yolk oozes out.

SPINACH RAVIOLI WITH SAGE BROWN BUTTER SAUCE

Splendido chef Giovanni Perticone doesn't tamper with a good thing. After all, what's better than his Spinach Ravioli in Sage Brown Butter Sauce? The dish incorporates only a few ingredients, but uses each to its best advantage. ❊ The most challenging aspect is making the pasta dough, which is a combination of semolina flour, eggs, and olive oil. He makes a simple filling of spinach, ricotta, mascarpone, and Parmesan. Finally, he adds the sauce: Butter, sage, and Grana Padano cheese. ❊ Perticone is a modern chef with a passion for the classics. In fact, at Splendido he's beginning to introduce some ancient recipes from Rome that predate the tomato. In his research he's found that the cuisine used fish sauce for flavoring, much like many Asian cultures do today. ❊ With his gift and passion he's turned this Pat Kuleto–designed restaurant in the Embarcadero into a top stop for Italian food. It's also one of the most dramatic restaurants, featuring unusual light fixtures, a domed brick ceiling at the entrance, rough stone columns, and an expanse of windows that overlook the Embarcadero.

Pasta
¾ pound semolina flour
¼ pound all-purpose flour
3 eggs
½ cup water
1 teaspoon olive oil
Pinch of salt

Filling
1 pound spinach, washed and stemmed
Salt
1 pound ricotta
3½ ounces mascarpone cheese
1 egg
1 ounce grated Parmigiano-Reggiano
Generous pinch of ground nutmeg
1 egg yolk, beaten to blend
All-purpose flour
Semolina flour

Sauce
10 tablespoons butter
10 fresh sage leaves
Salt
2 ounces grated Grana Padano cheese (see Note)
1 ounce shaved Grana Padano cheese (see Note)

—*To make the pasta:* Place the semolina and the all-purpose flours in the bowl of an electric mixer fit with the hook attachment. Mix on low speed to blend. Combine the eggs and the water in a small bowl. Gradually add to the flour mixture. Slowly drizzle the oil into the mixture while continuing to mix. Add the salt. Once the liquid is completely absorbed, form the dough into a ball, wrap in plastic, and refrigerate until the filling is made.

—*To make the filling:* Cook the spinach in a large pot of boiling salted water for 30 seconds. Drain. Immediately transfer the spinach to a bowl of ice water to stop the cooking. Drain. Dry the spinach thoroughly in a clean kitchen towel. Coarsely chop the spinach. In a medium bowl, stir together the ricotta and mascarpone until smooth. Stir in the egg, Parmigiano-Reggiano, and nutmeg. Fold in the spinach. Season to taste with salt.

—Use a pasta machine or rolling pin to roll out the dough as thin as possible. Cut the dough into 4 sheets measuring 18 inches by 6 inches. Using a teaspoon, make a row of filling down the center of 2 pasta sheets, spacing the filling 1½ inches apart.

—Brush around the mounds of filling with the beaten egg yolk. Quickly cover the 2 pasta sheets with the 2 remaining pasta sheets, forming 2 rows of ravioli. Lightly press around the mounds of filling, sealing the sheets of pasta together. Using a 3-inch ravioli cutter, cut the ravioli into squares. Arrange on a floured baking sheet. Sprinkle with semolina flour and keep refrigerated until ready to cook.

—*To make the sauce:* In a large sauté pan, melt the butter over medium heat and cook until golden brown, about 5 minutes. Add the sage leaves and cook until fragrant, about 2 to 3 minutes, making sure not to burn the leaves. Remove from the heat.

—Cook the ravioli in a large pot of boiling salted water until they rise to the surface, about 5 minutes. Drain. Transfer the ravioli to a serving bowl and sprinkle with salt and the grated cheese. Pour the browned butter over the ravioli and sprinkle the shaved cheese around the ravioli. Serve immediately.

Serves 4 to 6

Note: *Grana Padano cheese is similar to pecorino cheese and can be found at most upscale supermarkets.*

SECRETS OF SUCCESS:

Sautéing the sage leaves. The whole leaves are sautéed in the brown butter, flavoring the sauce and crisping the herb.

Four cheeses. The three cheeses in the filling and the fourth sprinkled on top marries various characteristics: nutty, tangy, creamy, and rich.

FETTUCCINE WITH SHIITAKE MUSHROOMS, ROASTED TOMATOES, AND ARUGULA

Simple is almost always the best way to go when preparing food, particularly pasta. Oftentimes restaurants add too much in an attempt to make dishes interesting. ✳ To get a "wow" experience, the ingredients need to be chosen carefully; otherwise, they either clash or become boring after a few bites. One of the best examples of picking the right stuff is found in Adolfo Veronese's Fettuccine with Shiitake Mushrooms, Roasted Tomatoes, and Arugula. The three dominant flavors marry flawlessly, creating a dish you just can't stop eating. ✳ Even though the added step of roasting the tomatoes is a key element in this recipe, the dish is still easy to prepare. ✳ Although Adolfo's closed in 1999, the recipe will live on for any cook wanting a great dish in a hurry without a lot of work.

10 Roma tomatoes
1 teaspoon salt, plus additional to taste
½ teaspoon freshly ground black pepper, plus
    additional to taste
3 tablespoons extra-virgin olive oil
3 garlic cloves, sliced
½ pound shiitake mushrooms, stemmed, caps
    cut into ½-inch pieces
½ cup dry white wine
Generous pinch dried red pepper flakes
1 tablespoon minced fresh parsley
1½ pounds fresh fettuccine
2 tablespoons butter
1 bunch arugula, tough stems removed (approxi-
    mately 6 cups of leaves, loosely packed)

—Preheat the oven to 450 degrees.

—Quarter the tomatoes and place them in a bowl with 1 teaspoon salt, ½ teaspoon black pepper, and 1 tablespoon of the olive oil. Toss well. Place the tomatoes on a baking sheet. Roast until the tomatoes are soft, juicy, and beginning to brown around the edges, about 20 to 25 minutes.

—Heat the remaining 2 tablespoons olive oil in a large pot over medium heat. Add the garlic and sauté until translucent, about 1 to 2 minutes. Add the mushrooms and sauté until tender, about 5 minutes. Add the wine, pepper flakes, roasted tomatoes, and parsley. Season to taste with salt and pepper. Toss briefly, then remove from heat.

—Cook the fettuccine in a large pot of boiling salted water until tender but still firm to bite. Drain. Toss the pasta with the roasted tomato mixture. Add the butter and arugula and toss until the butter melts and the arugula wilts slightly.

Serves 6

SECRETS OF SUCCESS:

The tomatoes. Seasoning the tomatoes and then roasting them helps concentrate the flavors so they stand up to the earthiness of the mushrooms and arugula.

The arugula. Tossing in a zesty ingredient like arugula and letting it wilt into the hot pasta brightens the dish and makes it more interesting.

The butter. Adding butter at the end of cooking enriches the dish and helps smooth and harmonize the flavors.

FETTUCCINE WITH ROCK SHRIMP AND ARUGULA

The combination of rock shrimp and arugula are magical in this pasta recipe by Vincenzo Cucco, chef/owner of Bacco. Like all good pasta dishes, it's relatively simple and all the other ingredients including tomato and wine support the main flavors. Butter finishes the dish to a wonderful smoothness. ❋ The pasta is a great way to start a dinner party or, since it can be tossed together in a half hour, it is a prime candidate for a work-night meal. ❋ These kinds of simple, satisfying dishes are part of the charm of this Noe Valley restaurant. The modern decor, spread over several storefronts, is painted a warm pumpkin color, creating a casual upscale environment for the food.

—Cook the pasta in a large pot of boiling salted water until tender but still firm to bite, about 2 minutes.
—Meanwhile, heat the oil in a large sauté pan. Add the shrimp and garlic and sauté for 1 minute. Using a slotted spoon, transfer the shrimp to a bowl. Add the wine to the pan and bring to a boil. Add the tomato; stir 2 minutes. Stir in the arugula and pepper. Season to taste with salt.
—Drain the pasta, reserving 1 cup of the cooking water. Add the pasta to the sauté pan. Add the butter and toss to coat, adding some of the pasta water if the mixture looks dry. Divide among 4 plates.

Serves 4

1 pound fresh fettuccine
Salt
¾ cup extra-virgin olive oil
1 pound fresh rock shrimp
2 teaspoons chopped garlic
1 cup dry white wine
1 large tomato, peeled, seeded, and cut into ½-inch dice (see page 363)
1 bunch arugula, cut into large pieces
½ teaspoon ground pepper
¼ cup (½ stick) unsalted butter, cut into small pieces

SECRETS OF SUCCESS:

Combining shrimp and arugula. The peppery qualities in the greens help to bring out a sweetness in the seafood.

The butter. It adds the finishing touch and brings it all together.

LINGUINE WITH LEMON CREAM

I'm in love with the Linguine with Lemon Cream at Mescolanza, a charming neighborhood Italian restaurant in the Richmond District. It's so easy—only six ingredients counting the pasta—but the end result is extraordinary. The flavors of cream, butter, and Parmesan set off the fresh lemon. ❊ In the restaurant, it's served without any garnish. At home, this pasta can become the base for myriad dishes. I love it with fresh lemon thyme or tarragon sprinkled on top. It's also exceptional with sautéed shrimp, broccoli rabe, or fresh white corn. ❊ The restaurant was purchased by Maria and Ruben Macedo in 1998, but they had been cooking there since it opened in 1987. ❊ Prices are reasonable and the recently redone interior makes this restaurant a cut above the typical neighborhood trattoria.

—Cook the linguine in a large pot of generously salted water until tender but still firm to bite, about 10 minutes.

—Meanwhile, combine the cream, lemon juice, and ½ teaspoon salt in a large saucepan over medium-high heat. Bring to a boil. Add the cheese and butter. Stir constantly until the sauce thickens, about 5 to 10 minutes.

—Drain the pasta. Transfer to a large serving bowl. Pour the sauce over; toss to coat. Season to taste with white pepper.

Serves 6

1 pound dried linguine
Salt for cooking pasta, plus ½ teaspoon
2½ cups heavy cream
Juice of 5 lemons
1 cup grated Parmesan cheese
¼ cup (½ stick) butter, cut into pieces
Freshly ground white pepper

SECRETS OF SUCCESS:

Lots of lemon. The juice of five lemons seems like a lot but it gives the sauce a fresh intensity without having to grate or chop the zest.

The utter simplicity. Better than the sum of its parts, the play between the cream, butter, Parmesan, and lemon juice is invigorating.

FUSILLI WITH EGGPLANT AND SMOKED MOZZARELLA

Since its inception nearly a decade ago, Pane e Vino has enjoyed the status of being one of the top neighborhood Italian restaurants in San Francisco, thanks to chef/owner Bruno Quercini. ❋ His earthy food has drawn customers far beyond the restaurant's Cow Hollow neighborhood. The homey interior, which includes a rustic table centered with a whole prosciutto cut to order, sets the tone. ❋ The Fusilli with Eggplant and Smoked Mozzarella has developed such a following that many people eat here just for this dish. It's a distinctive blend of garlicky tomato sauce, densely-textured fried eggplant, and creamy, smoky cheese. Since loads of garlic permeates the sauce and the eggplant, this is truly a dish for garlic fanatics.

Fusilli

1 eggplant, cut into ¼-inch-thick slices

8 tablespoons sea salt, plus additional for sprinkling

5 tablespoons olive oil

4 teaspoons finely chopped garlic

1 pound fusilli pasta

3 cups Neapolitan Tomato Sauce (recipe follows)

4 ounces smoked mozzarella, cut into ½-inch cubes

1 teaspoon freshly ground white pepper

2 to 3 tablespoons grated Parmesan cheese

2 teaspoons chopped fresh Italian parsley

Neapolitan Tomato Sauce

½ cup olive oil

½ cup garlic (about 2 medium heads), separated into cloves, peeled and chopped

½ cup roughly chopped fresh basil leaves

One 28-ounce can crushed tomatoes in puree

¼ teaspoon salt

¼ teaspoon ground white pepper

½ teaspoon sugar (optional)

—*To cook the fusilli:* Layer the eggplant in a colander, sprinkling sea salt between each layer, and place 4 plates on top to weigh it down. Let stand at least 8 and up to 12 hours to extract all the bitter juices. Cut the eggplant into ¼-inch slices.

—Bring a gallon of water and 8 tablespoons sea salt to a boil.

—Meanwhile, heat 1 tablespoon of the oil in a large skillet over medium-high heat. Add the garlic. Saute until lightly brown, about 3 to 5 minutes. Add remaining 4 tablespoons olive oil. Add the eggplant and sauté until golden brown, about 3 to 5 minutes. Transfer to paper towels to drain.

—Cook the pasta in the boiling salted water until tender but still firm to bite.

—Drain the pasta and return to the pan. Heat the Neapolitan Tomato Sauce in a small saucepan. Pour over the pasta. Add the eggplant, smoked mozzarella, and white pepper. Stir to combine and melt the cheese.

—Divide the pasta among 4 to 6 serving plates. Sprinkle with the Parmesan and parsley.

Serves 4 to 6

—*To make the sauce:* Heat the olive oil in a large sauce pan over high heat. Add the garlic and sauté until lightly browned, about 5 to 7 minutes. Strain the oil and discard the garlic. Return the oil to the pan and add the basil. Sauté until fragrant, about 1 minute. Add the tomatoes, salt, and pepper.

—Simmer uncovered until the sauce thickens slightly, about 30 minutes. Add sugar if the sauce is too acidic and simmer 10 minutes more.

—The sauce can be used immediately for the pasta, or refrigerated until ready to use.

Makes 3 cups

SECRETS OF SUCCESS:

Frying the garlic. The garlic is cooked until brown and then strained out of the oil, leaving its flavor behind. This oil flavors the tomato sauce.

Pressing the eggplant. Most recipes call for pressing the eggplant for only a short time. By doing it for at least 8 hours, all the juices are extracted, leaving a dense concentrated texture and no bitter taste.

ORECCHIETTE WITH BROCCOLI RABE AND POTATOES

Craig Stoll shows how easy it is to create magnificent pasta with only a little effort and a few ingredients. It's fast enough for a weeknight dinner, but complex enough for a dinner party. ❉ In this case, Stoll, who owns the popular Delfina restaurant in the Mission, uses orecchiette, the disk-shaped pasta that retains a chewy texture. The sauce is made from parsley, chile flakes, garlic, and anchovy fillets, which add a subtle depth of flavor to the blend. ❉ For interest, broccoli rabe and potato cubes are cooked in boiling water and set aside. Then the pasta is added and cooked part-way through. ❉ Stoll uses a clever technique that intensifies the flavor of the dish. The pasta, along with some of the water, is placed in a large sauté pan with the seasonings, where it finishes cooking. In the process the oil and other ingredients emulsify with the water to form a silken sauce that just coats the pasta. ❉ The chef also uses this technique with other pastas. Much of his cooking is inspired by his stint in Italy. Stoll worked at many large restaurants in the Bay Area, but was dissatisfied with what he could produce. He opened Delfina so he could serve the rustic food he loves to cook. The interior of the small restaurant has a casual industrial feel, with tables lining each wall leading back to a bar and an open kitchen.

4 tablespoons olive oil

¾ cup fresh white bread crumbs

Salt

¾ to 1 pound broccoli rabe (or broccolini)

2 garlic cloves, minced

2 canned anchovy fillets, drained and mashed to a paste

2 tablespoons minced fresh Italian parsley

1 tablespoon drained capers, chopped

¼ teaspoon dried red chile flakes

1 russet potato, peeled and cut into ½-inch dice

12 ounces orecchiette pasta

Freshly ground pepper

Grated Pecorino Romano cheese

—Heat 1 tablespoon of the oil in a medium sauté pan over medium heat. Add the bread crumbs and stir until golden brown, about 5 minutes. Remove from the heat.

—Bring a large pot of salted water to a boil.

—Finely chop the broccoli rabe by pressing the heads against a cutting board to compress the leaves. Starting from the flowering end, cut off ¼-inch pieces. Continue cutting the head, discarding the last inch or so of stem.

—Heat the remaining 3 tablespoons of oil over medium heat in a sauté pan large enough to hold the pasta. Add the garlic, anchovies, 1½ tablespoons of parsley, capers, and chile flakes. Cook until the ingredients are incorporated, but not letting the garlic brown, about 3 to 5 minutes. Remove from the heat.

—Place the broccoli rabe in a colander that fits inside the pot of boiling water. Submerge it in the boiling water for 1 minute. Remove the colander from the water and drain the broccoli rabe. Cool. Cook the potato the same way, until just tender, about 7 to 10 minutes.

—Add the pasta to the water and cook 7 minutes (the pasta will not be cooked through). Drain, reserving 4 cups of the cooking liquid.

—Add the broccoli rabe and potato to the sauce and set over high heat. Stir until broccoli rabe is coated. Season to taste with salt and pepper.

—Add the pasta and 2 cups of the reserved cooking liquid. Bring to a boil. Stir constantly until the pasta is cooked through and the liquid reduces and emulsifies with the oil to form a thin sauce that covers the pasta, adding more cooking liquid if the mixture becomes dry, about 5 minutes. Adjust the seasoning as needed. When finished there should only be a bit of sauce at the bottom of the pan.

—Transfer the pasta to large shallow bowls. Top with the toasted bread crumbs, remaining ½ tablespoon of parsley, and grated cheese.

Serves 4

SECRETS OF SUCCESS:

The anchovy fillets. Those who dislike anchovies will be tempted to leave them out, but that would be a mistake. You won't be able to taste them in the finished sauce but they add a complex background note that would be missing otherwise.

Finishing the pasta in the sauce. Boiling the partly cooked orecchiette with the seasonings and pasta water infuses the pasta with flavor and creates a silken sauce.

TRENNE WITH BRAISED LAMB SHOULDER, ARTICHOKES, AND ROASTED TOMATOES

Just about every restaurant in the Bay Area makes some kind of pasta, but the best effort often comes from Donna Scala, who with her husband, Giovanni, owns Bistro Don Giovanni in Napa. ❋ My favorite pick is the Trenne with Braised Lamb Shoulder, Artichokes, and Roasted Tomatoes. It's an incredibly flavor-packed sauce where the stock is reduced even before it's added to the browned cubes of meat. The mixture is baked and then the other ingredients are added. The sauce is again reduced until thick, then tossed with the triangular-shaped pasta tubes. If you can't find trenne, substitute another substantial pasta such as rigatoni or penne. ❋ Scala believes in the slow-cook method of making sauces, which extracts and melds all the components, just the opposite of the quick toss-together combinations favored by most restaurants. It's a time-consuming process, but these deeply satisfying flavors can't be produced any other way. ❋ These hearty dishes are served in modern surroundings with a peaked roof, an open kitchen visible behind glass, and a profusion of fresh flowers. The most coveted seats, however, are on the outdoor patio, which wraps around two sides of the building and includes a fireplace on one end and views of the vineyards on the other side.

Tomatoes
Olive oil
6 Roma tomatoes, halved
Salt and pepper
2 tablespoons sugar

Artichokes
2 cups water
2 cups dry white wine
Juice of 1 lemon
6 baby artichokes, trimmed and quartered
Salt and pepper

Lamb Sauce
2 quarts chicken stock
1 quart veal stock
3 tablespoons olive oil
2 pounds lamb shoulder, trimmed of fat and cut into ½-inch cubes
2 tablespoons toasted and ground fennel seed
Salt and pepper
½ cup fresh basil leaves, julienned
2 bay leaves
¼ cup pitted kalamata olives
1 pound trenne, rigatoni, or penne
¼ cup chopped fresh Italian parsley
¼ cup ricotta cheese

—*To make the tomatoes:* Preheat the oven to 250 degrees. Oil a baking sheet.

—Place the tomatoes cut side down on the prepared baking sheet. Brush with oil and season with salt and pepper. Sprinkle with the sugar. Roast for at least 4 hours or as long as overnight until the skins are shriveled and the tomatoes are only slightly moist. Remove from the oven. Peel the skin and discard. Place the flesh in a bowl. Cover and refrigerate until needed.

—*To make the artichokes:* Combine the water, wine, and lemon juice in a medium saucepan over medium heat. Bring to a simmer. Add the artichokes and simmer until tender when pierced with a fork, about 10 minutes. Drain. Season to taste with salt and pepper.

—*To make the lamb sauce:* Preheat the oven to 350 degrees. In a large saucepan, combine the stocks. Cook over high heat until reduced by three-quarters, about 30 to 45 minutes.

—In a large sauté pan, heat the oil over medium-high heat. Working in batches, add the lamb and brown on all sides. Using a slotted spoon, transfer the meat to a roasting pan. Add the fennel seeds to the roasting pan. Season to taste with salt and pepper. Add the reduced stock, basil, and bay leaves. Cover and cook in the oven until the meat is tender, about 30 to 40 minutes.

—Put the roasting pan on top of the stove over medium-high heat. Add the roasted tomatoes, artichokes, and olives and reduce to a thick sauce, about 10 minutes.

—Meanwhile, in a large pot of generously salted water, cook the pasta until tender but still firm to bite. Drain. Add to the sauce and toss to coat. Divide among 6 plates. Sprinkle with parsley and ricotta, and serve immediately.

Serves 6

> **SECRETS OF SUCCESS:**
>
> *Double reductions.* The stock is reduced before beginning the sauce, then again when the meat and tomatoes are added.
>
> *The tomatoes.* Slow roasting them in a warm oven until they are dry concentrates and intensifies the flavors. Adding sugar brings out their natural sweetness.

WARM WASABI HOUSE NOODLES WITH GRILLED PORK

Larry Tse, who opened his charming restaurant The House in North Beach in 1994, characterizes his food as a "modern and relevant expression of Asian-American food." ❋ The combinations he prepares are a cross-cultural blend that Tse prepared at home in his pre-restaurant days as an accountant. One of the most expressive examples is his Warm Wasabi House Noodles with Grilled Pork. The dish is a masterful study in contrasting tastes, textures, and temperature. The noodles take on smoky nuances from being stir-fried in a hot wok. The spicy warmth of wasabi adds even more complexity. The pork is grilled and placed on top of cool cucumbers to create a vibrant dish. ❋ Naming the restaurant The House was natural for Tse because he considers what he does as home cooking. The interior has a modern but comfortable feel and the care that Tse puts into his food is evident in the warm surroundings.

Pork

1 pound pork loin, sliced into ¼-inch-thick slices
1½ tablespoons minced garlic
2 teaspoons dark soy sauce
1 teaspoon crushed Korean red pepper flakes (or other dried red pepper flakes)
1 tablespoon minced fresh parsley
Freshly ground black pepper

Noodles

1 pound fresh wheat noodles, udon or Shanghai style (see Note)
2 tablespoons peanut oil
2 tablespoons minced garlic
2 tablespoons dark soy sauce
1 tablespoon light soy sauce
2 teaspoons premium oyster sauce
1 teaspoon sugar
Pinch of salt
4 teaspoons wasabi paste
1 tablespoon Asian sesame oil

1½ cups peeled, seeded, julienned cucumbers
Julienned green onions for garnishing
Sesame seeds for garnishing

—*For the pork:* Combine the pork with the garlic, soy sauce, red pepper, and parsley in a large bowl. Sprinkle with black pepper to taste. Cover and refrigerate for 20 minutes.

—*For the noodles:* Cook the noodles in a large pot of boiling water until tender, about 2 minutes. Drain and set aside.

—Preheat the grill (medium-high heat). Add 1 tablespoon of peanut oil to the marinating pork, then lift the pork from the marinade. Grill until cooked through, about 2 to 3 minutes per side. Transfer the pork to a platter. Cover loosely with foil to keep warm.

—Heat the remaining 1 tablespoon peanut oil in a large wok set over high heat. Add the garlic and stir 10 seconds. Add the cooked noodles, dark soy sauce, light soy sauce, oyster sauce, sugar, and salt. Stir quickly to combine. Remove from the heat.

—Mix the wasabi and sesame oil in a small bowl to blend. Add to the hot noodles; toss to coat. Transfer the noodles to a platter and cool until just warm.

—Arrange the cucumbers over the top of the warm noodles. Fan the pork over the cucumbers. Garnish with scallions and sesame seeds and serve.

Serves 4

Note: *Fresh wheat noodles are available in some supermarkets and at Asian markets.*

SECRETS OF SUCCESS:

A hot wok. Called "wok hay," stir-frying the noodles in an extremely hot wok adds a smoky flavor that can't be achieved any other way.

The temperature of the noodles. The noodles are allowed to sit after cooking so they're just warm, which intensifies the flavor and sets up a contrast to the cool cucumbers and the hot grilled pork.

SPAGHETTI ALLA VODKA

North Beach Restaurant's recipe for Spaghetti alla Vodka is 100 percent proof that simple is best. It has only eight ingredients in the sauce. Onion, cream, and butter weigh in on the sweet side of the equation. Vodka gives a peppery kick, and the Parmesan cheese fills in the flavor holes with its sharp, salty nuances. It's truly simple, and simply delicious. ❋ At the restaurant, the dish is served on plain white plates, but it's the type of recipe that adapts well to interpretation and additions. You can add herbs like rosemary or tarragon, vegetables such as peas or broccoli rabe, and crispy pancetta. ❋ Chef Bruno Orsi serves hundreds of plates of his straightforward pastas every day.

—Cook the spaghetti in a large pot of boiling salted water until tender but still firm to bite.

—Meanwhile, melt 4 tablespoons of the butter in a large, deep-sided pan over medium-high heat. Add the onion and sauté until translucent, about 5 minutes. Add the half-and-half and bring to a boil.

—Drain the spaghetti and transfer to the cream mixture. Add the cheese, vodka, and remaining 4 tablespoons of butter. Season to taste with salt and pepper. Simmer, stirring constantly, until well-blended, about 2 minutes. Adjust seasoning, if necessary.

—Divide among 4 warmed plates and serve.

Serves 4

1 pound spaghetti
Salt
8 tablespoons (1 stick) unsalted butter
1 medium onion, thinly sliced
3 cups half-and-half
1 cup grated Parmesan cheese
⅔ cup vodka
Freshly ground white pepper

SECRETS OF SUCCESS:

The vodka. Adding the vodka gives a spicy, complex kick to the straightforward blend and helps to balance the sweetness of the cream and onions.

SATSUMA POTATO GNOCCHI

Oritalia was a pioneering restaurant when it opened more than a decade ago, serving a blend of Asian and Italian food. It's a concept that soon caught on all over the country. ✷ How well this cross-cultural blend works is illustrated in the Satsuma Potato Gnocchi. Former chef Brenda Buenviaje replaced the traditional potatoes with Japanese yams, available in specialty produce sections. The yams give the gnocchi a subtle sweetness, and the starchiness makes for a firmer consistency than the potato version. ✷ They're so good they make a great side dish sautéed in a little butter. At the restaurant they're served with a galangal-lime beurre blanc, steamed asparagus, and sautéed Maine lobster.

—Cook the potatoes in a large pot of boiling water until tender when pierced with a fork. Drain. Cool slightly. When cool enough to handle but still hot, peel the potatoes. Rice the potatoes into a large bowl.

—Add the ¾ cup of flour, eggs, chives, cheese, salt, and pepper. Using your hands, combine until a soft dough forms, adding more flour if necessary.

—Working in small batches, roll the dough into ½-inch-wide ropes on a lightly floured surface. Cut the ropes into 1-inch pieces. Lightly dust with flour.

—Cook the gnocchi in a large pot of boiling salted water until they float to the top, about 2 to 3 minutes. Using a slotted spoon, transfer the gnocchi to a large bowl. Toss with melted butter or olive oil and serve immediately.

Serves 4 to 6

Note: *Satsuma potatoes are available at Japanese markets and at some specialty food stores.*

2 pounds Satsuma potatoes (see Note)
¾ cup (or more) all-purpose flour, plus additional for dusting
2 eggs
1 bunch fresh chives, minced
½ cup grated Parmesan cheese
1 teaspoon salt, plus more for the pasta water
½ teaspoon cracked white pepper
2 tablespoons melted butter or olive oil

SECRETS OF SUCCESS:

Japanese yams. They are sweeter than regular potatoes, making the gnocchi an ideal side dish for pork or game dishes.

POTATO GNOCCHI WITH SMOKED CHICKEN

So often, gnocchi tastes rubbery and dense, but the version served at Jackson Fillmore is different. The pillow-like puffs are tender with a mere touch of resistance. The addictive sauce combines tomatoes, heavy cream, and smoked chicken breast. The dish is topped with grated cheese and passed under the broiler just before serving so it's browned and bubbly. ✳ Chef/owner Jack Krietzman has turned this always-packed neighborhood trattoria into one of the most popular places for simple Italian food. While some combinations are traditional, the owner is always traveling to Italy to pick up new ideas, so the menu is always peppered with something new.

2 large potatoes

About 1½ cups all-purpose flour, plus additional for dusting

1 teaspoon kosher salt

¼ cup extra-virgin olive oil

½ cup chopped, smoked chicken breast (see Note)

½ cup diced tomato

1 garlic clove, minced

6 fresh basil leaves, chopped

½ cup heavy cream

Salt and freshly ground pepper

½ cup Fontina cheese, cut into ¼-inch cubes

3 tablespoons grated Parmigiano-Reggiano

2 tablespoons chopped fresh Italian parsley

—In a large pot of lightly salted water, boil the potatoes until tender when pierced with a fork. Drain. When cool enough to handle but still hot, peel the potatoes. Combine 1 cup of the flour and the Kosher salt in a large bowl. Rice the potatoes one at a time directly into the bowl. Mix with hands just until the dough comes together, adding as much of the remaining ½ cup flour as needed to create a soft dough. Be careful not to overwork the dough.

—Divide the dough into 4 pieces. Gently roll each piece out on a floured surface to form a long rope, about ½-inch thick. Cut each rope into ½-inch-long pieces. Sprinkle lightly with flour. Take a fork, and holding it so that the tangs are touching the cutting surface, gently rub each piece of dough along the tangs of the fork. An imprint of the tangs will be left on the gnocchi, giving it ridges. Set aside while you make the sauce.

—Heat the oil in a large broiler-proof skillet over medium-high heat. Add the smoked chicken, tomato, garlic, and basil. Bring to a boil. Add the cream. Season to taste with salt and pepper. Boil until slightly thickened, about 3 to 5 minutes.

—Preheat the broiler. Cook the gnocchi in a large pot of boiling salted water until they float to the surface of the water, about 3 minutes. Using a slotted spoon, transfer the gnocchi to the pan with the sauce. Add the Fontina cheese and remove from the heat. Sprinkle with the Parmigiano cheese. Adjust seasonings, if necessary. Put the pan under the broiler until slightly browned on top, about 1 to 2 minutes. Sprinkle with the parsley and serve immediately.

Serves 4 to 6

Note: *Smoked chicken breast can be found in the refrigerator section of some supermarkets. If not available, rotisserie or grilled chicken can be substituted.*

SECRETS OF SUCCESS:

The gratinee. Passing the dish under the broiler adds a finishing touch to the hearty dish.

Hot potatoes. Hot riced potatoes mixed into the flour mixture creates light and fluffy gnocchi.

PAN-FRIED GNOCCHI WITH SIRLOIN SAUCE

Chifeletti is a type of gnocchi prepared by Bruno Viscovi's grandmother when he was growing up in Albona, overlooking the Istrian Peninsula. She would always reserve a few of the small crescent dumplings and fry them as a special treat for him. ❉ When Viscovi opened Albona Ristorante Istriano near North Beach, he put them on the menu, accompanied by the beef sirloin sauce flavored with cumin. ❉ It's a wonderful dish, with the golden brown gnocchi playing off the rich beef sauce. Leftover sauce is ideal as a topping for pasta with fresh gratings of Parmesan cheese. ❉ Albona is the only restaurant on the West Coast specializing in this little-known Italian cuisine that has influences from countries such as Austria, Hungary, Croatia, and Turkey. The combinations are hearty, often with the unexpected addition of sweet spices such as nutmeg. ❉ Viscovi's unique food is served in a warm environment with accents of mahogany and beveled glass. And one of the biggest treats of all is that Viscovi is usually in the dining room, always willing to weave a romantic tale of his homeland.

Gnocchi

2 pounds russet potatoes

2 cups (or more) all-purpose flour, plus additional
    for dusting

½ teaspoon salt

⅛ teaspoon freshly grated nutmeg

2 tablespoons unsalted butter at room
    temperature

1 egg, beaten to blend

Sauce

¾ cup peanut oil

2 pounds beef sirloin, trimmed and cut into
    ½-inch cubes

1 onion, finely diced

1 carrot, finely diced

1 celery stalk, finely diced

½ cup finely chopped fresh Italian parsley

2 garlic cloves, minced

2 fresh oregano sprigs

2 fresh thyme sprigs

2 fresh rosemary sprigs

2 fresh marjoram sprigs

2 bay leaves

1 teaspoon porcini mushroom powder (see Note)

½ teaspoon salt

⅛ teaspoon dried red pepper flakes

1 cup dry red wine

¼ cup canned tomato sauce

½ teaspoon ground cumin

About 1 quart beef stock

2 tablespoons all purpose flour

1 quart vegetable oil for frying

—*To make the gnocchi:* Place the unpeeled potatoes in a large pot and add enough cold water to cover. Bring to a boil. Boil until the potatoes are easily pierced with a fork, about 45 minutes. Drain. Peel the potatoes by rubbing them in a towel while still hot. Pass through a potato ricer and spread onto a lightly floured surface.

—Sift 1¾ cups of the flour over the potatoes and sprinkle with the salt and nutmeg. Using your hands, incorporate the ingredients into a mound. Form a well in the center. Add the butter and egg.

—Briefly knead the mixture until it comes together, adding as much of the remaining ¼ cup flour as needed until a dough forms. With a rolling pin, roll the dough to a thickness of ½ inch. Using a 1½-inch round cookie cutter, cut out the dumplings and set them on a clean towel dusted with flour. Cover the dough with another towel and allow them to rest at room temperature while the sauce is being prepared.

—*To make the sauce:* In a large, heavy-bottomed skillet, heat ½ cup of the peanut oil. Working in batches, add the meat and cook until brown on all sides. Using a slotted spoon, transfer the meat to a strainer. Add the remaining ¼ cup peanut oil to the pan and heat over medium heat. Add the onion and sauté until translucent, about 3 to 5 minutes. Add the carrot and celery and sauté until golden brown, about 10 minutes, stirring frequently. Return the strained meat to the skillet and stir until warm. Increase the heat to high. Add the parsley, garlic, oregano, thyme, rosemary, marjoram, bay leaves, mushroom powder, salt, and red pepper flakes. Stir for 2 minutes.

—Gradually add the wine to the pan and boil until all of the liquid has evaporated, about 5 to 10 minutes. Lower the heat to medium. Add the tomato sauce and cumin. Add enough of the stock to barely cover the ingredients. Cover and simmer until the meat is tender, gradually adding more stock as needed. Remove from the heat; skim off the fat and transfer to a small bowl. Mix the flour into the fat to form a paste. Stir the paste into the sauce. Return to the heat and cook for 2 minutes. Remove from the heat. Cover the pot and set aside.

—In a heavy, high-sided pan, heat the vegetable oil over medium-high heat. Working in batches, add the gnocchi and fry until golden brown, about 5 to 7 minutes. Using a slotted spoon, transfer the gnocchi to paper towels and drain. Keep in a warm oven until all the gnocchi are cooked.

—Ladle ¾ cup of the sauce onto plates. Top with the gnocchi. Save the remaining sauce for future use with pasta.

Serves 2 to 4 as a main course; 6 as an appetizer

Note: *Porcini powder is available in specialty supermarkets.*

SECRETS OF SUCCESS:

Frying the gnocchi. Viscovi says he's never seen this technique used anywhere else; it was something his grandmother did. It makes the gnocchi crispy.

The sauce. The addition of porcini powder, red wine, a little tomato sauce, and crushed red peppers gives a complex depth of flavor.

WILD MUSHROOM RISOTTO

Maria Helm, formerly the chef at PlumpJack Café, makes the best risotto around. Even now that she's left, the recipe still shows up on the menu in different guises. ✻ One of the most popular variations is the Wild Mushroom Risotto made with caramelized onions and pancetta. With Helm's cooking technique, the rice has a rich depth of flavor, and a prized creamy, al dente texture. ✻ Helm recommends using Beretta Superfina Arborio Rice, which can be found at many supermarkets. ✻ Just about anything can be added to the basic risotto recipe. When using vegetables in the risotto, Helm suggests water or vegetable stock; seafood risotto should be made with shellfish stock because fish stock overwhelms the rice. Variations with meat can be made with chicken broth. I've even had some success using the Swanson's chicken broth in the box (much better than the canned version), diluting it by half. As the liquid boils down the flavors absorb and intensify. ✻ At the restaurant, the rice is cooked part way and then finished off when ready to serve, a trick that can be employed by the home cook who doesn't want to spend so much time in the kitchen while guests are in the living room. ✻ Aside from the Italian/Mediterranean food, PlumpJack has also become known for its wine list, where bottles are sold at a dollar above retail. It's the best bargain in the city, a double surprise because the restaurant is also one of the prettiest.

Mushrooms

1 cup diced pancetta

1 tablespoon butter

1 medium onion, finely diced

1 pound assorted wild mushrooms (such as shitake and crimini), cleaned and sliced

2 tablespoons chopped fresh thyme

Salt and pepper

Risotto

10 to 12 cups chicken stock

2 tablespoons butter

1 small onion, finely diced

1 cup dry white wine

6 cups arborio rice (preferably Beretta Superfina brand)

1 tablespoon chopped fresh Italian parsley

1 tablespoon chopped fresh chives

1 tablespoon chopped fresh chervil

1 teaspoon chopped fresh tarragon

Salt and pepper

—*To make the mushrooms:* Sauté the pancetta in a medium skillet over medium heat until slightly crisp. Using a slotted spoon, transfer the pancetta to paper towels and drain. Drain all but 1 tablespoon of the fat from the pan. Add the butter and melt over medium-high heat. Add the onion and sauté until golden brown, about 10 minutes. Add the mushrooms and thyme. Sauté until all the liquid evaporates, about 10 minutes. Season with salt and pepper. Stir in the pancetta. Transfer to a bowl and set aside.

—*To make the risotto:* Bring the stock to a boil in a medium saucepan. In a large heavy-bottomed saucepan over medium-high heat, melt the butter. Add the onion and sauté until translucent, about 5 minutes.

—Add the white wine and bring to a boil. Add the rice and stir to coat. Set a timer for 12 minutes. Add hot stock to the rice mixture 1 to 2 ladles at a time, stirring constantly. Add more as the rice absorbs the liquid.

—If you want, make this recipe ahead. When the 12-minute timer rings, remove the pan from stove and quickly spread the rice on a cookie sheet. When cool, place the pan in the refrigerator. Refrigerate herbs, mushroom mixture, and remaining stock.

—To continue, heat the stock in the pot over medium heat. Transfer the risotto to a large heavy-bottomed saucepan. Add 1 cup of stock, and stir constantly to heat through. Stir in the mushroom mixture and cook 6 minutes more, adding more stock as needed and stirring constantly.

—The rice should be creamy at this point. If not, add more stock and continue to cook. Stir in the parsley, chives, chervil, and tarragon. Season to taste with salt and pepper.

Serves 8

SECRETS OF SUCCESS:

The rice. Beretta Superfina takes a little longer to cook but produces a better texture.

Cooking ahead. The risotto can be cooked for 12 minutes, spread on a cookie sheet, and refrigerated until ready to use. It's then finished with the mushrooms and herbs.

VEGETABLES AND SIDE DISHES

STUFFED TOMATOES WITH GOAT CHEESE CRUST

I'm always pleasantly surprised when a restaurant goes the extra mile and tries to do something special with vegetables. Sure, lots of people are vegetarians or want to eat lighter, but too many places think no further than grilled vegetables or pasta primavera. ✳ At Bistro Viola in Berkeley, however, the vegetables star, either on their own or as a side dish. One of my favorite combinations created by Michael Zeitouni is the stuffed tomato, filled with haricots verts, potatoes, and fresh corn. The ingredients are cooked separately and then warmed in a ripe tomato shell, under a creamy blanket of goat cheese. ✳ The stuffed tomato can stand alone as a simple vegetable main course when served on a bed of frisee, or it can accompany roast chicken as it does in the restaurant. ✳ Bistro Viola, which opened in 1999, has a cozy neighborhood feel with polished birch plywood floors, an open kitchen, and a sleek stainless steel bar that dresses up the forty-seat dining room. There's also a thirty-five-seat patio, one of the few places for outside dining in Berkeley. The area is covered, and with the addition of space heaters, it's possible to eat al fresco much of the year. ✳ Zeitouni worked with George Morrone at the Blue Door in Miami and followed him back to San Francisco to work at One Market. The twenty-eight-year-old chef is certainly one to watch; he's turned this quiet neighborhood place into a destination.

This simple mixture is seasoned only with salt and pepper. However don't be afraid to use fresh herbs in the blend such as tarragon, thyme, or parsley.

4 large tomatoes
2 tablespoons olive oil
Salt and pepper
½ pound haricots verts or other thin young green beans
1 tablespoon butter
1 ear corn, kernels cut from cob
¼ cup water
1 fingerling potato, roasted or boiled and diced
4 ounces soft fresh goat cheese
1 head frisee

—Preheat the oven to 500 degrees. Core the tomatoes and clean out the interiors, leaving about a ½-inch wall around the edge of the tomato. Use 1 tablespoon of the oil to rub outside and inside the tomatoes. Generously salt and pepper both sides.

—Cook the haricots verts in a large pot of boiling salted water until just tender, about 4 minutes. Drain and rinse in cold water. Cut into 1-inch lengths and set aside.

—Melt the butter in medium sauté pan over medium-high heat. Add the green beans, corn, and water and cook 2 minutes. Add the diced potato and continue to cook until the liquid evaporates, about 1 minute. Season to taste with salt and pepper.

—Arrange the tomatoes in an ovenproof pan or baking sheet. Spoon the hot vegetables into the tomatoes. Divide the goat cheese over, pressing gently into the vegetables.

—Bake the tomatoes until hot, about 6 minutes.

—Meanwhile, toss the frisee in a large bowl with the remaining 1 tablespoon of oil. Season to taste with salt and pepper.

—Divide the lettuce among 4 plates. Top each with a stuffed tomato. Serve immediately.

Serves 4

SECRETS OF SUCCESS

Individual cooking. Cooking the vegetables separately and then warming them in the tomato keeps them tasting fresh.

The goat cheese. Just a small amount helps to turn a vegetable into a star, either as a side dish or a main course.

Fried Cardoons

An Italian friend remembers when her grandmother used to make fried cardoons. These are traditional in Italy, but in the Bay Area you don't find them much. In fact, I've only seen them at one restaurant: Absinthe. They're so delicious it's a wonder they don't replace fried calamari as a staple on menus. ❊ Most people are unfamiliar with cardoons, which look kind of like a stalk of celery on steroids. With a thick ribbed base and large leaves, there's a little preparation required. But they're no more work than artichokes, and the taste is similar. They're in season from late spring to the fall. ❊ At Absinthe, chef Ross Browne coats them with a buttermilk wash and a blend of flour and semolina, which adds a crunch to the batter. He then serves them with an anchovy mayonnaise. ❊ Browne, who was born in New Zealand, has worked at many Bay Area restaurants, where he was schooled in the ways of the Mediterranean. The restaurant is open late with a bar menu that's great for after the theater, ballet, or symphony. Named after the famous French liqueur, which is now banned, the restaurant has a fresh Art Deco feel.

Anchovy Mayonnaise

1 garlic clove, minced
¼ teaspoon salt, plus additional to taste
½ canned anchovy fillet, drained and finely chopped
1 egg yolk
½ cup extra-virgin olive oil
Fresh lemon juice

Cardoons

Juice of ½ lemon
1 medium bunch cardoons, trimmed of any leaves and spiny fibers
Salt
1 quart grapeseed or vegetable oil for frying
2 cups buttermilk
1 egg
4 cups all-purpose flour
1 cup semolina flour
Parmesan cheese for garnishing
Lemon wedges

—*To make the anchovy mayonnaise:* In a small bowl, mash together the garlic and ¼ teaspoon salt until a paste forms. Add the anchovy and egg yolk, mixing well. Gradually whisk in the oil until the mixture is the consistency of mayonnaise. Season to taste with lemon juice and additional salt, if necessary. Refrigerate until ready to use.

—*To make the cardoons:* Fill a bowl with cold water. Add the lemon juice. Cut the cardoons into 3-inch pieces and put in the lemon water to keep them from discoloring.

—Cook the cardoons in a large pot of boiling salted water until tender, about 45 minutes to 1 hour. Drain. Place the cardoons in a bowl of ice water until cool. Drain. Scrape off any remaining stringy fibers with a paring knife.

—Heat the grapeseed oil in a large deep-sided saucepan to 375 degrees.

—Whisk together the buttermilk and egg in a medium bowl. Add the cardoons and toss to coat. Drain the cardoons in a colander.

—In a separate bowl, mix the flour and the semolina. Toss the cardoons in the flour mixture, coating well. Shake off any excess flour.

—Working in batches, fry the cardoons in the oil until golden brown, about 3 to 5 minutes. Using a slotted spoon, transfer to paper towels to drain. Season with salt and grated Parmesan while still warm.

—Serve immediately on a paper bag–lined plate with the anchovy mayonnaise and lemon wedges.

Serves 6 to 8

SECRETS OF SUCCESS:

Choosing the cardoons. Try to find small to medium stalks that are solid. A hollow middle means that they are old.

Trimming the strings. Cardoons have ribs like celery that need to be removed.

Using an unsalted batter. Since the cardoons are parboiled before being fried, adding salt to the batter would draw out the moisture. Salt them after they're fried.

PARMESAN SPAGHETTI SQUASH

Spaghetti squash is an underutilized vegetable, and it's perplexing to try to figure out why that's so. The vegetable looks like its name: After cooking you use a fork to scrape the insides and it comes out looking like a perfect pile of angel hair pasta. With its pleasing crunch, spaghetti squash can be seasoned in many ways, both sweet and savory. ✤ At Bistro Zare, the casual restaurant opened in 1999 by Hoss Zare, it has found a permanent place on the menu. ✤ Zare first cooks the squash and then sautés it with butter, Parmesan, and just a pinch of nutmeg or a little truffle oil. It's hearty enough to be a meatless main course, but it also pairs well with grilled chops or even roasted chicken. ✤ Like pasta, spaghetti squash becomes a palette for other flavors, so you can vary the seasonings as you like.

—Pierce the squash 10 to 15 times with a fork. Cook the squash in a pot of lightly salted boiling water until soft to the touch, about 30 to 35 minutes. Drain. Cut the squash in half lengthwise. Remove the seeds. Using a fork, scrape the squash into strands. Transfer the squash strands to a medium sauté pan.

—Add the 2 tablespoons water to the pan and set over medium heat. Cook until the squash is tender, about 2 minutes. Add the butter and cheese; toss until the butter melts. Season to taste with salt and pepper. Transfer to a serving dish and drizzle lightly with truffle oil or nutmeg, if desired. Garnish with chopped chives.

Serves 6 to 8

1 spaghetti squash, about 3 pounds
Salt
2 tablespoons water
3 teaspoons butter
½ cup grated Parmigiano-Reggiano cheese
Pepper
Truffle oil or a pinch of ground nutmeg (optional)
Chopped fresh chives for garnishing

SECRETS OF SUCCESS:

Boiling the squash. In most recipes the squash is baked, but poking a few holes and boiling the unpeeled squash is easier and lends a crunchy-soft texture to the finished dish.

Cauliflower au Gratin

Vegetable gratins are great for company because they can be assembled earlier in the day and baked later. Bouchon's Cauliflower au Gratin is a lovely dish with cauliflower, cream, garlic, shallots, and horseradish, baked under a crust of cheese. ❊ It's the type of dish that's perfect for the restaurant—rich, delicious comfort food—and is just as good for the home cook. At Bouchon in Yountville, it comes to the table in an oval casserole, the top looking like a bubbling browned moonscape, and the smell permeates the air. ❊ If there are better ways to eat this workhorse vegetable, I don't know about it.

1 head cauliflower, cut into florets, stems chopped
Juice of ½ lemon
Salt
1 ½ tablespoons olive oil
1 tablespoon minced shallot
1 tablespoon minced garlic
1 cup vegetable stock or water
1 cup heavy cream
½ tablespoon prepared horseradish
Ground pepper
½ cup grated Gruyere cheese

—Preheat the oven to 425 degrees.

—Fill a large bowl with water. Add the cauliflower florets and lemon juice. Let stand 2 minutes. Drain. Transfer the florets to a pot of lightly salted boiling water and cook until tender, about 7 minutes. Drain and transfer to a large casserole dish.

—Heat the oil in a large sauté pan. Add the cauliflower stems, shallot, and garlic and cook until tender, about 5 minutes. Add the stock and cook until the liquid is reduced by half, about 3 to 5 minutes. Remove from heat and stir in the cream. Transfer to a blender and puree until smooth. Add the horseradish. Season to taste with salt and pepper.

—Pour the sauce over the florets and stir until coated. Top with the grated cheese. Bake until golden brown and bubbling, about 15 to 20 minutes.

Serves 8

SECRETS OF SUCCESS:

A lemon soak. The florets are soaked in lemon for a few minutes, which helps them to stay white and crisp.

Using the cauliflower stems. Cooking the cauliflower stems with the garlic and then pureeing them thickens the sauce and intensifies the flavors.

WHITE CORN AND GINGER SOUFFLÉ

Talk to Jacqueline Margulis, and she will tell you that the fear of falling soufflés is unfounded. Of course, she's been making them for more than twenty years and cracks more than a thousand eggs a week at her restaurant, Cafe Jacqueline. ❉ The entire menu at Cafe Jacqueline is made up of soufflés, save for a few soups and salads. What could be more romantic that sharing a savory soufflé to start and ending with a rich chocolate, lemon, or Grand Marnier soufflé? ❉ Margulis will tell you that just about anything can go in soufflés. One of the freshest combinations is her White Corn and Ginger Soufflé. Here the subtle play of flavors, mixed with mild Gruyère cheese, creates a delicious appetizer or light main course. ❉ The steps to success are easy: Make a béchamel—a flour and milk medley that serves as the soufflé base. Then add the vegetables and seasonings and stir in the egg yolks. Beat the egg whites to soft peaks and fold into the base. When it puffs up and becomes golden brown, it's ready to savor. ❉ The charming twenty-four-seat restaurant feels like a French cafe, with candles and a long-stemmed rose on each of the nine tables. The romantic room has a homey feel, thanks to the well-worn floors, tongue-and-groove paneling that looks as if it's seen a dozen coats of paint, and brass wall sconces.

1 teaspoon plus 2 tablespoons unsalted butter
2 tablespoons all-purpose flour
2 cups milk, warmed
Salt and ground white pepper
4 eggs, separated, at room temperature
1 cup grated Gruyère cheese
Kernels from 1 ear of white corn
1 tablespoon grated fresh ginger
2 garlic cloves, crushed

—Preheat the oven to 400 degrees.

—Grease an 8-inch soufflé dish with the 1 teaspoon butter.

—Melt the remaining 2 tablespoons butter in a medium saucepan over low heat. Add the flour and whisk for 2 minutes; do not let the mixture brown. Add the warmed milk and whisk until the mixture boils and is smooth and thickened, about 10 minutes. Season with salt and white pepper. Cool the soufflé base 10 minutes, then whisk in the egg yolks.

—Stir in the cheese, corn, ginger, and garlic.

—Using an electric mixer with clean dry beaters, beat the egg whites in a medium bowl until they form soft peaks. Using a rubber spatula, gently fold the whites into the soufflé base. Pour the mixture into the prepared soufflé dish. Bake until the top is puffed and brown, about 15 to 20 minutes. Serve immediately.

Serves 4

GORGONZOLA-POTATO GRATIN

This rustic gratin is designed to go with the Seared Black Pepper–Lavender Filet of Beef (see page 156) created by John McReynolds at Cafe La Haye in Sonoma. While it is a perfect accompaniment to that dish, it's equally good with roast chicken, pork, or other meat dishes. ❊ The thinly sliced potatoes are layered with garlic-infused cream and Gorgonzola, then baked until brown and bubbly. The potatoes and cream meld together and the gratin can either be cut into squares or spooned onto the plate. Any leftovers are great reheated in the microwave.

—Mix the cream, garlic, salt, and nutmeg in a small bowl. Let stand at least 1 hour at room temperature or up to 4 hours in the refrigerator. Strain out the garlic.

—Preheat the oven to 375 degrees. Generously grease a 13x9-inch baking dish with the butter.

—Slice the potatoes as thin as possible with a mandoline or by hand. Spread half the sliced potatoes evenly over the bottom of the prepared pan. Sprinkle half of the cheese over the potatoes. Cover with the remainder of the potatoes. Sprinkle the remaining cheese on top. Pour the garlic cream over potatoes.

—Bake until the potatoes are tender and the top is slightly brown, about 1 hour.

Serves 6 to 8

2 cups heavy cream
3 garlic cloves, chopped
2 teaspoons kosher salt
Pinch of ground nutmeg
1 tablespoon butter
5 large russet potatoes, peeled
⅓ pound Gorgonzola, crumbled

SECRETS OF SUCCESS:

Flavoring the cream. The garlic soaks in the cream, giving off a subtle uniform flavor.

Slicing the potatoes. Thinly sliced potatoes produce a more evenly flavored dish.

SAUTÉED MUSHROOMS

If you've been to Cha Cha Cha, one of the city's first Caribbean-inspired restaurants, you'll no doubt remember the sautéed mushrooms seasoned with sherry, garlic, and butter. They're truly memorable. ✻ They're great as an appetizer or party snack, but they also make an exciting side dish with grilled chicken or steak. The flavors of the garlicky mushrooms are so robust and the sauce is so good, you'll probably want to sop up the last bit with bread. ✻ All of Philip Bellber's creations are alive with flavor. Hailing from New York, he's a first generation Puerto Rican who's had the restaurant in the Haight-Ashbury since 1984. Only his food could be as colorful as the surrounding neighborhood. The noisy, vibrant restaurant echoes with a Latin beat, bright colors, and happy patrons.

—In a large, heavy skillet over medium-high heat, warm 2 tablespoons of the oil until it smokes. Add the mushrooms and sauté for 1 to 2 minutes, stirring constantly. Add the remaining 2 tablespoons oil, garlic, dried herbs, scallions, and red pepper flakes and sauté until the mushrooms brown, about 2 minutes.

—Add the sherry and cook until the liquid is reduced by half, about 3 to 5 minutes. Add the butter, a bit at a time, stirring to glaze the mushrooms. Season to taste with salt and pepper.

Serves 4

4 tablespoons olive oil
18 to 20 button mushrooms, stemmed
1 tablespoon minced garlic
Generous ¼ teaspoon dried basil
Generous ¼ teaspoon dried thyme
Generous ¼ teaspoon dried oregano
2 scallions (white part only), finely chopped
Pinch of dried red pepper flakes
½ cup dry sherry
4 tablespoons unsalted butter, cut into pieces
Salt and freshly ground pepper

SECRETS OF SUCCESS:

Smoking oil. Make sure the oil is hot so the mushrooms will brown.

Reducing the sherry. This intensifies the flavor, which is then smoothed out with butter swirled in at the last minute.

TORTILLA ESPAÑOLA

One of the must-have classic dishes served in all the Spanish tapas restaurants in the Bay Area is Tortilla Española. It's a potato-onion frittata held together with eggs. Served warm or at room temperature, it makes a wonderful appetizer, main course, or even a Sunday brunch dish. ✳ The best version belongs to Carlos Corredor at Timo's, a lively popular Mission District hangout. The place is crowded at all hours, mostly with a young crowd that's learning all about great Spanish food. Yellow and black table tops and bright colors all around add as much flavor to the surroundings as Corredor does to his food. ✳ The omelet, which is always on the menu, is made in a skillet on top of the stove. The thin slices of potatoes and onion are poached in oil, which is drained before the lightly beaten eggs are added. The mixture then cooks slowly over low heat. ✳ After it's lightly browned, the omelet is turned over and cooked long enough to brown the other side. When you slice into the frittata, you'll see layers upon layers of potatoes, onions, and eggs creating a dish that's much more exciting than the ingredients indicate.

About 1 quart plus 2 teaspoons olive oil
4 pounds large boiling potatoes, peeled and thinly sliced
2 medium white onions, thinly sliced
10 large eggs
Salt and pepper
Pinch of cayenne pepper (optional)
Spanish olives for garnishing

—Fill a deep-sided large saucepan about halfway with oil. Heat over low heat. Add the potatoes and onions. Poach until the potatoes are tender but not falling apart, about 20 minutes. Using a slotted spoon, transfer the potatoes and onions to paper towels and drain.

—Beat the eggs in a large bowl just long enough to mix the whites and yolks. Season with salt, pepper, and cayenne, if desired. Carefully fold in the potatoes and onions.

—In a 10-inch frying pan, heat the remaining 2 teaspoons oil over medium-high heat (do not use the oil the potatoes were cooked in) until smoking. Swirl to coat the sides of the pan. Add the egg mixture and carefully push down with a spatula to make the surface flat. Turn the heat down immediately to very low, cover the skillet, and cook until the bottom is golden brown, about 3 minutes.

—Uncover the skillet. Invert a plate over the skillet. Flip the omelet onto the plate. Slide the omelet back into pan, browned side up. Cover and cook until other side is golden brown, about 5 minutes. Turn the tortilla out onto a platter.

—Cut the tortilla into wedges. Garnish with olives. Serve warm or at room temperature.

Serves 12

SECRETS OF SUCCESS:

Selecting the right potatoes. Boiling potatoes are the best for this because they don't fall apart.

Beating the eggs. Beat just long enough to mix the yolks and whites. Overbeating will result in a rubbery consistency.

Cooking over low temperatures. The potatoes are literally poached in the oil (they don't absorb excessive amounts). A gentle temperature is also used to cook the frittata so it browns and evenly cooks the interior but doesn't become dry.

GREEN BEANS WITH CHILE OIL, PANCETTA, AND OYSTER SAUCE

When people think of Garibaldi's they remember one dish: the Green Beans with Chile Oil, Pancetta, and Oyster Sauce. Even as the restaurant has expanded—there's a location in Presidio Heights and another on College Avenue in Oakland—and chefs have changed, this dish has stayed on the menu. ✳ It's a simple mix that really tickles the taste buds. Crispy, salty pancetta sautéed with garlic and spicy chile oil smoothed out with oyster sauce make this a great appetizer or side dish. And the same preparation works equally well with asparagus. ✳ Both locations have an upscale look and an eclectic menu that veers to Italy, the Southwest, and Asia. It's the type of trendy but satisfying food that attracts a fiercely loyal neighborhood crowd.

—Cook the beans in a large pot of boiling water until crisp-tender, about 4 minutes. Drain. Transfer the beans immediately to a bowl of ice water to stop the cooking. When cool, drain and dry on paper towels.

—Heat the oil in a large skillet over medium heat. Add the pancetta and cook until brown and crisp. Using a slotted spoon, transfer the pancetta to paper towels and drain. Discard all but 2 tablespoons drippings from the skillet.

—Heat the 2 tablespoons of drippings in the skillet over medium-high heat. Add the garlic. Cook until lightly brown, about 2 minutes. Add the chile oil, oyster sauce, beans, and water and continue to stir until beans are evenly coated, adding more water if needed. Add the reserved pancetta and stir.

Serves 3

¾ pound fresh green beans (preferably Blue Lake), trimmed
2 tablespoons olive oil
3 slices pancetta, cut into ¼-inch pieces
3 garlic cloves, minced
2 teaspoons chile oil
3 tablespoons oyster sauce
4 tablespoons (or more) water

SECRETS OF SUCCESS:

The beans. Be sure to use Blue Lake or other young beans, which are sweeter than most.

The water bath. Plunging the beans into ice water not only immediately stops the cooking, but sets the bright green color.

POTATO SALAD WITH WHOLE-GRAIN MUSTARD

Most potato salads have an element of sweetness, but Gordon's uses savory ingredients to make one of the most fabulous around. It's a blend of mayonnaise, capers, mustard, tarragon, and loads of Italian parsley which lends a fresh, mild tang. ❈ Gordon's is a sophisticated country cafe in Napa Valley that's still undiscovered by the tourists, but packed with locals. It seems like all of Yountville is there in the morning, sitting at the communal pine tables eating pastry or eggs and drinking coffee. At lunch there are sandwiches and on some nights there's a fixed priced dinner that has become one of the treats of the Valley.

—Put the quartered potatoes in a large pot with enough salted water to cover by 1 inch. Bring to a boil. Reduce heat and simmer until the potatoes are tender when pierced with a knife but not falling apart, about 10 to 15 minutes.

—Meanwhile, combine the mayonnaise, parsley, tarragon, capers, red onion, both mustards, 1 teaspoon of salt, pepper, and water in a large bowl. Whisk to blend.

—Drain the potatoes. While they are still warm, add to the bowl with the dressing and toss gently to coat well. Cool to room temperature, then refrigerate until ready to serve.

Serves 8

4 pounds small red-skinned potatoes, quartered
1 teaspoon salt, plus additional for cooking potatoes
1 cup mayonnaise
1 cup chopped fresh Italian parsley
3 tablespoons chopped fresh tarragon
¼ cup drained capers
½ large red onion, thinly sliced
2 tablespoons whole-grain mustard
1 tablespoon Dijon mustard
1 teaspoon ground pepper
¼ cup water

SECRETS OF SUCCESS:

Savory ingredients. The blend of capers, mustard, tarragon, and parsley makes this an unusual potato salad.

Dressing the potatoes. Tossing the dressing with the hot potatoes infuses the flavor into the potatoes.

CARAMELIZED TURNIPS

The caramelized turnips at Delfina are a revelation: I never thought this every-day vegetable could taste so good. Chef/owner Craig Stoll first cuts the turnips into wedges and then roasts them in a warm oven. To produce a glass-like crust with a creamy interior, they are then sautéed in butter.

—Preheat the oven to 375 degrees.

—Cut off the stems and then cut the turnips into eighths from stem to root end. Place in a medium-size baking pan.

—Sprinkle the turnips with the salt and toss them with the oil to coat lightly. Roast the turnips until tender, about 40 minutes.

—Transfer the turnips to a large sauté pan. Add the butter and stir over medium heat until the butter melts and the turnips are browned, about 10 to 15 minutes.

Serves 2

2 medium turnips, peeled
1 teaspoon kosher salt
¼ cup olive oil
1 tablespoon butter

SECRETS OF SUCCESS:

Roasting and sautéing. The two-step process of roasting the turnips in the oven and then sautéing them in butter makes the difference.

BEANS WITH FETA

Few dishes are as satisfying as these Greek-style beans from Evvia, the upscale Greek restaurant in Palo Alto. ❋ Created by Jean Alberti, who is also the chef at its sister restaurant Kokkari in San Francisco, the hardest thing about making this recipe is finding butter beans, which are about the size and texture of dried lima beans. But don't sweat the small stuff; I've made them with smaller white beans and even cranberry beans with equal success. The only difference is that cooking times may vary, depending on the variety of bean. The beans are great as a vegetarian main course, or as a side dish to grilled or roasted meats.

—Place the beans in a large pot. Add enough water to cover the beans. Soak for at least 4 hours or overnight to soften. Drain and rinse the beans.

—Heat the oil in a large saucepan over medium-high heat. Add the onion and sauté until it begins to caramelize, about 5 to 7 minutes. Add the garlic and sauté 2 minutes. Add the tomatoes, beans, oregano, and bay leaf. Season to taste with salt and pepper.

—Add enough water to barely cover the beans. Gently simmer until the beans are just tender, about 1 to 1 ½ hours. If the mixture is too soupy, turn up the heat and boil until most of the liquid has evaporated. Cool.

—Preheat the oven to 350 degrees. Transfer the bean mixture to a casserole and top with feta cheese and chopped parsley. Bake until the beans are warm and the feta melts, about 15 to 20 minutes.

Serves 6

1 pound large dried butter beans (or other dried beans)
10 tablespoons olive oil
1 large onion, thinly sliced
2 garlic cloves, minced
1 pound ripe tomatoes, peeled, seeded, and diced (see page 363)
1 teaspoon dried oregano or 1 tablespoon chopped fresh oregano
1 bay leaf
Salt and pepper
6 ounces Greek feta, crumbled
1½ tablespoons chopped fresh Italian parsley

SECRETS OF SUCCESS:

Cooking beans with the flavorings. This helps to infuse more flavor into the beans.

Cooling the beans before baking. This process adds an even more concentrated flavor, with the alluring contrast of the feta cheese melted over the top.

CRISP ROASTED POTATOES

This recipe for roasted potatoes is so simple, you'll wonder how they could be so good, but Maurizio Bruschi's creations are distinctive. The exterior is as crisp as glass and the interior is almost as smooth as mashed potatoes.

—Preheat the oven to 450 degrees. Line a large sheet pan with foil.

—Dry the potatoes well. Cut into 6 to 8 slices per potato. Place the potatoes the prepared pan. Brush the potatoes with the oil. Sprinkle with salt, pepper, and rosemary. Bake for about 15 minutes. Using a spatula, turn. Bake until almost tender, about 10 minutes more. Remove the potatoes from the oven and allow to cool for 5 to 10 minutes.

—Increase the oven temperature to 500 degrees. Put the potatoes back into the hot oven and cook until crisp and brown, about 3 to 5 minutes more, watching them carefully so they don't burn. Serve hot.

Serves 4

2 ½ pounds russet potatoes, peeled
10 tablespoons extra-virgin olive oil
Salt and freshly ground pepper
Chopped fresh rosemary

SECRETS OF SUCCESS:

Double roasting. The potatoes are roasted until almost done, removed from the oven, and then returned for a final crisping.

GREEN BEANS WITH NEW POTATOES

This simple but hearty casserole that makes a great side dish or a meatless main course comes from Tibet. It was created by Tsering Wangmo at Lhasa Moon, San Francisco's only Tibetan restaurant. ❊ The beans and potatoes are stir-fried with a little oil, soy sauce, and tomato. The seasonings are straightforward with a little kick from fresh ginger, garlic, onion, red pepper, and jalapeño.

—Slice the potatoes into sticks about the same size as the green beans. Set aside.

—In a medium pan, heat the oil over high heat. Add the onion, garlic, paprika, and ginger and sauté until onion is soft, about 5 minutes. Add the potatoes, jalapeño, and tomato and stir-fry until the tomato is dry, about 5 minutes. Add the beans and water and simmer until the beans and potatoes are just tender, about 8 minutes. Stir in the soy sauce and red pepper. Season to taste with salt.

Serves 4

SECRETS OF SUCCESS:

Cutting the potatoes. Cutting the potatoes into sticks about the same size as the green beans makes for a pretty presentation and an integrated taste.

2 large potatoes, peeled
1 tablespoon oil
½ onion, chopped
2 garlic cloves, finely chopped
½ teaspoon paprika
1-inch piece of fresh ginger, peeled and finely chopped (see page 362)
1 jalapeño chile, seeded and coarsely chopped
½ tomato, chopped
1 pound string beans, cut diagonally into 1½-inch pieces
¼ cup water
1 teaspoon soy sauce
½ small red bell pepper, thinly sliced
Salt

LONG BEAN AND OKRA SAMBAL

Chris Yeo established what was one of the first restaurants featuring food from Singapore and Malaysia, served in a quaint environment designed to look like a courtyard. ❊ While Yeo adds a personal touch to the food, much of it is based on classic preparation such as in the Long Bean and Okra Sambal. ❊ With something this good, who needs innovation? The combination of the crunchy long beans, which look similar to regular green beans but are nearly three feet long, and the distinctive okra is wonderful. The flavor is enhanced with dried shrimp, jalapeño, garlic, shallots, and a little oyster sauce. ❊ It creates a spicy dish that's great with something as simple as roast chicken. It can also be a satisfying main course with steamed rice.

1½ tablespoons dried shrimp (see Note)
5 red jalapeño chiles, seeded
4 walnut-sized shallots or 2 medium onions, sliced
5 garlic cloves, sliced
1 tablespoon plus ⅓ cup water
¼ cup vegetable oil
9 ounces long beans, cut into 2-inch lengths
½ pound okra
1 tablespoon oyster sauce
1 teaspoon sugar
½ teaspoon salt

—Place the dried shrimp in a small bowl. Add enough warm water
   to cover. Let stand for 10 minutes. Drain. Finely mince the shrimp
   in a blender or mini food processor and set aside.
—Grind the chiles, shallots, and garlic to a smooth paste in a blender
   or food processor. Add a tablespoon more of water if needed to
   facilitate the blending.
—Heat the oil in a large wok or saucepan over medium heat. Add
   the ground chile mixture and fry, stirring frequently, until it is
   completely combined with the oil and has the consistency of dry
   porridge, about 3 to 5 minutes.
—Increase the heat to medium-high. Add the minced shrimp; cook
   until the mixture is crumbly, about 1 to 2 minutes.
—Add the beans and okra; stir-fry 5 minutes. Add the ⅓ cup water,
   oyster sauce, sugar, and salt. Stir-fry until the sauce reduces
   enough to glaze the vegetables and the vegetables are tender,
   about 5 minutes.

Serves 4

Note: *Dried shrimp is available at Asian markets.*

> **SECRETS OF SUCCESS:**
>
> *The chile mixture.* This ground, fragrant paste called *rempah* is stir-fried until it blends with the oil to form a sauce that coats the vegetables.
>
> *A bit of sugar.* A teaspoon of sugar, added near the end of cooking, does a miraculous job of taming the harshness of the chiles and rounding out the flavors.

WHITE VEGETABLE PUREE

When you're tired of the basic mashed potatoes, this White Vegetable Puree from LuLu will reinvigorate your palate. ❊ Potatoes are mashed with onions, celery root, turnips, and parsnips and seasoned with a mixture of olive oil and butter. The flavors meld so you won't be able to distinguish the individual components. ❊ This pureed vegetable dish also keeps three or four days in the refrigerator. It can be reheated on the stove, in the oven, or in the microwave with no loss of flavor.

—Preheat the oven to 300 degrees.

—Place the onions, leeks, garlic, 2 tablespoons of the oil, and the water in an oven-proof skillet or baking dish. Season with salt and pepper. Bake covered until the onions are soft and translucent, but not brown, about 1 hour. Remove from the oven and set aside, leaving the cover on.

—Meanwhile, combine the potatoes, celery root, turnips, and parsnips in a large pot. Cover with water and add a couple tablespoons of salt. Bring to a boil and reduce heat to a simmer. Cook until the vegetables are tender, about 15 to 20 minutes. Drain, reserving 2 cups of the cooking liquid.

—Run the boiled vegetables and the cooked onion mixture through a food mill. Transfer to a larger bowl. Add the remaining olive oil and the butter and stir until thoroughly blended. Adjust the texture with as much of the reserved cooking liquid as needed to make a light and fluffy mixture. Adjust the seasoning with salt and pepper.

Serves 4 to 6

3 white onions, halved
2 leeks, white parts only, roughly chopped
8 garlic cloves, peeled
⅓ cup fruity extra-virgin olive oil
¼ cup water
Salt and pepper
1 pound russet potatoes, peeled and quartered
½ pound celery root, peeled and quartered
½ pound turnips, peeled and quartered
½ pound parsnips, peeled and roughly chopped
3 tablespoons unsalted butter

SECRETS OF SUCCESS:

The food mill. Running all the vegetables through the mill adjusts the textures and melds the flavors.

Steaming the onions, leeks, and garlic. Placing the ingredients in oil and water and baking in the oven produces a creamy mild sweetness.

BLANCHED GREENS WITH SESAME DRESSING

The Blanched Greens with Sesame Dressing at O Chame in Berkeley is a versatile salad or side dish with any meal, including a Western-style grilled chicken or steak. ❋ The chilled greens are tossed with a simple dressing that includes soy, rice vinegar, and toasted sesame seeds. The dressing can be served with spinach, chard, or even wilted salad greens. It's also excellent with green beans or asparagus, served either hot or cold. ❋ The best fish stock to use for this recipe is the soup base for the Udon Noodle Soup with Smoked Trout (page 72), also from O Chame. If you don't have time to make it, you can use chicken stock.

—Combine the sesame seeds, stock, vinegar, mirin, and soy sauce in a small bowl. Stir the dressing to blend.
—Blanch the greens in a large pot of boiling water just until wilted, about 30 seconds.
—Drain. Transfer to a large bowl filled with ice water to cool. Drain. Gently squeeze out the water. Refrigerate the greens and dressing separately until ready to serve.
—Toss the greens in a large bowl with the dressing and serve.

Makes 4 servings

¾ cup (about 2½ ounces) toasted sesame seeds
5 tablespoons fish stock or chilled chicken stock
2 tablespoons rice vinegar
2 tablespoons mirin
2 tablespoons soy sauce
2 pounds greens (such as spinach, chrysanthemum greens, mustard greens, or baby tatsoi)

SECRETS OF SUCCESS:

Squeezing the greens. Extracting the moisture allows the blanched greens to absorb the dressing.

The sesame dressing. The balance of salty and sweet, with the added nutty crunch of sesame seeds, creates a refreshing side dish.

SPICY PICKLED CABBAGE SLAW

Stephen Ganner created this Spicy Pickled Cabbage Slaw to accompany his Tamarind-Guava Barbecued Spareribs (page 142). ✹ The piquant crunchy cabbage salad, which marinates overnight in pickling juices, is a great foil to the tropical-inspired ribs, but it's also a versatile addition to other main courses. It's especially great for a picnic or outdoor party, and it's sensational with grilled chicken or sausage.

—To make the pickling juice: Place all the ingredients for the pickling juice except for the onion in a large saucepan and bring to a boil. Remove from the heat and cool to room temperature. Strain. Add the sliced red onion to the pickling juice and set aside for at least 4 hours.

—To make the slaw: Combine both cabbages, the bell peppers, poblano, jalapeños, and pickling juices with onions in a large bowl. Mix well and let stand at room temperature at least 4 hours or refrigerate up to 24 hours.

—Just before serving, strain the slaw, discarding the pickling juices. Stir in the maple syrup. The pickled slaw can be served chilled or at room temperature.

Serves 4

SECRETS OF SUCCESS:

Pickling the vegetables. Making the pickling juices and letting the sliced onions marinate longer gives the onions a more interesting flavor and texture.

The maple syrup. Most recipes use sugar, but the maple syrup adds a rich earthiness to the cabbage.

Pickling Juice
1 cup water
1 cup cider vinegar
10 whole black peppercorns
1 teaspoon mustard seeds
1 teaspoon peeled and minced fresh ginger
1 jalapeño chile, seeded and minced
¼ cup sugar
2 tablespoons kosher salt
1 whole clove
1 red onion, thinly sliced

Slaw
½ head red cabbage, cut into ⅛-inch-thick strips
½ head green cabbage, cut into ⅛-inch-thick strips
1 red bell pepper, cut into ⅛-inch-thick strips
1 yellow bell pepper, cut into ⅛-inch-thick strips
1 poblano chile, seeded and deveined, cut into ⅛-inch-thick strips
2 jalapeño chiles, seeded and minced
¼ cup maple syrup

CIPOLLINE IN AGRODOLCE

The sweet and sour onions at Vineria are one of my favorite accompaniments. They're great as an appetizer, as a snack with a glass of wine, or as a counterpoint to the main course. ❉ The preparation is straightforward, but the taste is exciting. The small onions are cooked until tender, then simmered in balsamic and other ingredients to achieve the "agrodolce" or sweet-sour balance. Then, just before serving, they're tossed with salt, olive oil, and a shower of fresh oregano. ❉ Partners Susanna Borgatti and Wally Tettamanti opened Vineria in the Mission several years ago as a follow-up to their popular L'Osteria del Forno. Here there's the same homey feeling, but a little more room, including a large wine bar.

—Place the onions in a bowl of cold water for about 10 minutes to loosen the skins. Drain, then peel with a sharp knife.

—Place the onions in a 10-inch skillet with just enough water to cover. Bring to a simmer over medium heat and cook 15 minutes, adding more water if necessary to keep the onions covered. Add the vinegar, sugar, and 1 tablespoon salt. Lower the heat and gently simmer until the onions are translucent and soft when pierced with a fork, about 45 minutes.

—Transfer the onions to a bowl. Season with additional salt if necessary. Toss with the olive oil and oregano.

Serves 4

1 pound cipolline onions
½ cup balsamic vinegar
1 tablespoon sugar
1 tablespoon (or more) salt
3 tablespoons extra-virgin olive oil
1 tablespoon minced fresh oregano

SECRETS OF SUCCESS:

A slow simmer. Simmering the onions slowly in the vinegar allows them to pickle.

Fresh oregano. It's rare that this herb gets to star and it's a marvelous balance to the sweet-and-sour onions.

Tomato-Tamarind Okra

Yahya Salih has been bringing his creative interpretation of Middle Eastern cuisine to the Bay Area for more than a decade. One of the most interesting and versatile dishes at YaYa Cuisine is the Tomato-Tamarind Okra, a thick, exotic-tasting vegetable stew. ✻ The okra is long-cooked and allowed to boil down with tomato sauce, tamarind, garlic, and curry powder to form a thick sauce-like texture. It can be served alone as a side dish, but it makes a marvelous meatless main course when it's spooned over couscous or used as a dip for grilled vegetables. It can also serve as a sauce/relish for grilled chicken breast, pork, or steak. It's great made ahead and keeps well in the refrigerator for nearly a week. ✻ YaYa Cuisine has moved to three different locations over the last decade. It started South of Market, then moved to the Sunset District, and now Salih caters to the lunch and dinner crowds in the Financial District. ✻ The interior has an exotic feel thanks to deep blue walls and a mural representing the Fertile Crescent. A castle-like structure adds interest to another wall, and the soft lighting contributes to the clandestine mood.

1 pound small bright green okra
3 ½ cups water
2 cups canned tomato sauce
2 tablespoons tamarind paste or the juice of ½ lemon
4 large garlic cloves
1 teaspoon curry powder (optional)
Salt and pepper

—Trim the stems off the okra just above the ridge about ¼ inch down from the tip of the stem.

—Place the okra and 1½ cups water in a medium saucepan. Bring to a boil over high heat. Cover, reduce heat, and simmer until the okra changes color to olive green and the liquid evaporates, about 45 minutes. Do not worry if the liquid evaporates and the okra browns slightly; it will take on a pleasant smoky flavor. Remove from the heat.

—In a large saucepan, combine the remaining 2 cups of water, tomato sauce, and tamarind paste. Bring to a boil over high heat. Boil 5 minutes. Strain. Add to the okra. Add the garlic and curry, if desired. Season to taste with salt and pepper. Simmer over medium-low heat for 30 to 45 minutes until the sauce is thickened, stirring gently and occasionally.

Serves 4

SECRETS OF SUCCESS:

Trimming the okra. The secret to eliminating the "slime" from okra is to cut the stem in precisely the right place. Approximately ¼ inch down from the tip of the stem is a crosswise ridge. Cut through the okra just above that ridge in order to expose the tiny holes around the circumference. When the okra cooks, the "slime" will be released through those holes.

The ingredients. The combination of okra, tomato, and tamarind makes for an aromatic, intriguing taste.

Cooking the okra. The vegetable is cooked for an hour and a half, making a thick rich stew.

GARLIC BROCCOLI RABE

Hoss Zare has a way with vegetables, and they often star on the plate at his namesake restaurant in the Financial District. His lusty style even translates to the vegetables that have enough backbone to stand up to anything. ❋ A good example is the broccoli rabe, also known as rapini, which is increasingly showing up in mainstream markets. Looking like delicate broccoli with leafy, pungent leaves, it's been a staple in the Italian diet for generations. Zare uses balsamic vinegar, anchovies, and garlic to produce a marvelous side dish. After the broccoli rabe is sautéed and seasoned, it's sprinkled with toasted bread crumbs for an additional crunch. ❋ This has become one of the most popular dishes at his restaurant, which has a romantic cave-like feel.

—Heat the oil in a large sauté pan over medium-high heat. Add the broccoli rabe. Sauté for 2 minutes. Add the garlic and anchovies. Season to taste with salt and pepper. Sauté until broccoli rabe is tender, about 5 to 7 minutes. Remove from heat. Drizzle the broccoli rabe with the balsamic vinegar and add 1 to 2 tablespoons of water if needed to moisten.

—Transfer the broccoli rabe to a serving bowl. Top with bread crumbs and serve.

Serves 4 to 6

4 teaspoons extra-virgin olive oil
3 bunches broccoli rabe, trimmed
2 garlic cloves, finely chopped
4 canned anchovy fillets, drained and finely chopped
Salt and pepper
3 teaspoons aged balsamic vinegar
¼ cup toasted bread crumbs

SECRETS OF SUCCESS:

The flavorings. Balsamic vinegar, anchovies, and garlic give this a bold Italian spin that transforms the natural bitterness in the vegetable.

The bread crumbs. This added flourish sprinkled on top lends a marvelous crunch.

Asparagus and Leek Escabeche

Few preparations of asparagus are as delicious as this recipe from Zibibbo, especially in the off season when the spears aren't as flavorful. ❋ They are sautéed with leeks and seasoned with thyme, garlic, and chiles. Then the vegetables are doused in dry sherry and red wine vinegar, and the liquid is quickly reduced to form a glaze. ❋ Chef Jody Denton suggests serving this dish with slices of crusty bread.

—In a large sauté pan over low heat, heat the olive oil and asparagus together, rolling the asparagus around as the pan heats up. Once the asparagus begins to sizzle slightly, add the leek and garlic. Season with salt and pepper. Continue to gently stir until the leek begin to soften, about 3 to 5 minutes. Add the chiles and thyme and increase the heat to high.

—When the pan is sizzling, add the sherry and vinegar and boil until only a few tablespoons of liquid remain, about 5 to 7 minutes. Stir in the chopped parsley and serve.

Serves 4 to 6

3 tablespoons extra-virgin olive oil

2 bunches medium asparagus spears, trimmed to about 4 inches in length

1 small leek, (white part only) thinly sliced

3 tablespoons thinly sliced garlic (preferably spring garlic, if available)

Salt and pepper

8 whole small dried red chiles

Leaves from 4 fresh thyme sprigs, chopped

½ cup dry sherry

¼ cup red wine vinegar

1 tablespoon chopped fresh Italian parsley

SECRETS OF SUCCESS:

Adding the sherry and vinegar. These elements not only add flavor, they "pickle" the asparagus, keeping it slightly crisp.

Cooking the asparagus and oil together. Letting the two ingredients heat up together makes for an evenly tender spear.

SESAME SPINACH ROLLS WITH SOY-LIME VINAIGRETTE

When you're tired of serving the same pile of vegetables, Hawthorne Lane's Sesame Spinach Rolls will pull you out of the rut. ❄ They take a little effort to prepare, but the presentation is fabulous. First cabbage leaves are steamed and set aside. Then the spinach is seasoned, cooked, and dried. The mixture is placed on the cabbage leaves, which become wrappers for the log-shaped package. Each log is cut into six medallions, and served with a soy-lime vinaigrette. They're served at room temperature so they can be made ahead and sliced before serving. ❄ This spinach dish is designed to be served with the restaurant's Miso-Glazed Black Cod (see page 190), but it's also good with many preparations of chicken and fish. ❄ Any remaining vinaigrette keeps in the refrigerator for up to 2 days and can be drizzled over fish or chicken.

Spinach Rolls

2 large savoy cabbage leaves
Salt
2 tablespoons plus 1 teaspoon olive oil
1 shallot, minced
1 garlic clove, minced
5 cups loosely packed spinach leaves, washed, dried, and stemmed
Pepper
1 tablespoon sesame seeds, lightly toasted

Vinaigrette

3 tablespoons fresh lime juice (from about 2 limes)
2 tablespoons soy sauce
2 tablespoons rice wine vinegar
½ shallot, minced
1 small garlic clove, minced
Salt and pepper
⅓ cup peanut oil
½ teaspoon Asian sesame oil

—*To prepare the spinach rolls:* Blanch the cabbage leaves in a medium saucepan of boiling salted water until limp. Drain. Spread each leaf ribbed-side up on a cutting board and, using a sharp knife, trim the thickest part of the center rib flat with the leaf. Blot the leaves dry and set aside.

—Heat 2 tablespoons of the oil in a large saucepan over medium-high heat. Add the shallot and garlic; cook just long enough to release the aroma, about 30 seconds. Add the spinach and stir quickly to coat the leaves with the oil. Cook until the spinach becomes completely limp, about 5 minutes. Season to taste with salt and pepper. Remove from the heat and cool.

—Squeeze out all the liquid from the spinach. Divide the spinach in half and roll each half into a 1-inch-diameter cylinder. Wrap each cylinder tightly in the blanched cabbage leaves. Rub the leaves lightly with the remaining 1 teaspoon of oil, then roll in sesame seeds to coat.

—If made ahead, wrap the rolls in plastic wrap until ready to serve.

—*To make the vinaigrette:* Combine the lime juice, soy sauce, vinegar, shallot, and garlic in a small bowl; stir to combine. Season to taste with salt and pepper. Gradually whisk in the peanut and sesame oils until emulsified. Adjust seasoning if needed.

—*To serve:* Cut each spinach log into 6 medallions, using a sharp knife. Arrange on small plates and drizzle with the vinaigrette. Serve more vinaigrette in individual dipping bowls, if desired.

Serves 4

> **SECRETS OF SUCCESS:**
>
> *Pressing the spinach.* Be sure to get all of the moisture out of the spinach so the rolls won't be soggy and can be cut into medallions.

SPINACH WITH APRICOTS AND RAISINS

I've seen spinach with currants and pine nuts at many Spanish tapas restau-rants, but the use of apricots and raisins used at Timo's gives the earthy greens a unique, vibrant flavor. ✳ Of course there's another difference here. Most recipes call for olive oil, but Carlos Corredor stretches the bounds of the cuisine and uses brown butter, which adds a softer, nuttier nuance to the blend.

—Blanch the spinach in a large pot of lightly salted boiling water until slightly wilted, about 2 minutes. Drain. Transfer the spinach to a bowl of ice water to stop the cooking process. Drain. Squeeze out as much liquid as possible from the spinach. Set aside.

—In a large sauté pan, melt 3 tablespoons of the butter over medium heat. Cook until the butter is hazelnut brown in color, about 5 minutes. Add the spinach and reduce the heat to low. Dot the remaining butter and half of the pine nuts, raisins, and apricots on the spinach. Lightly season with salt. Turn the spinach over with a spatula and sprin-kle with the remaining pine nuts, raisins, and apricots. Season with a bit more salt if needed. Continue to cook over low heat, turning occasionally, until all the butter has melted and the spinach is heated through. Serve immediately.

Serves 4

½ pound fresh spinach, washed and
    stemmed
Salt
6 tablespoons butter
2 tablespoons pinenuts, toasted
2 tablespoons raisins
2 tablespoons chopped dried apricots

SECRETS OF SUCCESS:

Blanching the spinach. This makes cook-ing easier, plus it ensures that any remaining dirt has been washed out.

The apricots and browned butter. Both of these ingredients are nontraditional, but they are a marvelous counterpoint to the spinach.

ALMOND CURRANT COUSCOUS

When a colleague tried the Almond Currant Couscous at Greens, she didn't want to stop eating it. "Just give me some milk to pour over it," she said, "and I'll eat it for breakfast." ✽ It really is that good. ✽ The cooking method used by Annie Somerville keeps each grain distinctive, while the addition of currants and cinnamon permeates the grains. The couscous is great by itself or served under the grilled Vegetable Brochettes with Marinated Tofu (see page 214). You can vary the seasonings by adding ¼ cup chopped dried apricots in place of the currants, or you can use cumin in place of the cinnamon.

—In a medium skillet with a tight-fitting lid, melt the butter over medium heat. Add the couscous and almonds and stir until the grains are fragrant and heated through, about 4 to 5 minutes. Remove from the heat.

—Bring the water to a boil in a small saucepan. Stir in the currants, cinnamon, and ¼ teaspoon salt. Pour over the couscous. Cover the skillet and let stand for 20 minutes. Fluff the couscous with a fork and season with additional salt if needed. Serve immediately.

Serves 4 to 6

2 tablespoons unsalted butter
1½ cups instant couscous
¼ cup whole blanched almonds, toasted and chopped
1½ cups water
¼ cup dried currants
½ teaspoon cinnamon, preferably fresh ground
¼ teaspoon (or more) salt

SECRETS OF SUCCESS:

Toasting the couscous. Toasting the couscous in butter gives it a nutty flavor and keeps the grains separate.

Flavoring the water. Adding the cinnamon and currants to the water for the couscous, rather than stirring the flavorings in near the end, produces a more uniform taste.

BUTTERMILK PANCAKES

Several people in the Food department thought they had the best recipe for buttermilk pancakes, until they tasted this version from Bette's Oceanview Diner in Berkeley. ❋ Owner Bette Kroening has been making these for nearly twenty years. They have become so popular that she even started a line of packaged mixes that can be bought all around the Bay Area. ❋ What makes these so good—as well as every one of the all-American specialties at the diner—is they are made fresh. The baking soda, baking powder, and buttermilk work to make them lighter and fluffier than just about any you'll find.

2 cups all-purpose flour
2 tablespoons sugar
2 teaspoons baking powder
1 teaspoon baking soda
½ teaspoon salt
2 eggs
2 cups buttermilk
½ cup milk
¼ cup unsalted butter, melted
Choice of berries, sliced bananas, raisins, or
    chopped toasted nuts (optional)
Oil for the griddle

—In a large bowl, combine the flour, sugar, baking powder, baking soda, and salt. In another bowl, lightly beat the eggs, buttermilk, milk, and melted butter to blend. Just before you are ready to make the pancakes, add the liquid ingredients to the dry ingredients all at once, stirring just enough to mix. The batter should be slightly lumpy.

—If you want to add fruit or nuts, stir them in now, or sprinkle them into the pancakes while they are on the griddle.

—Heat a lightly oiled griddle or heavy skillet over medium-high heat (375 degrees on an electric griddle). Pour ¼ cup batter per pancake onto the skillet, spacing the pancakes apart so they do not run together. When bubbles cover the surface of the pancakes and the undersides are lightly browned, turn and cook until lightly browned on the bottom, about 2 minutes.

—Serve immediately on warmed plates with the topping of your choice.

Serves 4 (Makes about 24 four-inch pancakes)

> **SECRETS OF SUCCESS:**
>
> *The ingredients.* The baking powder, baking soda, and buttermilk work together to make the pancakes light and fluffy.
>
> *Leaving the lumps.* The batter begins to react the minute the wet ingredients are added. Stir quickly and don't overmix. There should still be lumps in the batter.

PECAN STICKY BUNS

Danny Wilser makes the best sticky buns—fat, gooey, and studded with large pecan halves. And what's even better is that it's a relatively simple recipe to make at home. ❊ Wilser and his partner, Robert Merryman, have created the top home-cooking spot in San Francisco at Ella's. They serve excellent dinners, but the place is best known for breakfast. On weekends the line begins to form a half hour before the doors open. ❊ The interior, too, is a cut above the coffee-shop cafe. The terra-cotta walls are set off by impressive flower arrangements at the counter in front of the open kitchen. Large draped windows overlook the corner of Presidio and California, making a bright and airy impression. At night, it takes on a cozy glow from candles on each table.

Dough

4 cups bread flour
1 tablespoon sugar
1 scant tablespoon (1 envelope) active dry yeast
2 teaspoons salt
1¼ cups warm milk
1 egg
¼ cup (½ stick) unsalted butter at room temperature

Syrup

12 ounces brown sugar
6 tablespoons (¾ cup) unsalted butter
¼ cup water
3 tablespoons light molasses

Sticky Buns

¼ cup (½ stick) unsalted butter, melted
¾ cup sugar
¾ teaspoon cinnamon
1 tablespoon grated orange zest
1 cup pecan halves

—*To make the dough:* Place the flour, sugar, yeast, and salt in the mixing bowl of an electric mixer fitted with a dough hook. Add the milk, egg, and butter. Mix for 7 minutes on low speed until a soft, sticky dough forms. Cover the bowl with plastic wrap and set aside in a warm, draft-free place until doubled in volume, about 30 to 45 minutes.

—*To make the syrup:* In a small saucepan, combine the brown sugar, butter, water, and molasses. Bring to a boil, stirring constantly. Cook to 242 degrees on a candy thermometer, about 8 to 10 minutes. Remove from heat and cool slightly.

—*To make the sticky buns:* Preheat the oven to 375 degrees. Pour a little of the melted butter into a 9x13-inch baking dish. Use a brush to grease the bottom and sides well.

—On a lightly floured surface, roll the dough into an 8x14-inch rectangle.

—Pour the remaining melted butter onto the dough and use a brush to butter the dough completely. Combine the sugar and cinnamon. Sprinkle the cinnamon-sugar and orange zest evenly over the dough. Pour half of the syrup into the prepared pan. Pour the other half of the syrup over the dough. Sprinkle half of the pecans over the dough and the other half in the pan.

—Starting at one long side, roll the dough to form a log. Cut the roll into 6 equal pieces. Place pieces, cut-side down, in the baking dish. Let stand for 5 minutes.

—Bake until the buns are evenly browned and seem firm in the center, about 45 minutes. Remove from the oven. Turn the baking pan upside down onto a sheet pan. Let the buns stand 1 minute. Remove the baking pan.

Serves 6

SECRETS OF SUCCESS:

Molasses. Much of the seductive flavor in the sauce comes from rich molasses, rather than granulated or brown sugar.

Orange zest. The zest gives the sticky buns a clean, fresh flavor.

WAFFLES WITH CARAMELIZED PECANS

Zazie is the perfect bistro, nestled into Cole Valley, a quiet residential neighborhood. You have several choice options, depending on your mood: You can sit at a table in front, inside the thirty-seat restaurant, or on the umbrella-shaded patio in back. ❋ Breakfast and brunch becomes high art here. Warming lattes are served in over-sized bowls, and the breakfast fare is marvelous. My favorite is the light and airy waffles, topped with maple syrup and sugary pecan halves. ❋ The restaurant, named after a Louis Malle film "Zazie dans le Metro," features simple straightforward food with a French flair. While several chefs have come and gone, the waffles remain a stellar standout.

½ cup warm water, about 110 degrees
½ cup active dry yeast
2 cups milk
2 cups all-purpose flour
½ cup (1 stick) unsalted butter, melted
1½ teaspoons vanilla extract
1 teaspoon salt
¼ teaspoon hazelnut extract
1 teaspoon plus ½ cup sugar
2 eggs
¼ teaspoon baking soda
Oil for greasing
2 cups pecan halves
1 tablespoon water
Maple syrup

—In a large bowl, combine the water and yeast. Set aside until the yeast dissolves and the mixture is foamy, about 5 minutes.

—Add the milk, flour, butter, vanilla, salt, hazelnut extract, and 1 teaspoon sugar to the yeast mixture. Stir to blend. Cover the bowl with plastic wrap and set aside overnight at room temperature.

—Heat your waffle iron according to the manufacturer's instructions. Just before cooking the waffles, whisk the eggs and the baking soda into the yeast mixture.

—Oil a large baking sheet. Combine the pecans, water, and remaining ½ cup sugar in a large sauté pan over medium-high heat. Stir occasionally until the sugar caramelizes, about 5 minutes. Pour the caramelized nuts out onto the prepared cookie sheet, spreading evenly. Allow the nuts to cool about 5 to 10 minutes.

—When the waffle iron is hot, pour on about ½ cup batter and close the lid. After 2 or 3 minutes, lift the top of the iron carefully to see if the edge of the waffle is golden brown. If it's still pale, close the lid and cook for another minute.

—To serve, place the waffle on a plate with a generous amount of caramelized pecans and serve with maple syrup.

Serves 8

SECRETS OF SUCCESS:

The batter. Setting aside the yeast batter in a warm place overnight creates a waffle that has a crisp exterior and an incredibly tender interior.

Caramelized pecans. The nuts add a spectacular taste and texture to the waffles.

CARAMELIZED ONION WAFFLE WITH SMOKED SALMON AND RADISH SALAD

I have a confession to make: I'm not wild about brunch. If I have to review a brunch place, I generally try to go late enough so I can segue into lunch. Brunch dishes simply don't excite me. ❋ But I was totally captivated by the Caramelized Onion Waffle with Smoked Salmon and Radish Salad at Kelly's Mission Rock. It's one of the most innovative dishes I've seen in some time. And to enjoy it on the wood deck overlooking the Bay Bridge is absolutely magical. ❋ Of course most of us don't have that kind of view at home, but the waffle part of the equation is easy for the home cook. First the caramelized onions are added to the waffle batter. Then when the hot crisp waffle comes off the iron, it's paved with smoked salmon and drizzled with lemon cream. The waffle is crowned with a well-dressed knob of frisee, endive, radish sprouts, and radishes. ❋ The waffle is the handiwork of Kelly's opening chef, Richard Crocker, who worked for five years at Boulevard before leaving in 1998 to open this redo of Mission Rock Resort. The seedy, but popular, place was taken over by Jim Kelly, who used to own Pat O'Shea's. He's revamped the entire structure with an industrial-meets-nautical look, which sets the right tone for a working wharf.

Lemon Cream
1 cup sour cream
¼ cup whole milk
Zest of 1 lemon
3 tablespoons fresh lemon juice

Radish Salad
1 to 2 bunches radishes, trimmed
2 heads Belgian endive, halved, cored, and
　　separated into leaves
1 head frisee, trimmed of outer green leaves
　　and cored
One 3½ ounce package radish sprouts
5 tablespoons fresh lemon juice
2 tablespoons extra-virgin olive oil
Salt and pepper

Waffles
3 tablespoons butter
2 medium yellow onions, finely diced
2 cups all-purpose flour
½ cup chopped fresh mixed herbs (such as
　　parsley, thyme, chives, tarragon, and chervil)
1½ tablespoons baking powder
1 tablespoon ground black pepper
1 teaspoon salt
1½ cups milk
2 eggs at room temperature
⅓ cup melted butter
Vegetable oil for greasing
¼ pound thinly sliced smoked salmon or gravlax

—*To make the lemon cream:* Whisk the sour cream, milk, lemon zest, and lemon juice in a small bowl to blend. Refrigerate until ready to use.

—*To make the salad:* Thinly slice the radishes on a mandoline. Combine the radishes, endive, frisee, and radish sprouts in a large bowl.
—In a separate bowl, whisk together the lemon juice and olive oil. Season to taste with salt and pepper. Set salad and dressing aside separately.

—*To make the waffles:* Melt the 3 tablespoons butter in a large skillet over medium heat. Add the onions and sauté until golden and caramelized, about 10 minutes. Set aside to cool.
—In a large bowl, combine the flour, herbs, baking powder, pepper, and salt. In a separate bowl, combine the milk, eggs, and melted butter. Fold the wet ingredients into the dry ingredients, being careful not to overmix. Fold in the caramelized onions. The batter should be slightly lumpy.
—Heat a waffle iron according to the manufacturer's instructions. Brush the grill lightly with vegetable oil. Cook the waffles until golden brown, about 3 to 5 minutes. Brush the grill with oil between each waffle.
—Place a waffle in the center of each of 6 plates. Drape salmon on the waffles around the edges. Drizzle with lemon cream. Toss the salad with the dressing. Top each waffle with some of the salad.

Serves 6

SECRETS OF SUCCESS:

The waffles. Adding the caramelized onions to the waffles and topping them with smoked salmon is a brilliant idea.

The salad. Well dressed and cool, the salad creates a wonderful counterpoint to the hot crisp waffle and the silky, salty salmon.

MUSHROOM QUICHE

For all the talk about the return of classic combinations, eyebrows still raise and people smirk when anyone mentions quiche. It's still such a cliché that only the most confident chef will put it on the menu. Fortunately, Joseph Keller is the confident sort, and his restaurant, Bouchon in Yountville, makes the best one I've tasted. ❊ The pastry is buttery and almost flaky, and the filling tastes like a cross between a flan and a crème brûlée. It's studded with a plethora of sautéed mushrooms, but if you're feeling creative you can add just about anything you like as long as the volume is about the same. ❊ Keller, who hails from the East Coast, came to the Napa Valley to open this classy French brasserie with his brother Thomas, the chef/owner of the French Laundry. ❊ The restaurant, which opened in 1998, was an immediate hit; it didn't hurt that the chic interior was designed by Adam Tihany, the man behind Spago Palo Alto and Le Cirque 2000 in New York, to name a few. What he produced was an authentic-looking brasserie, complete with zinc bar, pressed tin ceiling, and a chalkboard for the daily specials.

Pastry

Butter for greasing

1 cup all-purpose flour, plus additional for
    dusting

½ cup cake flour

⅛ teaspoon baking powder

Pinch of salt

1 cup (2 sticks) unsalted butter, cut into pieces

¼ cup water

Quiche

3 eggs

1 cup milk

1 cup heavy cream

Salt and pepper

Pinch of ground nutmeg

1 teaspoon minced fresh thyme

2 tablespoons butter

2 shallots, sliced

1 cup chanterelle mushrooms, stemmed and
    chopped

1 cup oyster mushrooms, stemmed and chopped

½ cup crimini mushrooms, stemmed and
    chopped

—*To make the pastry:* Preheat the oven to 400 degrees. Butter a 10-inch diameter springform pan with 2-inch-high sides. Dust with flour, shaking out excess.

—Combine the 1 cup all-purpose flour, cake flour, baking powder, and salt in a large bowl. Using a pastry blender, thoroughly cut in the butter until the mixture resembles peas. Add the water. Stir gently just until the mixture comes together, being careful not to overmix the dough.

—Gather the dough into a ball. Flatten into a disk. Roll out the dough on a lightly floured surface to about a ⅛-inch-thick round. Transfer the dough to the prepared pan. Prick the dough all over with a fork. Line with parchment paper or aluminum foil. Fill the pan halfway up with dry beans to prevent the pastry from bubbling up. Bake for 15 to 20 minutes until golden brown. Transfer the pan to a baking rack to cool. Remove the beans and paper or foil. Maintain oven temperature.

—*To make the quiche:* Whisk the eggs, milk, and cream in a large bowl to blend. Season to taste with salt, pepper, and nutmeg. Stir in the thyme. Set aside.

—In a large sauté pan, melt the butter over medium heat. Add the shallots and all the mushrooms and sauté until the shallots are translucent, about 5 minutes. Drain off any excess liquid.

—Place the mushrooms in the cooled pastry shell. Pour the egg mixture over, filling to the top. Bake until the filling is set, about 30 to 40 minutes. Cool 10 minutes before serving.

Serves 8

SECRETS OF SUCCESS:

The filling. The proportions—2 cups of liquid to 3 eggs—produce a custard that is creamy and moist.

A hot oven. Many custards are done in a water bath, but this version not only abandons that step, it also bakes at 400 degrees. It works because of the amount of cream and milk.

Flour and butter. To achieve the creamy consistency, the fine-textured cake flour and a high proportion of butter are used.

CARAMELIZED ONION FOCACCIA

I've had focaccia all over the Bay Area, and one of the best versions comes from Rose's Cafe. My favorite—they make several kinds—is a simple mixture of caramelized onions that's spread over the top. Once you've mastered the bread, you can top it with just about anything you like. ❋ What makes this one different is the crisp crust, so there's a slight crackle when you take the first bite, giving way to a spongy light interior. ❋ Creating the focaccia is a two-step process: First you have to make the starter and let it rest in the refrigerator overnight. The next day you can make your dough and toppings. ❋ The great thing is you can bake the focaccia and freeze them. They are excellent reheated in a 350-degree oven. ❋ The focaccia is only one specialty at this charming cafe in the Marina, owned by Reed Hearon. With outdoor seating—a great place to bring your dog—it captures the casual spirit of the Italian trattoria where people can come for a cappuccino and pastry or linger over a full meal.

Starter Dough
¼ teaspoon active dry yeast
½ cup warm water, about 110 degrees
1½ cups cool water
1½ pounds all-purpose unbleached flour

Topping
¼ cup olive oil
2 white onions, halved and thinly sliced
2 garlic cloves, crushed
4 fresh thyme sprigs
¼ cup red wine vinegar

Focaccia
2⅓ cups warm water, about 110 degrees
1½ teaspoons active dry yeast
7½ ounces starter dough
¼ cup olive oil, plus more for oiling pans and brushing dough
2 pounds and 1 ounce all-purpose unbleached flour
2 teaspoons salt

—*To make the starter dough:* Dissolve the yeast in the ½ cup warm water in the bowl of a heavy-duty mixer. Let stand until foamy, about 5 minutes.

—Add the cool water and flour and mix with the paddle attachment until smooth, about 4 to 5 minutes. Transfer to a large bowl. Cover and refrigerate overnight, until nearly doubled in size.

—*To make the topping:* Heat the oil in a large sauté pan over medium-high heat. Add the onions, garlic, thyme, and vinegar and cook until the onions are caramelized to a deep golden brown, stirring often, about 15 minutes.

—*To make the focaccia:* Whisk the warm water and yeast in the bowl of a heavy-duty mixer until the yeast dissolves. Add the 7½ ounces of starter dough and mix with your fingers until blended. Discard any remaining starter dough. Whisk in the ¼ cup oil.

—Add the flour and salt. Using the paddle attachment, mix until the dough is smooth, about 7 minutes.

—Place the dough in an oiled bowl. Cover and let stand in a warm draft-free place until doubled in volume, about 1½ to 2 hours. Divide the dough into 4 equal balls. Place each in a well-oiled 8-inch cake pan. Gently stretch the dough out to the edge of the pan. Brush each with olive oil and top with one-fourth of the caramelized onions. Cover with greased plastic wrap. Let rest in a warm place until the dough is relaxed and bubbles form, about 45 minutes.

—Preheat the oven to 425 degrees.

—Using your finger, make deep indentations every 1½ inches over the entire surface of the dough. Bake 5 minutes.

—Spray a little water on the bottom of the oven to create steam. Reduce the oven temperature to 400 degrees. Bake for 10 to 15 minutes longer until the focaccia are golden brown on top and bottom.

Makes 4 focaccia

SECRETS OF SUCCESS:

Spraying the oven. Spraying the bottom of the oven with water during the first few minutes of baking creates steam that produces a crisper crust.

The caramelized onions. Make sure the onions are nicely browned, which creates a sweet, rich flavor, setting up a pleasant contrast with the red wine vinegar.

CRISPY BREADSTICKS

Brix is a beautiful restaurant in St. Helena serving delicious, innovative East-West food. Unfortunately, I always fill up on the breadsticks—I even ask for seconds—and then pick at the rest of the meal. ✳ The breadsticks from former chef Tod Michael Kawachi are thin, crisp, and salty, with an almost nutty flavor. ✳ The 100-seat dining room, broken up by partitions, is given an expansive feel with a peaked wood ceiling and airy yellow and green color scheme. Ironwork branches and leaves form the backs of chairs, which are surprisingly comfortable. A large open kitchen, featuring a wood-fired oven, stretches along two walls. ✳ It all works to create a visual package that fits the casual sophistication of the valley.

1½ teaspoons active dry yeast
¾ cup lukewarm water, about 100 degrees
2½ cups all-purpose flour, plus additional for dusting
2 tablespoons olive oil, plus more for oiling
2¼ teaspoons salt
¼ cup grated Parmesan cheese
¼ teaspoon ground black pepper
⅛ teaspoon cayenne pepper

—In a large bowl, dissolve the yeast in the lukewarm water. Let stand until mixture is foamy, about 5 minutes. Add the 2½ cups flour, 2 tablespoons olive oil, and 1½ teaspoons of the salt and mix by hand using a rubber spatula until a smooth dough forms. Cover the bowl with plastic wrap and let stand in a warm, draft-free place until doubled in size, about 30 minutes.

—Preheat the oven to 350 degrees.

—In a small bowl, combine the cheese, black pepper, cayenne, and remaining ¾ teaspoon salt. Set aside.

—Line a large baking sheet with parchment paper. Divide the dough into four pieces and roll each piece on a lightly floured surface into a rectangle about ¼ inch thick and 14 to 16 inches long. Sprinkle the dough with the cheese mixture and fold in half. Roll the dough out again to its previous size. Cut the dough into very thin, long strips measuring ⅛ inch wide by about 16 inches long. Place the pieces on the prepared baking sheet and bake until golden, about 10 to 12 minutes. Serve at room temperature.

Makes about 4 dozen breadsticks

SECRETS OF SUCCESS:

The seasoning. The Parmesan cheese, salt, pepper, and cayenne are sprinkled on the dough, folded, and rolled, trapping the cheese in the middle. This adds flavor and prevents the cheese from burning.

Two kinds of pepper. Cayenne and black pepper give the thin breadsticks a double whammy.

FRIED OLIVES

Fried olives are something that not too many people had heard of before Tavolino opened in 1998, and they've created a taste sensation. ✲ It's a simple mixture of green olives stuffed with an anchovy and garlic mixture. The olives are coated in flour, eggs, and bread crumbs before being fried until golden. ✲ The combination of warm, salty, and crunchy created by former chef David Stevenson is irresistible. These almost beg to be eaten with a martini or a glass of fruity white wine. The only problem is you won't want to stop.

½ cup oil-packed anchovy fillets, drained
1 garlic clove, chopped
1 slice French bread, crust removed
1 tablespoon fresh lemon juice
½ teaspoon ground black pepper
50 small pitted green olives
½ cup all-purpose flour
1 cup panko bread crumbs (see Note)
8 egg whites
1 teaspoon water
2 cups canola oil
Lemon wedges for garnishing

—In a food processor, puree the anchovies, garlic, bread, lemon juice, and pepper to create a smooth paste. Place the mixture into a medium-sized zip-lock bag. Snip off ⅛ inch of one corner, creating an opening. Gently squeeze the bag to fill the holes in the olives with the anchovy mixture.

—Place the flour in a small bowl. Add the olives and toss to coat. Remove the olives from the flour and shake off excess.

—Place the panko in a medium bowl. In another medium bowl, beat the egg whites with the water until the mixture is slightly foamy.

—Place about 10 olives in a strainer and dip the strainer in and out of the egg white mixture to coat the olives. Allow the excess to drain off. Toss the olives in the bread crumbs and set aside on a cookie sheet. Continue this procedure until all the olives are coated. Let the olives dry for 30 minutes.

—Heat the oil in a 4-quart saucepan to 350 degrees. Working in batches, place the olives in a metal strainer and dip the strainer into oil to completely cover the olives. Deep fry until the olives are golden brown, about 4 minutes.

—Remove the strainer from the oil and shake off excess. Set the olives in the center of a medium platter. Garnish with lemon wedges.

Serves 4

Note: *Panko bread crumbs are available at Asian markets or in the Asian foods section of some supermarkets.*

SECRETS OF SUCCESS:

The anchovies. Taste the anchovy to make sure it isn't too fishy; the flavor varies widely between brands.

The drying time. Letting the olives dry for 30 minutes after coating helps to set the breading, creating a firmer crust.

The coating. Egg whites and fine bread crumbs make for a lighter, crisper coating.

SALSA ROJA

At Cafe Marimba, owner Louise Clement features more than fifty different salsas that change daily. ❈ One of the most popular is Salsa Roja, where the tomatoes, poblano chiles, onion, and garlic are charred or roasted and then blended together. ❈ The Salsa Roja is fairly mild, so feel free to add more jalapeños to taste. It's great with tortilla chips and particularly good served with beef.

—Char the poblano and jalapeño over the flame of a gas burner or in a broiler until blackened on all sides. When cool enough to handle, remove the stem. Slice the chiles in two and remove the seeds and any tough membranes.

—Roast the tomatoes, onion, and garlic under a broiler until softened and browned, about 20 minutes.

—Place the chiles, tomatoes, onion, and garlic in a blender and use the pulse button to coarsely chop the ingredients. Or crush by hand by using the back of a spoon. Either way, the salsa should remain chunky.

—Transfer to a bowl and stir in the cumin and oregano. Season to taste with salt. Thin with water if necessary.

1 medium poblano chile
1 jalapeño pepper
8 medium Roma tomatoes
1 white onion, sliced
5 garlic cloves, peeled
¼ teaspoon ground cumin
¼ teaspoon dried oregano, toasted
Kosher salt

Makes about 2 cups

> **SECRETS OF SUCCESS:**
>
> *Roasted ingredients.* Roasting all the ingredients brings out a rich, smoky quality.

SALSA VERDE

For a light, fresh flavor there's Salsa Verde, made with tomatillos, a green veg-etable that resembles tomatoes and is available at most major grocery stores. ❈ Cafe Marimba's Salsa Verde is great with tortilla chips and excellent with grilled chicken or pork.

—In two batches, puree the tomatillos, garlic, cilantro, and jalapeños in a blender or food processor until smooth. Transfer to a bowl. Thin with water if necessary. Season to taste with salt.

Makes about 2 cups

15 tomatillos, husked, washed, and halved
8 garlic cloves, peeled
½ bunch fresh cilantro
2 jalapeños, seeded and sliced
Kosher salt

SECRETS OF SUCCESS:

Raw ingredients. All the ingredients are raw and pureed until smooth, creating an exciting, pungent blend.

KIROV LEMONADE

Jeremiah Tower, who has sold Stars, is known as a great cook. ❈ But he also has a passion for mixology. "I dream up new cocktails, then come in and try them with the bartenders once a month or so," Tower once explained. ❈ His most popular drink at Stars was the Kirov Lemonade, which he created in 1990 for the Bolshoi Ballet Company, who was performing near his restaurant in San Francisco. ❈ The drink is a combination of Stoli Limonaya and lemon juice over ice. Stars, which underwent a remodel to freshen the interior, has remained one of the prime places to go before or after a performance around the Civic Center area.

—Fill a cocktail shaker with ice. Add the Limonaya, lemon juice, and sugar. Shake well. Fill a bucket glass (a short glass that looks similar to a shot glass but holds about 9 ounces) with ice. Strain the contents of the shaker into the glass. Top with seltzer water. Garnish with a lemon wedge.

Serves 1

Ice
3 tablespoons (1½ ounces) Stoli Limonaya
3 tablespoons (1½ ounces) fresh lemon juice
¾ teaspoon (scant) superfine sugar
Seltzer water
Lemon wedge

SECRETS OF SUCCESS:

The vodka. Be sure to use lemon vodka to get the intensity of lemon on lemon.

SATURN COCKTAIL

Jason Sheehan created the Saturn Cocktail at Mercury. With white upholstery and lots of mirrors, it's a festive place to spend an evening. ❋ For this cocktail Sheehan mixes lemon and lime juice with vodka and Cointreau in an ice-filled shaker. It's then poured into a chilled martini glass rimmed in sugar and garnished with an orange twist.

—Fill a cocktail shaker and a martini glass with ice. Pour the 1 tablespoon of lime juice, lemon juice, simple syrup, Cointreau, and vodka over the ice in the shaker. Shake vigorously.

—Place the sugar on a plate. Discard the ice in the glass. Wet the rim with the remaining lime juice. Press the rim of the glass down into the sugar. Twist gently to evenly coat the rim in sugar.

—Strain the cocktail into the glass and garnish with the orange twist, if desired.

Serves 1

Note: *To make simple syrup, combine equal amounts of sugar and water in a small saucepan over high heat. Stir until the sugar dissolves. Bring to a boil, reduce the heat, and simmer for 5 minutes. Remove from heat and cool. Store in the refrigerator.*

Ice
1 tablespoon fresh lime juice, plus a little extra for the rim of the glass
1 tablespoon fresh lemon juice
½ to 1 teaspoon simple syrup (see Note)
1 ounce (2 tablespoons) Cointreau
2 ounces (¼ cup) premium vodka
Super-fine sugar to coat the rim of the glass
Orange twist for garnish (optional)

SECRETS OF SUCCESS:

A chilled glass. The drink needs to be ice cold.

Good liquor. Be sure to use premium vodka and Cointreau, rather than a generic triple sec.

IMA GIMLET

Jean Tartaglia had a dream of opening a restaurant that would be a gathering place for drinks and good food. With Mecca, in the Upper Market area, he realized his dream. ❖ The huge bar in the center, with dining tables on two sides, give people the best of both worlds. Those dining can watch the bar action or the open kitchen that's tucked away in the back, while those having drinks can enjoy the bustling atmosphere. ❖ The drinks served here are some of the best in town: a great cosmopolitan, old fashioned, or my favorite, an Ima Gimlet that produces a gentle twist on the traditional gimlet. The sugar-rimmed glass adds just the right sweetness to the tart lime, mint, and vodka. The only problem is you don't want to stop with one drink. ❖ Those who don't come for the drinks, come for the contemporary American fare crafted by chef Mike Fennelly. Fresh shellfish, including oysters on the half shell, are a specialty. You can also get Asian-inspired dumplings and Italian-inspired pizza that may be topped with prosciutto and spinach or sausage and onions. And they all go great with the Ima Gimlet.

Ice

12 fresh mint leaves

5 tablespoons (2½ ounces) vodka

1 tablespoon (½ ounce) triple sec

Juice of 1 large lime

½ tablespoon simple syrup, or more to taste
   (see Note)

Super-fine sugar for coating the rim of the glass

Lime slice

Straw (optional)

—Fill a cocktail shaker with ice. Add the mint leaves, vodka, triple sec, lime juice, and syrup. Shake well.

—Place the sugar on a plate. Rub the lime slice on the rim of a wineglass and turn the glass over in the plate of sugar to coat the rim. Twist gently to evenly coat. Fill the glass with ice. Strain the contents of the shaker into the glass. Garnish with the lime and serve with a straw, if desired.

Serves 1

Note: *To make simple syrup, combine equal amounts of sugar and water in a small saucepan over high heat. Stir until the sugar dissolves. Bring to a boil, reduce the heat, and simmer for 5 minutes. Remove from heat and cool. Store in the refrigerator.*

SECRETS OF SUCCESS:

Fresh mint leaves. This variance from the classic gimlet really gives the drink a wonderful lift.

RUBY RED SANGRIA

Charanga is the type of Pan-Latin restaurant that wants to make you reach for a glass of sangria. It's little wonder then that they serve the best in the city. Most versions are watered down or lightened up, but chef Gabriela Salas, who hails from Costa Rica, uses only fruit and sugar to flavor the red wine. ✣ In fact the blend is a simple mix of Taylor Hearty Burgundy, Valencia orange, Granny Smith apple, lemon, and sugar. It's potent stuff and goes well with the food at this innovative restaurant that derives its name from a Cuban style of music and dance. Partner Rita Abraldes is Cuban-American, so they both bring their heritage to the restaurant. While the interior is bare bones and noisy, the food is excellent and prices are under $10.

—Divide the wine between 2 pitchers. Divide the fruit and sugar between the pitchers. Stir until sugar dissolves. Chill and serve.

Makes 2 pitchers to serve 6 to 8

SECRETS OF SUCCESS:

Taylor Hearty Burgundy. It's true. Of all the inexpensive box wines on the market, this has the most character. It's smooth and not too tannic.

The citrus fruit. The whole diced fruit, pith and peel included, intensifies the flavor.

Sangria will keep in the refrigerator for several days.

3 bottles (750 ml each) Taylor Hearty Burgundy wine
1 Valencia orange, cut into ½-inch dice
1 Granny Smith apple, cut into ½-inch dice
1 lemon, cut into ½-inch dice
½ cup sugar

CUCUMBER VODKA

The name of the restaurant—Infusion—gives you a clue about what to order. On any night you can find up to a dozen different flavored, or infused, vodkas: jalapeño, watermelon, pineapple, vanilla, and my favorite—cucumber. ❋ The clear liquid takes on the pure, intense flavor of cucumber. It's great served as an ice-cold apéritif from the freezer or over ice. It's also great in a Bloody Mary. ❋ The technique is simple and effortless. All you need is the flavoring agent and a good-quality vodka. Period. ❋ These infusions are the backbones of Infusion, a trendy South-of-Market restaurant that features a robust, eclectic menu and live entertainment. Spice is used liberally in the food, and these refreshing flavored vodkas help cool the palate.

—Place the cucumber slices in a large, clean glass container and pour the vodka over. Cover the container and store at room temperature for 2 weeks.
—When the vodka is ready, strain through a fine mesh sieve lined with a paper coffee filter or 2 thicknesses of damp cheesecloth.
—Pour into a clean bottle (the original vodka bottle is fine), seal tightly, and store in the freezer.

Makes 1 (750 ml) bottle

Serve straight up like a martini, use in a Bloody Mary, or mix with club soda over ice.

3 to 4 hothouse cucumbers, peeled and cut into ⅛-inch rounds
1 (750 ml) bottle vodka

SECRETS OF SUCCESS:

The flavoring. The cucumber adds an exciting, refreshing note to the vodka.

The freezer. Storing the vodka in the freezer, where it becomes thick and syrupy, makes it even more refreshing.

DESSERTS

APPLE GALETTE

Apple galettes are popular in restaurants all around the Bay Area, but the version done by Mark Drazek at Zax is the best. ❋ The reason is that the dough has lots of butter, which makes for a rich flaky crust. More butter is added to the apple filling and the dough is folded around it, leaving a hole in the center. The pastry and fruit merge into a delicious whole that's best when still warm from the oven. ❋ It's one of the signature desserts of this charming North Beach–area restaurant that's owned by Drazek and his wife, Barbara Mulas. He handles the desserts and salads, while she concentrates on the main courses. Together they produce food that's unbeatable.

Dough
2 cups all-purpose flour, plus additional
    for rolling
Pinch of salt
1 cup (2 sticks) chilled unsalted butter, cut
    into cubes
3 tablespoons ice water

Filling
6 large, tart apples (such as Granny Smith or
    Pippin), peeled and cut into ⅛- to ¼-inch
    slices
½ cup sugar, plus additional for sprinkling
½ teaspoon ground cinnamon
½ cup (1 stick) unsalted butter, melted

Vanilla or caramel ice cream

—*To make the dough:* Sift the flour and salt into a bowl. Add the butter and quickly cut it into the flour mixture with a pastry blender or two dull knives until the mixture is the texture of cornmeal. Sprinkle in the ice water and mix quickly with a fork just until the dough comes together.

—Divide the dough into 6 equal pieces, flatten each piece into a disk, and wrap individually in plastic wrap. Refrigerate the dough for at least 4 hours and up to 2 days.

—Just before assembling the galettes, remove the dough from the refrigerator and soften slightly.

—*To make the filling:* Preheat the oven to 425 degrees. Mix the apples, sugar, and cinnamon in a large bowl.

—On a lightly floured surface, roll out each piece of softened dough to a 7-inch diameter circle, about ⅛-inch thick. Spoon filling in the center of each, leaving a 3-inch border.

—To shape the galette, with your hands side by side, gently lift two inches of the edge of the dough with both hands. Fold the dough in your right hand over the filling and then fold the dough in your left hand over the filling, forming a pleat of dough. Continue this motion 6 to 8 times around the edge of the galette until all the dough is pleated around the filling, leaving an exposed center of filling.

—Brush the edges of the dough with the melted butter and sprinkle with sugar. Place the galettes on a sheet pan lined with parchment paper and bake until the crust is golden and the filling begins to bubble, about 35 minutes.

—Serve warm with vanilla or caramel ice cream.

Serves 6

SECRET OF SUCCESS:

Unsalted butter. This produces a rich, flaky, and buttery crust that melds with the tart, sweet apples.

Chilling the dough. This makes it easier to handle and helps ensure a flaky crust.

APPLE CRISP

Everyone I know who's tried Kerry Heffernan's Apple Crisp says it's the best they've tasted. The secret is in the topping. There's twice as much as just about any recipe I've encountered. And why not? Isn't that what people really love? ❋ The topping is made with flour, oats, and lots of butter, with a judicious amount of sweet spices. The filling is plump with Granny Smith apples, lending a firm texture and tart taste. ❋ After an hour of baking, the crisp emerges from the oven browned, bubbling, and absolutely delicious. Serve it warm with a scoop of vanilla ice cream in the center of each dish. ❋ The apple crisp is one of the most popular choices at Oakland's Autumn Moon Café, owned by Heffernan and Wendy Levy. They have created a charming space that is loosely based on a movie theme, with classic posters and photos all around the various dining rooms. ❋ The food celebrates American classics, but whatever you order, be sure to end with the crisp.

1¾ cups all-purpose flour
1¼ cups oats
2¼ cups plus 2 tablespoons sugar
⅛ teaspoon ground allspice
⅛ teaspoon ground nutmeg
2⅛ teaspoons ground cinnamon
1 cup (2 sticks) chilled unsalted butter
5 Granny Smith apples, peeled and sliced
2 teaspoons fresh lemon juice
Nonstick vegetable oil spray
Vanilla ice cream

—Preheat the oven to 350 degrees.

—Combine the flour, oats, 2¼ cups sugar, allspice, nutmeg, and ⅛ teaspoon of the cinnamon in a large mixing bowl. Using the large holes of a grater, grate the butter into the bowl. Using your fingertips, mix just until it begins to come together, being careful not to overmix.

—In another large bowl, toss the apples with the remaining 2 tablespoons sugar and 2 teaspoons cinnamon, and the lemon juice.

—Spray an 8x8-inch pan (or larger) with vegetable oil spray. Transfer the apple mixture to the pan and sprinkle with the topping.

—Bake uncovered until the topping is golden brown and the apples are tender, about 30 to 35 minutes. Serve warm with a scoop of vanilla ice cream.

Serves 6 to 8

SECRETS OF SUCCESS:

Lots of topping. It's not too much. It creates a warm crunchy foil to the gooey apples.

Grating the cold butter. Grating the chilled butter for the topping on the large holes of a grater makes it easier to incorporate into the flour mixture.

BUTTER PECAN PIE

Tony Gulisano may have his heart in Italy, but he has a way with American desserts. At his new Park Chow, a sister restaurant to his moderately priced Chow in the Castro, the chef serves a spectacular version of pecan pie. ✳ The problem with most pecan pie recipes is that they are so rich and sweet that the nuts seem like an afterthought. Gulisano's version is perfectly balanced, and the filling is cooked, giving it a silken texture. During baking the pecans rise to the top.

Crust
1½ cups unbleached all-purpose flour, plus
    additional for rolling
1 teaspoon sea salt
¾ cup (1½ sticks) chilled unsalted butter, cut
    into cubes
¼ cup ice water

Filling
1½ cups pecans (halves and pieces)
1 cup C & H golden brown sugar
1 scant cup light corn syrup
½ cup (1 stick) unsalted butter
1 tablespoon all-purpose flour
¼ teaspoon sea salt
3 eggs, lightly beaten
1 teaspoon vanilla extract

Vanilla ice cream or lightly whipped cream

—*To make the crust:* Combine the 1½ cups flour and the salt in a food processor and mix briefly. Gradually add the butter to the flour mixture while pulsing the processor on and off, until the butter is cut into pieces the size of small peas. With the processor running, gradually add the ice water and process until large clumps form. Remove the dough from the processor, shape into a ball, and flatten into a disk. Wrap in plastic and refrigerate 1 hour.

—Let the dough soften slightly at room temperature. Roll the dough on a lightly floured surface into a 13-inch round. Carefully transfer the dough to a 9-inch pie pan. Trim any dough hanging over the edge. Crimp the edges decoratively. Freeze for 10 minutes.

—*To make the filling:* Preheat the oven to 425 degrees. Combine the pecans, brown sugar, corn syrup, butter, flour, and salt in a heavy-bottomed pan over medium heat. Bring to a boil, stirring constantly. Remove from heat. Cool 15 minutes.

—Whisk the eggs and vanilla into the filling. Pour the filling into the pie shell.

—Bake 10 minutes. Reduce the oven temperature to 325 degrees. Bake until the custard has set and the nuts rise to the surface, about 30 to 40 minutes. Transfer to a rack and cool.

—Serve with ice cream or lightly whipped cream.

Serves 8

SECRETS OF SUCCESS:

Boiling the filling. Pecan pie filling is rarely cooked before being baked in the shell. It's a technique usually reserved for cheese pies.

Freezing the pie shell. The unbaked dough is placed in the freezer so that when the filling is poured in, the crust will stay firm.

The brown sugar. Pure cane sugar, such as C & H, has a reliable flavor and texture.

BOSTINI CREAM PIE

No, Bostini Cream Pie is not a misprint. It's not Boston Cream Pie, but Kurtis Baguley's luscious dessert is always incorrectly identified. ❋ In fact, the Bostini Cream Pie is the pastry chef's take on the famous dessert. And, frankly, pie is a misnomer, too. It's actually a cake, or in this case, it's orange chiffon cake on top of rich custard covered with a warm chocolate glaze. If I had to choose one dessert to dig into night after night, it would probably be this one. ❋ This dessert wowed more than 100 food editors a couple of years ago when they met in the Napa Valley. The combination is nothing short of ethereal. ❋ While Baguley has left the restaurant, his legacy remains in the form of the Bostini Cream Pie.

Custard
¾ cup whole milk
2¾ tablespoons cornstarch
9 egg yolks, beaten to blend
1 whole egg
3¾ cups heavy cream
½ cup plus 1 tablespoon sugar
½ vanilla bean

Orange Chiffon
Nonstick vegetable oil spray
1½ cups cake flour
¾ cup super-fine sugar
1½ teaspoons baking powder
¼ teaspoon salt
¾ cup fresh orange juice
⅓ cup canola oil
⅓ cup beaten egg yolks (about 3 to 4 large yolks)
1½ tablespoons grated orange zest
1 teaspoon vanilla extract
1 cup egg whites (about 8 large)
1 teaspoon cream of tartar

Chocolate glaze
1 cup (2 sticks) unsalted butter
8 ounces semisweet chocolate, finely chopped

—*To make the custard:* Whisk the milk and cornstarch in a large bowl until smooth. Whisk in the yolks and whole egg until the mixture is smooth.

—Combine the cream and sugar in a large saucepan over medium heat. Add the vanilla bean. Bring to a boil. When the mixture just boils, whisk in the egg mixture, stirring constantly until the mixture is thick enough to coat the back of a spoon, about 10 minutes. Strain the custard. Pour into eight 7-ounce custard cups. Chill.

—*To make the orange chiffon:* Preheat the oven to 325 degrees. Spray eight more 7-ounce molds with nonstick cooking spray (they must be the same size as the molds used for the custards).

—Sift the cake flour, sugar, baking powder, and salt into a large bowl. Add the orange juice, oil, egg yolks, zest, and vanilla. Stir until smooth, but do not overmix.

—Using an electric mixer, beat the egg whites in a large bowl until frothy. Add the cream of tartar and beat until soft peaks form. Gently fold the beaten whites into the batter. Divide the batter among the prepared molds (they will be filled almost to the top). Place the molds on a baking sheet.

—Bake until the cakes bounce back when lightly pressed with a fingertip, about 25 minutes. Do not overbake. Transfer the baking sheet to a rack and cool. Remove the cakes from the molds when cool. Cover the cakes with plastic.

—*To make the glaze:* Melt the butter in a small saucepan over medium-low heat until just about to bubble. Remove from the heat; add the chocolate and stir until melted and smooth. Pour through a strainer and keep warm.

—Cut a thin slice from the top of each cake to create a flat surface. Place a cake flat side down on top of each custard. Cover the tops with warm chocolate glaze. Serve immediately.

Serves 8

SECRETS OF SUCCESS:

The fine texture. Cake flour, super-fine sugar, and beaten egg whites produce a finely textured cake.

The presentation. The custard goes on the bottom of the individual ramekins, then the cake, and finally the chocolate glaze, which should drizzle down the side of the cup.

BANANA CREAM PIE

If I had to name one dessert that I crave above the rest, it's the Banana Cream Pie at Liberty Café. It doesn't even matter that banana is far from my favorite fruit—when it's paired with the rich cool custard, frothy whipped cream, and flaky crust at Liberty Café, it's nothing short of perfect. ❉ What makes it so special is how owner Cathie Guntli has tweaked a great recipe with a better crust and a rich cream filling. But the all-American cafe does the same with many of its specialties. ❉ After three years as the pastry chef at Zuni Cafe, Guntli decided it was time to open her own restaurant. She found a cozy thirty-two-seat space in Bernal Heights. While not fancy, the interior has a homey quality that fits the demeanor of the food. ❉ In recent years the restaurant has expanded and now features an outdoor patio and wine bar, and a bakery where you might even be able to find the Banana Cream Pie to take home, if it's not already sold out. But now you can have it any time with this recipe.

Crust
2 cups all-purpose flour, plus additional for rolling
1 teaspoon salt
¼ cup chilled solid vegetable shortening
¼ cup (½ stick) chilled unsalted butter
4 to 8 tablespoons ice water

Pastry Cream
2 cups whole milk
½ vanilla bean, split lengthwise
½ cup sugar
¼ cup all-purpose flour
2 tablespoons cornstarch
3 eggs
3 tablespoons unsalted butter

Topping
1 cup heavy cream
2 tablespoons sugar
½ teaspoon vanilla extract

4 to 5 bananas, peeled and cut into ¼-inch slices
Chocolate shavings for garnishing

—*To make the crust:* In the bowl of a food processor fitted with a metal blade, combine the flour and salt. Add the shortening and butter and pulse the processor on and off until the mixture is the size of peas. Add the water a tablespoon at a time, processing only until the dough begins to come together. Form the dough into a ball. Flatten into a disk. Wrap in plastic and refrigerate until chilled, at least 1 hour.

—Preheat the oven to 350 degrees. Remove the chilled dough from the refrigerator; soften slightly if necessary. Roll out the dough on a lightly floured surface to a 10-inch round, about ⅛-inch thick. Transfer to a 9-inch pie dish. Crimp the edges decoratively. Line the dough with foil and pie weights or dry beans to keep the crust from bubbling up during baking. Bake until the edges of the crust are lightly browned, about 10 to 15 minutes. Remove the weights and foil and continue to bake for 5 to 7 minutes until the whole crust is golden brown. Transfer to a rack and cool completely.

—*To make the pastry cream:* Pour the milk into a large saucepan over low heat. Scrape in the seeds from the vanilla bean; add the bean. Heat until warm. Stir in ¼ cup of the sugar and continue to warm until small bubbles form around the edge of the pan, about 5 to 7 minutes.

—Meanwhile, in the bowl of an electric mixer, beat the flour, cornstarch, eggs, and remaining ¼ cup sugar until smooth.

—Slowly whisk the warmed milk into the egg mixture. Return the mixture to the saucepan. Stir over low heat until thick and slightly bubbly, about 10 minutes. Remove from heat. Strain into a large bowl. Add the butter and stir until melted. Press plastic wrap directly onto the surface of the pastry cream to prevent a skin from forming. Cool. Refrigerate until cold.

—*To make the topping:* Beat the cream, sugar, and vanilla in a large bowl until stiff peaks form.

—Spread a thin layer of pastry cream on the bottom of the crust. Top with a layer of bananas. Continue to layer the bananas and pastry cream until you reach the top of the crust, finishing with the pastry cream to prevent the bananas from turning brown. Top with the whipped cream and garnish with chocolate shavings.

Serves 8 to 10

SECRETS OF SUCCESS:

The crust. Using a combination of butter and shortening gives a crisper texture and richer flavor.

The custard. Butter melted into the hot custard at the end lends a silken texture.

The whipped cream. An alternative to meringue, the lightly sweetened cream adds another rich, cool element.

BANANA CREAM TART WITH COCONUT CARAMEL SAUCE

One of the most requested restaurant dessert recipes at *The Chronicle* is the Banana Cream Tart with Coconut Caramel Sauce at Grand Cafe. ❉ The crust is made with graham crackers and macadamia nuts, then baked. Then smooth custard, lightened with whipped cream, is alternated with layers of sliced bananas. Finally, the custard is unmolded and drizzled with a golden caramel sauce made with sugar and coconut milk.

Crust
Oil for greasing
1½ cups graham cracker crumbs
½ cup finely ground macadamia nuts
½ cup (1 stick) unsalted butter, melted and
    cooled
1 tablespoon sugar

Sauce
2 cups sugar
1¼ cups canned unsweetened coconut milk

Custard
1½ cups sugar
⅓ cup plus 1 tablespoon cornstarch
¼ teaspoon salt
3 cups cold whole milk
2 egg yolks
2 tablespoons unsalted butter
2 teaspoons vanilla extract

Topping
1 cup heavy cream
1 teaspoon powdered sugar, sifted

2 ripe but firm bananas, peeled and sliced

—*To make the crust:* Preheat the oven to 350 degrees. Oil a large baking sheet. Arrange eight 3-inch ring molds with hinges on the baking sheet. Combine the graham cracker crumbs, nuts, melted butter, and sugar in a medium bowl. Pat into ring molds. Bake until lightly brown, about 8 to 10 minutes. Cool, leaving the ring molds in place.

—*To make the sauce:* Place the sugar in a small heavy-bottomed saucepan over medium-high heat and stir constantly until it becomes golden brown in color. Be careful to not let the sugar burn. Carefully add the coconut milk, stirring vigorously. Cook over medium heat until the sauce thickens slightly, about 3 to 5 minutes. Set aside.

—*To make the custard:* Combine the sugar, cornstarch, and salt in a large saucepan. Whisk in the cold milk until the mixture is completely smooth. Place the saucepan over medium-low heat and stir until the mixture is warm. Whisk the egg yolks in a small bowl to blend. Stir a small amount of the hot milk mixture into the egg yolks to temper. Then pour the egg yolk mixture back into the milk mixture and cook until it is quite thick, whisking vigorously, about 10 minutes. Remove from the heat. Stir in the butter and vanilla. Pour the custard in a bowl and press plastic wrap directly on the surface of the custard to prevent a skin from forming. Cool the custard completely.

—*To make the topping:* Beat the cream to soft peaks in a large bowl. Fold ⅓ cup of the cream into the cooled custard. Beat the powdered sugar into the remaining whipped cream.
—Slide a spatula under each ring mold and move each to a serving plate. Inside the rings, alternate layers of bananas and custard, finishing with custard on the top. Carefully unhinge and remove the rings. Spoon the coconut caramel sauce around and over the custard.
—Garnish with the sweetened whipped cream.

Serves 8

SECRETS OF SUCCESS:

Small ring molds. This allows you to spoon in the filling and unhinge the sides. These molds are available at specialty foods or equipment stores.

Browning the sugar. The sugar should turn golden brown before being mixed with the coconut milk to form a rich but simple sauce.

SNICKER'S PIE

Snicker's Pie has a deeper meaning to Mimi Silbert, the founder of Delancey Street, the country's largest self-help residential program for people trying to rebuild their lives. ✳ The pie is great, featuring a graham cracker crust with chocolate fudge, cream cheese, and pieces of Snicker's Bars, but it also represents the culmination of Silbert's dream of opening the restaurant and residential facility. Each night as Silbert, who began the foundation in 1972, worried about finances and design details, she consoled herself with fudge, Snicker's Bars, and cheesecake. "We developed this pie as a victory consolidation to save calories and celebrate the completion of our home," she says. ✳ Calorie-saving is relative, as you'll see when you fork into this rich pie. After the crust is made, the fudge layer is blended together and baked. Then the Snicker's Bars are added, topped off with the cheesecake. It's baked again and drizzled with chocolate syrup. ✳ The restaurant, which opened in 1991, has large windows overlooking the Embarcadero, and the plain interior is warmed up with displays of fresh produce and arrangements of fresh flowers all around the restaurant. The menu features home cooking from around the world. ✳ The entire staff—including waiters, cooks, and bus boys—are among the 500 residents in the program, and they've been trained by some of the city's best chefs and restaurateurs who occasionally volunteer their time to help.

Crust
Butter for greasing
2 cups graham cracker crumbs
4 teaspoons brown sugar
½ cup (1 stick) unsalted butter, melted

Fudge Layer
½ cup (1 stick) unsalted butter, cut into 8 pieces
4 ounces semisweet chocolate, chopped
1 ounce unsweetened chocolate, chopped
6 tablespoons all-purpose flour
½ teaspoon baking powder
⅛ teaspoon salt
½ cup sugar
1 large egg
1 egg yolk
1 teaspoon vanilla extract
2 cups ½-inch pieces of Snicker's Bars (about 8½ ounces)

Cream Cheese Layer
10 ounces cream cheese at room temperature
⅓ cup sugar
1 large egg
1 teaspoon vanilla extract

Topping
2 ounces milk chocolate, chopped
3 tablespoons heavy cream

—*To make the crust:* Preheat the oven to 350 degrees. Butter a 9-inch deep-dish glass pie pan.

—In a medium bowl, combine the graham cracker crumbs and the brown sugar. Stir in the melted butter until well incorporated. Press the mixture evenly onto the bottom and up the sides of the prepared pan. Bake until the crust is set, about 5 minutes. Transfer to a rack and cool. Maintain the oven temperature.

—*To make the fudge layer:* In the top of a double boiler set over simmering water, combine the butter, semisweet, and unsweetened chocolate. Stir until melted and smooth. Remove from over the water and cool slightly.

—Sift the flour, baking powder, and salt into a medium bowl.

—Using an electric mixer, beat the sugar, egg, and yolk in a large bowl until slightly thickened, about 1 minute. Add the vanilla and the cooled chocolate mixture and mix until well blended. Add the dry ingredients and mix just until combined.

—Pour the fudge mixture into the crust. Bake until a skewer inserted into the center comes out with moist batter still attached, about 15 minutes. If the crust browns too quickly, cover with foil. Transfer the pan to a rack. Cool for 10 minutes. Evenly arrange the Snicker's Bars over the fudge layer.

—*To make the cream cheese layer:* Using an electric mixer, beat the cream cheese and sugar in a medium bowl until smooth. Add the egg and vanilla and beat until smooth. Carefully spread the mixture over the Snicker's Bars. Bake until the cream cheese layer is set, about 15 minutes. Cool on a rack.

—*For the topping:* Stir the milk chocolate and cream together in the top of a double boiler set over simmering water. When just melted and smooth, remove from heat. Dip a spoon into the mixture and drizzle decoratively over the pie.

—Refrigerate the pie until well chilled. Serve cold. The pie can be prepared up to 3 days ahead. Cover loosely with foil and keep refrigerated.

Serves 12 to 16

SECRETS OF SUCCESS:

The layers. Fudge is baked in the shell, topped with Snicker's, and then covered with a cheesecake filling. The filling is baked again, which helps unify the layers and produces a complex, rich pie.

BUTTERMILK SHORTCAKE WITH STRAWBERRIES AND MEYER LEMON SYRUP

Even those who love strawberry shortcake have to admit that it's not always perfect; usually there's one element that disappoints. In the case of Rivoli's Buttermilk Shortcake with Strawberries and Meyer Lemon Syrup, all the components are right on target. ❊ Chef/owner Wendy Brucker has created a shortcake with a tangy sweetness and a crumbly sconelike texture; the strawberries are enhanced by cooking and pureeing part of the berries to make a sauce, and the whipping cream is embellished with crème fraîche. To top it off, the plate is drizzled with a Meyer Lemon Syrup. It's perfect.

Shortcakes

2 cups all-purpose flour

3 tablespoons sugar, plus additional for
    sprinkling

2 teaspoons baking powder

1 teaspoon baking soda

½ cup (1 stick) chilled unsalted butter, cut into
    ¼-inch pieces

¾ cup buttermilk

Strawberry Filling

4 cups sliced fresh strawberries

½ cup sugar

Pinch of salt

Squeeze of fresh lemon juice

Cream

1 cup heavy cream

1 cup crème fraîche

1 teaspoon vanilla extract

2 tablespoons sugar

Syrup

½ cup sugar

½ cup water

2 tablespoons grated Meyer lemon or
    other lemon zest

Powdered sugar for dusting

—*To make the shortcakes:* Preheat the oven to 375 degrees. Line a baking sheet with parchment paper. Sift together the dry ingredients into a bowl. Add the butter and mix with your fingers until it is broken up and the mixture has the texture of wet sand. Add the buttermilk and gently mix in.

—Shape the dough into 6 shortcakes on the prepared baking sheet by using a 4-inch ring mold and easing the dough into the ring with the aid of a soup spoon dipped into hot water.

—Place the baking sheet on another baking sheet. This keeps the bottom of the shortcakes from burning.

—Sprinkle the tops of the shortcakes with additional sugar. Bake until golden, about 10 minutes. Cool on a baking rack. Slice the shortcakes in half and store in a covered container if made ahead.

—*To make the filling:* Combine 1 cup of the strawberries and the sugar, salt, and lemon juice in a small saucepan. Cook over medium heat for 20 minutes. Puree and strain. Cool to room temperature. Stir in the remaining strawberries.

—*To make the cream:* Combine the cream, crème fraîche, vanilla, and sugar in a large bowl; beat until medium peaks form.

—*To make the syrup:* Combine the sugar, water, and zest in a small saucepan; bring to a simmer over medium heat. Cook for 5 minutes. Cool to room temperature.

—*For each serving:* Place the bottom half of a shortcake on a dessert plate, cut side up. Top with a generous spoonful of the strawberries, then a large dollop of whipped cream, and finally more strawberries. Crown with the top half of the shortcake, and drizzle with a portion of Meyer Lemon Syrup. Dust with powdered sugar.

Serves 6

SECRETS OF SUCCESS:

Berry puree. Even less than spectacular berries are delicious when they're mixed with a sweetened cooked puree.

The whipping cream. Mixing the crème fraîche into the whipping cream gives the topping extra heft.

Lemon syrup. This extra garnish brings all the elements together.

Two baking pans. Baking the shortcakes on two baking pans stacked together keeps the bottoms from becoming too brown.

CLAFOUTI

One of the most popular restaurant desserts recently has been *clafouti,* a fruit mixture that can be as smooth as custard or as dry as a cake. Generally they all have one thing in common, and that's the fruit that's incorporated into the batter. ❊ To me, the rich cake-like clafoutis are the best, and Casa Orinda's version created by Sharon McCoy is at the top of my list. ❊ It's an easy dessert to produce, and it can be in the oven in a matter of minutes. A cup of butter is melted in the bottom of the pan, then a batter is poured in and topped off with fruit— for this recipe we used peaches and raspberries, but just about any fruit will work, especially stone fruits including plums, nectarines, or apricots. ❊ It comes out golden brown, moist, and buttery. Try serving it with either whipped cream or a scoop of vanilla ice cream. ❊ These types of homey desserts are the backbone of the offerings at Casa Orinda, which has been in business since the 1930s and is owned by John Goyak.

1 cup (2 sticks) unsalted butter
2 cups all-purpose flour
2 cups sugar
4 teaspoons baking powder
½ teaspoon salt
1½ cups milk
1½ to 2 cups sliced peeled fresh peaches
    (see Note)
½ cup fresh raspberries
Lightly sweetened whipped cream or ice cream

—Preheat the oven to 350 degrees. Put the butter into a 13x9x2-inch baking pan and place in the oven until the butter has just melted. Remove the pan from the oven and set aside.

—Whisk the flour, sugar, baking powder, and salt in a large bowl to blend. Add the milk and stir briskly until well blended. The batter will be thin.

—Pour the batter over the melted butter in the baking dish. Using a rubber spatula, cut through the batter a couple of times to incorporate the butter and push the batter into the corners of the pan.

—Drain any liquid from the peaches and arrange them evenly over the batter (they'll sink to the bottom). Add the raspberries the same way.

—Bake until the entire top is golden brown, about 50 minutes.

—Serve warm with the lightly sweetened whipped cream or ice cream.

Serves 10 to 12

Note: *To peel peaches, blanch in a pot of boiling water for about 15 seconds. Remove from water and slip off the skins.*

> **SECRETS OF SUCCESS:**
>
> *The butter.* Don't skimp on the amount or use margarine; the butter gives it a rich nutty flavor that can't be achieved by any other means.

FRESH APPLE CAKE

The Fresh Apple Cake at Cafe for All Seasons in San Francisco's West Portal neighborhood is one of those desserts that brings back memories of home. It doesn't matter that we probably never had anything this good at home—it's still a nice fantasy. ❈ The beauties of this cake from chef/owner Donna Katzl are twofold: It's easy to make, and it tastes just as good a day or two after baking as it does right from the oven. In addition, the caramel sauce adds another dimension. It's used to glaze the cake, and it can be gently warmed again and spooned over and around each slice to add a just-baked quality. ❈ I've had caramel sauces that were complicated to make and didn't taste half as good. This one is a simple blend of butter, brown sugar, and cream, and once you try it you'll be hooked. If you don't want to just eat it from a spoon, try pouring it over ice cream. ❈ This dessert is the type of soul-satisfying food that has made Cafe for All Seasons one of most popular neighborhood cafes in the Bay Area. Katzl, who owns the restaurant with her husband, Frank Katzl, studied with James Beard. His all-American sensibilities are apparent in her menu and in the cafe's decor, which features an open kitchen and casual but pleasant surroundings.

Cake
Butter and flour for preparing pan
2 cups sugar
1½ cups Wesson oil
3 eggs
3 cups all-purpose flour
2 teaspoons ground cinnamon
1 teaspoon baking soda
½ teaspoon salt
½ teaspoon ground nutmeg
3 cups coarsely chopped Granny Smith apples
    (unpeeled)
1 cup chopped walnuts
2 teaspoons vanilla extract

Caramel Sauce
1 cup (2 sticks) unsalted butter, cut into pieces
2 cups (packed) light brown sugar
1 cup heavy cream

—*To make the cake:* Preheat the oven to 325 degrees. Butter and flour a 10-inch Bundt pan.

—Using an electric mixer, beat the sugar and oil in a large bowl. Add the eggs, one at a time, beating well after each addition.

—Sift the flour, cinnamon, baking soda, salt, and nutmeg into the egg mixture. Beat thoroughly. The batter will be very stiff.

—Fold the apples and walnuts into the batter with a spatula, then stir in the vanilla. Spoon the batter into the prepared pan. Bake until a toothpick inserted near the center of the cake comes out clean, about 1¼ hours. Place the pan on a rack. Cool for about 1 hour.

—*To make the caramel sauce:* Melt the butter in a heavy-bottomed saucepan over medium heat. Add the brown sugar and stir until it dissolves. Add the cream, whisking to form an emulsion. Remove from heat.

—To unmold the cake, run a knife around the edges of the pan and gently turn the cake onto a platter.

—Pour about ½ cup of the warm sauce over the cake to form a glaze. Serve immediately, with a little of the remaining sauce spooned over each slice, or let the cake cool completely. The sauce keeps well in the refrigerator, but it should be reheated before serving. You can use a microwave oven, or reheat on top of the stove over low heat. Whisk well before spooning over wedges of cake.

Serves 12

COCONUT PECAN CAKE WITH CARAMEL MOUSSE

Santa Fe Bar and Grill in Berkeley has a long, distinguished history that includes well-known chefs Mark Miller and Jeremiah Tower. Several other chefs and owners have moved in and out of the restaurant's picture since then, but the place still thrives. Now it's owned by Ahmad Behjati, who expanded the gardens outside and remodeled the interior. ❊ One of the best desserts on the menu is the Coconut Pecan Cake featuring layers of creamy caramel mousse and a topping of coconut and pecans, similar to the filling found in a German chocolate cake. It's an unbeatable combination.

Pecan Cake
Butter for greasing
1 cup toasted pecans
1 cup powdered sugar
6 eggs
¼ cup all-purpose flour
6 egg whites
¼ cup granulated sugar
¼ cup (½ stick) unsalted butter, melted

Caramel Mousse
½ cup sugar
1 teaspoon fresh lemon juice
1 tablespoon plus ¼ cup water
1 cup heavy cream
1 sheet gelatin (or 1 teaspoon powdered gelatin)
1 tablespoon brandy
½ teaspoon vanilla extract

Coconut Pecan Topping
½ cup milk
½ cup sugar
2 egg yolks, beaten to blend
¼ cup (½ stick) unsalted butter
½ teaspoon vanilla extract
¾ cup unsweetened shredded coconut
½ cup toasted chopped pecans

—*To make the cake:* Preheat oven to 375 degrees. Butter an 11x17-inch cake pan. Line with parchment paper. Combine the pecans and powdered sugar in the bowl of a food processor fitted with a metal blade. Process until finely ground. Transfer the nut mixture to the bowl of a mixer. Add the eggs and beat for 6 to 8 minutes, or until doubled in volume. Fold in the flour and set aside.

—In a clean mixing bowl, whip the egg whites to soft peaks using an electric mixer with clean dry beaters. Gradually add the granulated sugar and beat until stiff peaks form. Fold the whites into the batter. Fold in the melted butter. Pour into the prepared pan. Bake until the center springs back when lightly touched, about 10 to 12 minutes. Transfer to a rack to cool. (The cake can be made 1 day in advance. Cover with plastic and store at room temperature.)

—*To make the caramel mousse:* In a heavy-bottomed saucepan over medium heat, combine the sugar, lemon juice, and 1 tablespoon of water and cook until the sugar becomes dark amber in color, about 5 to 7 minutes. Remove from the heat and slowly add ¼ cup of the cream. Whisk the caramel until smooth.

—Combine the gelatin and remaining ¼ cup water in a medium bowl. Let stand 3 to 5 minutes until the gelatin dissolves. Stir in the hot caramel, brandy, and vanilla. Using an electric mixer, beat the remaining ¾ cup of cream in a medium bowl until soft peaks form. Fold into the mousse.

—Invert the cooled cake onto a cookie sheet turned upside down. Remove the pan and the parchment. Cut the cake in half crosswise so that you have two pieces of cake measuring approximately 8-by-12 inches. Spread one layer with the caramel mousse and stack the other layer atop the filling. Place in the refrigerator while you make the topping.

—*To make the topping:* Combine the milk, sugar, yolks, butter, and vanilla in a small saucepan over medium heat. Stir until thickened, about 5 minutes. Remove from the heat. Stir in the coconut and pecans.

—Remove the cake from the refrigerator and pour the topping over the center of the cake. Use a metal spatula to spread the topping evenly over the top and sides of cake. Return the cake to the refrigerator for several hours or overnight to set.

Serves 8

SECRETS OF SUCCESS:

Keeping it light. The stiffened egg whites help to lighten the cake and the whipped cream gives the caramel mousse an equal lightness.

WARM CHOCOLATE CAKE

Warm chocolate cake with a gooey runny center has become a standard on Bay Area menus, but the first place I tasted it was at LuLu. The trend caught on quickly, with as many variations as there are letters in the alphabet, but I still like this version best. ✳ The outside looks like a cake with a thin shell. Once you cut into it, however, the center begins to ooze. In so many versions, the inside tastes like underdone batter, but in this one it tastes like frosting. It's interesting to compare it with the cake served at Left Bank (see page 342), which has a little flour that forms a thicker shell and a firmer center than this one.

Butter and flour for preparing ramekins
1 cup (2 sticks) unsalted butter
8 ounces unsweetened chocolate, chopped
8 ounces bittersweet Valrhona chocolate
¼ cup unsweetened cocoa powder
1 tablespoon vanilla extract
⅛ teaspoon salt
1 egg, separated
1 teaspoon cream of tartar
¾ cup sugar
Powdered sugar for dusting

—Butter and flour four to six 4-ounce ramekins. In the top of a double boiler set over simmering water, combine the butter, both chocolates, and the cocoa powder. Stir until melted and smooth. Remove from over water. Cool to just above room temperature.

—In a small bowl, whisk the vanilla, salt, and egg yolk to blend. Stir into the chocolate mixture.

—Using a whisk, whip the egg white and cream of tartar in a large bowl to stiff peaks, then fold in the sugar.

—Gently fold about a quarter of the whipped egg white into the chocolate to lighten it. Then fold the chocolate into the remaining white. Gently spoon the batter into the prepared ramekins. Cover and refrigerate for at least 2 hours or up to overnight.

—Preheat the oven to 400 degrees.

—Take the ramekins directly from the refrigerator and place them in the oven. Bake until the tops begin to crack and the centers are still soft, about 15 to 20 minutes. Remove from the oven and invert the ramekins onto serving plates. Gently lift the ramekins; the cakes should remain on the plates. If they stick in the ramekins, run a paring knife around the edge of the ramekin and unmold the cakes. Dust with powdered sugar and serve warm.

Serves 4 to 6

> **SECRETS OF SUCCESS:**
>
> *Refrigerating the batter.* Chilling the mixture at least two hours helps to keep the center soft and silken.
>
> *Baking in a hot oven.* Although it only bakes 10 minutes, the high temperature helps to quickly form a "shell" on the outside.

GERMAN CHOCOLATE CAKE

German chocolate cake is a classic, but Mary Jo Thoresen, who oversees the pastry kitchens at both Enrico's and Bandol, has improved this ever-popular cake. ❊ She creates four layers of moist, finely textured cake and spreads each with a rum glaze and the gooey coconut pecan mixture. Then when she finishes assembling the layers, she caps it all with a rich chocolate icing. ❊ With all of these layers, she's able to give people what they crave: the buttery, candy-like filling. It's so delicious that you can't stop eating it. ❊ The cake is part of the dessert offerings at Enrico's, a wildly popular restaurant located on the Bohemian Broadway strip. The restaurant boasts San Francisco's best outdoor patio and a view of the garish neon strip advertising strip clubs and other night-time entertainment. It sounds a little seedy, but the area is undergoing a revival (Black Cat is directly across the street) and people are having fun coming to the naughty side of Broadway. ❊ Aside from this voyeuristic view, Enrico's offers good Italian/Mediterranean–inspired food prepared by chef/owner Rick Hackett and live entertainment. ❊ People may come once for the entertainment, but they'll come back for Thoresen's desserts.

Cake
Butter for greasing
2 ounces unsweetened chocolate, chopped
2 ounces semisweet chocolate, chopped
¼ cup water
1 cup (2 sticks) unsalted butter at room
    temperature
1½ cups sugar
4 eggs at room temperature, separated
2 cups all-purpose flour
1 teaspoon baking soda
1 teaspoon baking powder
½ teaspoon salt
1 cup buttermilk
1 teaspoon vanilla extract

Filling
1 cup heavy cream
1 cup sugar
3 egg yolks
1 cup pecans, toasted and coarsely chopped
1⅓ cups unsweetened coconut, lightly toasted
6 tablespoons (¾ stick) unsalted butter
½ teaspoon salt

Syrup
¾ cup sugar
1 cup water
Rum to taste

Chocolate Icing
8 ounces semisweet chocolate, chopped
1 cup heavy cream
3 tablespoons unsalted butter
2 tablespoons light corn syrup

—*To make the cake:* Preheat the oven to 350 degrees. Butter two 9-inch cake pans and line them with parchment paper, including a collar around the sides.

—In the top of a double boiler set over barely simmering water, combine the unsweetened chocolate, semisweet chocolate, and water. Stir until the chocolate is melted and the mixture is smooth. Remove from over water; cool to room temperature.

—Using an electric mixer, beat the butter and 1¼ cups sugar in a large bowl until light and fluffy. Slowly mix in the chocolate mixture. Add the egg yolks one at a time, mixing thoroughly after each addition.

—In a separate bowl, sift the flour, baking soda, baking powder, and salt. Mix the buttermilk and vanilla in a small bowl. Add the dry ingredients to the chocolate mixture in three additions alternately with buttermilk mixture.

—In a separate bowl and using clean dry beaters, beat the egg whites until foamy. Add the remaining ¼ cup sugar and beat to medium-firm peaks.

—Gently fold the egg whites into the batter. Pour the batter into the cake pans, dividing equally. Bake until a skewer inserted into the center of the cake comes out clean, about 25 to 30 minutes. Cool completely on a rack.

—*To make the filling:* Combine the cream, sugar, and egg yolks in the top of a double boiler set over simmering water. Stir constantly until the mixture reaches 170 degrees, about 10 minutes. Remove from over water and pour through a fine strainer into a bowl. Add the pecans, coconut, butter, and salt and stir until the butter melts. Cool to room temperature.

—*To make the syrup:* Combine the sugar and water in a small saucepan. Stir over medium-low heat until the sugar dissolves. Cool to room temperature. Add rum to taste.

—*To make the icing:* Place the chocolate in a heat-proof bowl. Bring the cream just to a simmer in a small saucepan over low heat. Pour it over the chocolate. Add the butter and corn syrup. Stir (do not whisk) until smooth. Cool to a spreadable consistency.

—*To assemble the cake:* Turn the cooled cakes out of the pans. Carefully peel off the parchment. Using a long serrated knife, carefully cut each cake horizontally into two layers. Place the bottom layer on a plate, brush lightly with the rum syrup, and spread one quarter of the filling all the way to the edge of the cake. Place a second layer on top and repeat the process. Continue until all four layers are stacked and covered with filling. Ice the sides of the cake with the chocolate icing.

—If you wish, put some icing in a pastry bag fitted with a tip of your choice and pipe a border around the edges of the cake. Refrigerate until well chilled before serving.

Serves 8 to 10

SECRETS OF SUCCESS:

Cutting the cake. Splitting each cake in two layers helps to distribute the filling throughout.

The syrup. Each layer is brushed with a rum syrup which helps to keep the cake moist and adds additional complexity.

WARM CHOCOLATE CUPCAKE SUNDAE WITH HOT FUDGE SAUCE

The memory of devil's food cake often is better than the reality. The problem: the cake is either too dry or too gooey, too sweet or too bitter. ❖ Fortunately, the version served at Lark Creek Café in Walnut Creek is just right. We're talking balance, an important but elusive achievement in cooking. At the restaurant, a more casual offshoot of Bradley Ogden's Lark Creek Inn in Larkspur, the cupcake is served warm. It has a wonderful moist crumb and an intense, earthy flavor that can stand up to ice cream and chocolate sauce. ❖ The cake, like many of the dishes at the restaurant, is an all-American hit. Ogden loves homey dishes. But this isn't just a diner; the look is sleek and sophisticated, just like the cooking.

Sauce
12 ounces bittersweet chocolate, chopped
⅓ cup unsweetened cocoa powder
¾ cup light corn syrup
½ cup heavy cream
⅓ cup sugar
Pinch of salt
6 tablespoons unsalted butter, cut into pieces
1 teaspoon vanilla extract

Cupcakes
Nonstick vegetable oil spray
1 cup all-purpose flour
⅔ cup sugar
½ cup unsweetened cocoa powder
¾ teaspoon baking soda
¼ teaspoon baking powder
¼ teaspoon salt
2 eggs
¾ cup buttermilk
¼ cup sour cream
6 tablespoons (¾ stick) unsalted butter, melted
½ cup peeled and grated raw red beets

Vanilla bean ice cream
Whipped cream for garnishing

—*To make the sauce:* Melt the chocolate in the top of a double boiler over simmering water, stirring until smooth. Stir in the cocoa powder. Remove the mixture from over water.

—In a 1-quart non-corrosive saucepan over low heat, combine the syrup, cream, sugar, and salt. Stir until sugar dissolves. Simmer over low heat about 5 minutes. Remove from the heat. Stir in the butter and vanilla. Pour the sugar mixture into the chocolate and stir to blend. If not using immediately, cool. (The sauce can be stored in the refrigerator for up to 5 days.)

—*To make the cupcakes:* Preheat the oven to 350 degrees.

—Spray 8 muffin cups with nonstick spray. In a large bowl, sift together the flour, sugar, cocoa powder, baking soda, baking powder, and salt.

—In the bowl of an electric mixer, beat the eggs and buttermilk until blended. Add the sour cream, mixing only until streaks begin to disappear. Add the melted butter and mix until just combined. Stir in the dry ingredients. Gently fold the beets into the batter. Fill each muffin cup halfway with the batter. Bake until the top springs back when touched, about 20 to 30 minutes. Transfer the pan to a rack and cool slightly.

—Reheat the fudge sauce, if necessary, in a double boiler over simmering water for 10 minutes. Split the warm cupcakes in half. Arrange the bottom layer of the cakes in serving dishes. Place a scoop of vanilla bean ice cream on each bottom layer. Cover the ice cream with the top layer of cake. Ladle 2 ounces of hot sauce over the top and garnish with a dollop of whipped cream.

Serves 8

> ### SECRETS OF SUCCESS:
>
> *A secret ingredient.* A half cup of raw beets gives the cake a rich, deep color, a moist texture, and an earthy undercurrent that brings out the best in the chocolate.
>
> *Multiple dairy products.* Most cakes have butter or buttermilk, but this one has three dairy ingredients, which adds a complex flavor and texture.

CHOCOLATE FONDUE

Fondue, which conjures up thoughts of the 1970s, is an effortless way to dine at home. It gives people something to do—dip morsels of food into a hot liquid—and it forces people to slow down. The results are a relaxed evening and great conversation. Still passé, you say? Well, consider this: For the Swiss, it has never gone out of style. And when you go to Matterhorn Swiss restaurant, you'll find lots of variations. ✳ One of the best and easiest fondues is made with bitter-sweet chocolate smoothed with cream. It's perfect for dipping cubes of pound cake and fresh fruit like strawberries, peaches, apples, and pears. The kid in us will also love dunking marshmallows into the warm sauce. ✳ It's not only fun, it's also one of the easiest desserts to prepare. At Matterhorn, the warm mix-ture is accented with a bit of liqueur such as Grand Marnier. While orange is always a great addition, you can also use kirsch (cherry) or any other flavor. You can also leave the liqueur out altogether. ✳ If you threw away your fondue pot when you retired your avocado-colored refrigerator, don't fret—you can use a chafing dish, warming plate, or a portable camping burner set on very low heat. ✳ At the restaurant, owned by Andrew and Brigitte Thorpe, you can begin the meal with a cheese or meat fondue and end with the chocolate. ✳ The interior of Matterhorn feels like a Swiss chalet with knotty-pine paneling and cozy booths. All you need is the snow on the win-dowsill, and it will feel like Christmas all year around.

¾ cup heavy cream

12 ounces bittersweet chocolate, finely chopped (preferably European chocolate such as Lindt, Valrhona, or Carma)

1 to 2 tablespoons liqueur, such as Grand Marnier or framboise (optional)

Dipping ingredients such as seasonal fruit, cut into chunks; angel food cake or poundcake, cut into cubes; cookies, such as gingersnaps; marshmallows

—Heat the cream in a heavy-bottomed saucepan. Remove from heat and add the chocolate.

—Let stand until the chocolate softens, then add the liqueur and whisk until smooth.

—Transfer the chocolate mixture to a ceramic fondue pot or double boiler and keep warm over very low heat. Serve immediately with the dipping ingredients alongside.

Serves 6

SECRETS OF SUCCESS:

Indirect heat. The chocolate is never melted directly over a burner or even in a double boiler. Instead, the cream is heated before the chunks of chocolate are put in to soften. No other cooking is required.

The best chocolate. Use good-quality European chocolate to produce a rich and satisfying flavor.

The right temperature. Keep chocolate sauce warm over very low heat so the mixture doesn't curdle or separate.

PASSION FRUIT CHEESECAKE

What do you serve at a cross-cultural restaurant that specializes in the cuisine of two cultures not known for elaborate desserts? That was Billy McVicker's dilemma as pastry chef at Oritalia, which features a blended Italian/Asian cuisine. ✳ The solution: a cheesecake made with cream cheese, sour cream, and passion fruit puree. It has a tropical flavor and an American richness, topped with a thin layer of tangy crème fraîche. If the passion fruit puree is hard to find, other fruit puree can be substituted: mango, guava or even strawberry.

Crust
½ cup ground pistachios
2 tablespoons sugar
6 tablespoons (¾ stick) unsalted butter, melted
¼ cup all-purpose flour
Butter for greasing

Filling
8 ounces cream cheese (preferably Gina Marie)
    at room temperature (see Note)
½ cup sugar
2 teaspoons cornstarch
1 large egg
1 ½ teaspoons vanilla extract
½ cup sour cream
¼ cup passion fruit puree or other fruit puree
    (see Note)

Topping
½ vanilla bean, split lengthwise
½ cup crème fraîche
Sugar

Fresh berries for garnishing

—*To make the crust:* Combine the pistachios, sugar, butter, and flour in the bowl of an electric mixer fitted with a paddle attachment. Mix over low speed until blended. Cover with plastic wrap and chill 30 minutes.

—Preheat the oven to 325 degrees.

—Lightly butter a 9½-inch springform pan. Gently press the chilled crust mixture onto the bottom and up the sides of the pan. The crust should be about ⅛-inch thick. Bake until lightly browned, about 7 minutes. Transfer the pan to a rack and cool completely. Reduce oven temperature to 300 degrees.

—*To make the filling:* Beat the cream cheese and sugar in a large bowl until fluffy. Add the remaining filling ingredients one at a time, beating well and scraping down the sides of the bowl with a rubber spatula after each addition. Mix until smooth. Strain to remove any lumps.

—Pour the filling into the crust (the crust will be ¾ full). Bake for 15 to 20 minutes or until the center puffs slightly. Remove from the oven and immediately place in the refrigerator until fully chilled, about 2 hours.

—*To make the topping:* Scrape the seeds from the vanilla bean into a medium bowl; discard the bean. Add the crème fraîche, and sugar to taste. Whisk until soft peaks form.

—Remove the sides from the springform pan and evenly spread the topping over the cheesecake.

—Garnish with fresh berries.

Serves 6 to 8

Note: *Gina Marie cream cheese is available in specialty cheese shops. If passion fruit puree is unavailable, pureed fresh mango, guava, or strawberry can be substituted.*

> **SECRETS OF SUCCESS:**
>
> *The flavoring.* The passion fruit gives this creamy dessert an unusual but satisfying appeal.
>
> *Slow cooking.* The 300-degree oven gently sets the cheesecake.

CRÈME BRÛLÉE

Crème brûlée is probably the number one dessert on San Francisco–area menus, and the best of the lot can be found at Foothill Cafe, located in the Carneros region of the wine country. ❊ Underneath the thin layer of caramelized sugar is vanilla-rich custard that's cool and barely set. The amazing texture comes from using only cream and egg yolks, instead of the usual whole eggs, and then baking the custard in a slow oven. ❊ Chef Jerry Shaffer worked at Masa's before going out on his own in this quaint restaurant, located in a strip mall. The place isn't fancy—it's a storefront, after all—but it has captured the hearts of locals who would like to keep it as a Napa Valley secret. ❊ But Shaffer's food is too good. His homespun American combinations are unsurpassed, as is his crème brûlée.

1 quart heavy cream
1 vanilla bean, split lengthwise
¼ teaspoon lemon zest
Pinch of salt
8 egg yolks
¼ cup vanilla sugar (see Note)
2 tablespoons Cognac
Sugar in the raw or granulated pure cane sugar
    for topping

—Bring the cream to a boil in a heavy medium saucepan. Add the vanilla bean, lemon zest, and salt. Remove from heat and steep for 30 minutes. Remove and reserve the vanilla bean.

—Preheat the oven to 275 degrees.

—Combine the yolks and vanilla sugar in a large bowl and whisk for 1 minute. Slowly add the warm cream to the eggs. With the edge of a knife, scrape the seeds from the reserved vanilla bean into the mixture. Discard the bean. Strain the liquid. Stir in the Cognac and let the custard rest for 10 minutes. Skim any foam from the surface. Pour the mixture into eight 6-ounce ramekins.

—Place the ramekins in a large baking pan. Carefully pour enough boiling water around the ramekins in the pan to come about halfway up the ramekins.

—Bake until the custards are set, about 30 to 45 minutes. Cool in the refrigerator.

—Top with a generous even layer of sugar in the raw or granulated sugar. Caramelize the top with a propane torch by passing the tip of the flame over the surface of the crème brûlée until the sugar bubbles and darkens to a deep golden brown.

Serves 8

Note: *To make vanilla sugar, place a whole vanilla bean in 2 cups of sugar and store in an airtight container at least 3 weeks.*

SECRETS OF SUCCESS:

Slow baking. Cooking the custard in a hot-water bath in a 275-degree oven produces a creamier texture.

Vanilla sugar. The sugar helps to infuse a deep, intense vanilla flavor throughout.

BITTERSWEET CHOCOLATE POT DE CRÈME

The Bittersweet Chocolate Pot de Crème at 42 Degrees is a misnomer. Pots de crèmes are generally baked custards, and this is like a stovetop pudding, but who wants to quibble with a dessert this good? ❋ Anne Walker's chocolate concoction is probably the best chocolate dessert I've tasted. That's pretty high praise, but then this is a pretty spectacular dessert. ❋ The chocolate chunks are stirred into a hot mixture of eggs and cream at the end of cooking, producing an intensely flavored pudding. Similar versions at other restaurants are too sweet, making the combination seem one-dimensional. At 42 Degrees the sugar is in perfect balance with the cream, eggs, and bittersweet chocolate. ❋ The restaurant, which formerly housed Cafe Esprit, has a spirited ambiance, with a loft-like feel where walls of windows roll up to bring the outdoors in. A mezzanine that hangs above the bar and open kitchen affords a view of the dining room below. ❋ Known for rustic Mediterranean food and live music nightly, the restaurant also features a bar menu that always includes the pot de crème.

4 cups heavy cream
1¾ cups half-and-half
½ cup sugar
Pinch of salt
18 egg yolks
12 ounces bittersweet chocolate (preferably Callebaut), finely chopped
1 teaspoon vanilla extract
Lightly sweetened whipped cream (optional)

—In a large saucepan, combine the cream, half-and-half, ¼ cup of the sugar, and the salt. Bring to a simmer.

—In a mixing bowl, whisk the egg yolks and remaining ¼ cup of sugar until blended. Pour a few tablespoons of the hot cream mixture into the egg yolks to help temper them. Then pour the yolk mixture into the hot cream mixture. Stir over medium heat until the pudding thickens enough to coat the back of a spoon, about 10 minutes.

—Place the chocolate in a large bowl. Pour the hot pudding over. Add the vanilla and whisk until the chocolate melts and the mixture is blended. Strain the mixture through a sieve. Pour into 8-ounce ramekins. Refrigerate until fully chilled, at least 2 hours. Serve with lightly sweetened whipped cream, if desired.

Makes 14 pots de crèmes

SECRETS OF SUCCESS:

The chocolate. We've tried it with different brands, but Callebaut is the best for this recipe.

The yolks. This rich pudding has a huge amount of egg yolks, which makes a richer pudding.

Tempering the yolks. Adding a few spoonfuls of hot liquid to the yolks prevents them from curdling when added back into the hot liquid.

CHOCOLATE FONDANT WITH ORANGE–BLACK PEPPER CRÈME FRAÎCHE

"Not another flourless chocolate cake!" I thought as I dutifully ordered the Chocolate Fondant at Left Bank in Menlo Park. I really didn't want it but couldn't see a way around it. Besides, the accompaniment sounded intriguing: Orange–Black Pepper Crème Fraîche. ❈ When the cake arrived I wondered how I could have doubted the talents of owner Roland Passot, who also owns La Folie in San Francisco and Left Bank in Larkspur. ❈ The cake has a dense chocolate-truffle texture, but tastes "finished" unlike so many raw and undercooked versions I've encountered. Passot's cake is kind of like eating a warm gooey truffle, and the flavored crème fraîche adds a tangy, spicy dimension that makes the chocolate taste even richer.

Fondant

6 ounces chopped bittersweet chocolate

1 cup (2 sticks) unsalted butter, cut into cubes, plus 2 tablespoons at room temperature

8 eggs

1 cup granulated sugar

½ cup all-purpose flour

½ cup unsweetened cocoa powder

12 toasted hazelnuts or brandied cherries

Crème Fraîche

2 cups crème fraîche

1 tablespoon orange zest

2 tablespoons sifted powdered sugar

1 teaspoon whole pink peppercorns, freshly ground

1 teaspoon whole black peppercorns, freshly ground

—*To make the fondant:* Melt the chocolate and the 1 cup butter in a small saucepan over low heat, stirring until smooth. Pour into a large bowl. In another large bowl, whisk the eggs and sugar to blend. Fold in the flour. Fold the egg mixture into the chocolate mixture. Cover and refrigerate about 2 hours.

—Preheat the oven to 400 degrees. Brush the bottom and sides of eight 4-ounce ramekins with the remaining 2 tablespoons butter. Dust with cocoa powder.

—Transfer the chilled batter to a pastry bag with a plain tip. Pipe half of the chocolate mixture into the ramekins, filling each halfway. Drop 3 hazelnuts or cherries into each ramekin, then pipe the remaining chocolate over. Place the ramekins on a sheet pan. Bake the fondants until firm to the touch and just beginning to pull away from the sides of the ramekins, about 12 to 14 minutes. Transfer to a baking rack.

—*To make the crème fraîche:* Using an electric mixer, beat the crème fraîche until soft peaks form. Stir in the zest, powdered sugar, and peppercorns.

—Loosen the edges of the fondants with a sharp knife and unmold them onto plates. Serve with a spoonful of crème fraîche.

Serves 8

> **SECRETS OF SUCCESS:**
>
> *High temperature.* Baking at 400 degrees produces the crisp exterior and creamy, molten interior.
>
> *The crème fraîche.* Both the orange and the black pepper have an affinity for chocolate and make the flavors seem more intense.
>
> *Peppercorns.* Adding both pink and black peppercorns gives more complexity.

COFFEE AND DOUGHNUTS

Coffee and doughnuts may be a classic combination, but it takes on added allure when it's on the menu at The French Laundry, considered by many critics to be one of the top restaurants in the United States. ❋ Tucked away in an historic stone laundry in the wine country, it's the closest thing the United States has to a three-star French country restaurant. Chef/owner Thomas Keller made such a splash when he took over this veteran location in 1994 that three years later he won the James Beard Award as the country's best chef. ❋ It's that good. No matter what you order on the fixed price menus, Keller gives you a bonus, and the small innovative courses keep coming, each better than the last. ❋ In case you haven't figured it out, Keller's version of Coffee and Doughnuts isn't typical. It's small doughnuts placed around a cup filled with a cappuccino semifreddo. ❋ Part of the fun of eating at The French Laundry is trying to figure out what Keller will name various specialties. Keller's a serious cook, which you'll understand the minute you take your first bite. But he just doesn't want his customers to take things too seriously.

Starter
2¼ teaspoons (or 1 envelope) active dry yeast
5 ounces warm water (about 110 degrees)
1 cup all-purpose flour

Cappuccino Semifreddo
1 teaspoon instant espresso powder
⅓ cup boiling water
10 egg yolks
1¼ cups sugar
½ vanilla bean, split lengthwise
1 cup heavy cream
4 ounces egg whites (about 8 extra-large)

Doughnuts
2¼ teaspoons (or 1 envelope) active dry yeast
2 tablespoons warm milk, about 110 degrees
1 cup (or more) all-purpose flour, plus additional for rolling
2 tablespoons plus 1½ cups sugar
1½ teaspoons salt
4 ounces egg yolks (about 8 extra-large)
¼ cup (½ stick) unsalted butter, melted
1 quart vegetable oil
¾ teaspoon ground cinnamon

—*To make the starter:* Mix the yeast with the water in a small bowl. Set aside until foamy, about 10 minutes. Transfer to the bowl of an electric mixer and add the 1 cup of flour. Using a dough hook, mix until the ingredients are thoroughly blended. Cover with plastic wrap and refrigerate for 12 hours or overnight.

—*To make the semifreddo:* Stir the espresso powder and boiling water in a small bowl until the espresso powder dissolves. In the bowl of an electric mixer, beat the yolks and ¼ cup of the sugar until the mixture is thick and pale in color, about 5 minutes. Scrape in the seeds from the vanilla bean. Discard the bean. Add the espresso mixture and mix well. Place the bowl in a larger bowl filled with ice.

—In a medium mixing bowl, beat the cream with ¼ cup of the sugar until soft peaks form. Gently fold into the yolk mixture.

—In another large bowl, beat the egg whites with the remaining ¾ cup sugar until stiff peaks form. Fold the whipped whites into the yolk-cream mixture and incorporate well. Pipe or spoon the semifreddo into demitasse cups or 4-ounce ramekins. Place in the freezer and freeze for 50 minutes or longer (remove from the freezer 30 minutes before serving if frozen longer).

—*To make the doughnuts:* Mix the yeast with the warm milk in a small bowl and let stand until foamy, about 10 minutes. Combine the flour, 2 tablespoons sugar, and salt in a mixing bowl. Using an electric mixer with a dough hook, begin to mix the dough. Add the yeast mixture, yolks, and melted butter, and continue to knead until all of the ingredients are blended. Add the starter and mix until well blended, about 10 minutes.

—Roll the dough out on a well-floured surface to ¼-inch thickness. If dough is too sticky, knead in additional flour. Cut into desired shapes (a 2½-inch cookie cutter works well) or divide the dough into walnut-size balls. Place the doughnuts on a baking sheet. Cover with a damp towel and refrigerate at least 30 minutes and up to 1 hour. Remove from the refrigerator, remove the towel, and set in a warm draft-free place until doubled in size, about 30 minutes.

—Meanwhile, in a deep sauté pan or wok, heat the oil to 325 degrees. Mix the remaining 1½ cups of sugar with the cinnamon in a small bowl to blend.

—Working in batches, fry the doughnuts until golden brown, turning once, about 1 to 2 minutes. Using a slotted spoon, transfer the doughnuts to paper towels and drain.

—Roll the hot doughnuts in the cinnamon-sugar and serve immediately with the semifreddo.

Makes 18 to 20 two-inch doughnuts and 10 to 12 semifreddos.

SECRETS OF SUCCESS:

The presentation. Making the doughnuts into round balls and serving the semifreddo in coffee or demitasse cups adds a whimsical note to any meal.

The semifreddo. The rich egg mixture isn't cooked; it's frozen and then allowed to thaw for half an hour so it's icy cold and creamy.

BAKED LEMON PUDDING

Tart lemon and tangy buttermilk is a combination that can't be beat. Those two ingredients make a luscious pudding at Buckeye Roadhouse, which sits just across the Golden Gate Bridge in Mill Valley. ❄ Because of the addition of flour, the top becomes cake-like during baking while the bottom is smooth and intensely citrus. ❄ It's the type of dessert that entices you to pull off Interstate 101 as you painfully commute inch by inch toward home. After a few minutes alone with this creamy dessert, you'll be ready to head on. ❄ Cindy Pawlcyn took the American concept she pioneered at Fog City Diner and Mustards a step further at Buckeye to produce an upscale restaurant with rustic food. The interior looks like an Aspen ski lodge with peaked ceilings and a massive stone fireplace.

Butter for greasing
⅔ cup plus ¼ cup sugar
½ cup all-purpose flour
1½ cups buttermilk
½ cup fresh lemon juice
1½ tablespoons grated lemon zest
¼ cup (½ stick) unsalted butter, melted
3 eggs, separated

—Preheat the oven to 350 degrees. Butter a 1½-quart casserole.

—Whisk the ⅔ cup sugar and the flour in a large bowl. Add the buttermilk, lemon juice, and zest, and whisk until smooth. In a separate bowl, whisk the melted butter with the egg yolks. Add a little buttermilk mixture to the warm eggs and stir to temper. Then add the eggs back into the buttermilk mixture and stir to blend.

—Using an electric mixer, beat the egg whites on high speed until foamy. Gradually add the remaining ¼ cup sugar, continuing to beat until soft peaks form. Fold the beaten whites into the lemon mixture in 3 additions until the batter is thick and smooth.

—Pour into the prepared casserole. Place the casserole in a large baking pan. Add enough water to come halfway up the sides. Bake until the top of the pudding is golden, about 50 minutes. If after 50 minutes the top of the pudding is not brown, place under a broiler for about 1 minute until it begins to turn color.

Serves 8

SECRETS OF SUCCESS:

The flour. The small amount of flour gives the creamy tart dessert a slightly cake-like texture on top and a pudding consistency underneath.

The buttermilk. This tangy ingredient is responsible for the lovely texture and rounded flavor.

CHOCOLATE BREAD PUDDING WITH SUNDRIED CHERRIES

Lissa Doumani may have given up the pastry kitchen for the front of the house when she opened Terra with her husband Hiro Sone, but she still oversees the desserts. ✱ One of the most popular and delicious concoctions is the Chocolate Bread Pudding with Sundried Cherries. While other versions are dry, this one is intensely rich and moist, and it's given distinction from both the sundried cherries and a hefty dose of Cognac.

3½ cups ¼-inch bread cubes from a batard loaf
   with crusts removed
½ cup sundried cherries
⅓ cup Cognac
8 ounces bittersweet chocolate, chopped
3 large eggs, beaten to blend
1 cup heavy cream
½ cup sour cream
½ cup sugar
1 teaspoon vanilla extract
¼ teaspoon ground cinnamon
1 cup crème fraîche or sour cream
1 tablespoon powdered sugar
6 fresh mint sprigs for garnishing

—Arrange the bread cubes on a sheet pan and let sit uncovered overnight to dry.

—Preheat the oven to 350 degrees. In a small bowl, soak the cherries in the Cognac for 20 minutes to soften.

—Melt the chocolate in the top of a double boiler set over simmering water, stirring until smooth. Remove from over water. In a large bowl, stir the eggs, cream, sour cream, sugar, vanilla, and cinnamon until smooth. Whisk in the warm chocolate. Fold in the bread and the cherries with Cognac. Let stand until the bread fully absorbs the custard and no white from the bread is showing. Divide the mixture among six 10-ounce individual soufflé dishes or one 2-quart soufflé dish. Place the soufflé dish(es) in a large baking pan. Fill the pan halfway with boiling water.

—Bake the pudding until it is very firm and no longer jiggles, about 45 minutes. Remove from the water and cool slightly. (The baking can be done a day in advance. Cover and refrigerate, then rewarm in a 250-degree oven about 15 minutes before serving.)

—In a small bowl, whisk the crème fraîche and powdered sugar until soft peaks form. Place a large dollop on top of each serving and garnish with a sprig of mint. Serve warm.

Serves 6

SECRETS OF SUCCESS:

Sun-dried cherries. Plumped in Cognac, these add a wonderful surprise to the luscious chocolate dessert.

The topping: The tart crème fraîche is needed to balance the richness of the dessert, preventing it from becoming overwhelming.

PEAR BRIOCHE BREAD PUDDING

One of the most talked-about desserts from readers of *The Chronicle* is the Pear Brioche Bread Pudding at Bistro Don Giovanni in the Napa Valley. ❋ The dessert incorporates a buttery blend of fruit, dried cherries, and spices. You can sneak it cold for breakfast, but it's best warm with a caramel swirl or vanilla ice cream.

1 cup (2 sticks) unsalted butter
1 vanilla bean, split lengthwise
1 loaf brioche (about 4 cups), cut into ½-inch
    cubes
3 cups heavy cream
1 cup milk
1¼ teaspoons ground ginger
¼ teaspoon ground cinnamon
¼ teaspoon ground nutmeg
1 cinnamon stick
1 star anise piece
¼ teaspoon salt
1 cup sugar
12 egg yolks
5 firm pears (such as Bartlett or Comice), peeled
    and cubed
1 cup dried tart cherries
Vanilla ice cream

—Preheat the oven to 350 degrees.

—Melt ¼ cup of the butter in a small saucepan over low heat. Scrape in the seeds from the vanilla bean; discard the bean. Toss the vanilla butter with the brioche in a large bowl. Spread the bread onto a sheet pan and toast in the oven until golden and crisp, about 15 to 20 minutes. Set aside. Reduce the oven temperature to 325 degrees.

—Combine the cream, milk, ginger, cinnamon, nutmeg, cinnamon stick, star anise, and salt in a medium saucepan over medium-high heat. Bring just to a boil. Remove from the heat and add the sugar, whisking until completely dissolved. Whisk the yolks in a large bowl to blend. Gradually whisk 1 cup of the hot cream into the yolks. Return the mixture to the saucepan with the remainder of the cream mixture. Strain through a fine sieve into a large bowl. Place the bowl in a larger bowl of ice water to cool.

—In a large sauté pan over medium-high heat, melt the remaining ¾ cup butter. Add the pears and sauté until soft but still retaining their shape, about 5 minutes. Remove from the heat. Stir in the cherries.

—Transfer the toasted bread to a 9x13 baking dish. Stir in the fruit. Pour the custard over the top. Push the bread under the custard so that all the bread is well soaked.

—Place the baking dish in a larger pan. Fill the larger pan halfway up the sides with water. Bake until the custard sets, about 35 to 45 minutes. Serve warm with vanilla ice cream.

Serves 6 to 8

> **SECRETS OF SUCCESS:**
>
> *Toasting the bread.* Tossing the cubes of brioche with vanilla butter and toasting them gives an added complexity.
>
> *A rich custard.* A dozen egg yolks and three cups of cream make for a smooth rich blend that contrasts with the toasted bread.

SUMMER BERRY PUDDING

Loretta Keller first tasted Summer Berry Pudding when she was the chef at Stars Cafe in the early to mid-1980s. She fell in love with the way it showcased the abundance of berries at the height of the summer season. ❊ So when she left to open Bizou, she adapted the recipe for her own use. The pudding has a dense, berry-saturated texture that you don't find in most versions of this dessert. The berries are cooked first until they begin to break up. The bread is soaked in the juices and layered with the berries in a glass or ceramic mixing bowl. The top is then gently pressed for up to 24 hours with a three-pound weight, so the mixture becomes dense and heavy with the syrup. ❊ When ready to serve, the pudding can be unmolded for an impressive presentation. ❊ The recipe calls for an unusually large number of berries (14 pints), but don't skimp. It makes the pudding exceptionally good.

4 pints fresh strawberries, hulled and quartered
1 cup (or more) sugar
¼ cup (or more) fresh lemon juice
5 pints fresh raspberries
5 pints fresh blackberries
¼ cup Cassis liqueur
1 loaf sliced pain de miel or Pepperidge Farm sliced white bread, crusts removed, slices halved
¼ cup heavy cream

—In a large saucepan over medium heat, cook the strawberries, 1 cup of sugar, and ¼ cup of lemon juice for 10 minutes. Add the raspberries and blackberries and cook until the berries begin to break up. Stir in the liqueur. Remove from heat and cool. If necessary, add more sugar or lemon juice to adjust the flavor.

—To assemble the pudding, put the berry compote in a shallow pan. Dip enough of the bread slices into the berry juice to cover the bottom of a 2-quart ceramic or glass mixing bowl. Using a slotted spoon, spoon some of the berries onto the bread. Continue this layering until all of the bread, berries, and juices have been used, finishing with bread and leaving a couple inches of space at the top since the pudding requires pressing and it may overflow. Cover with plastic wrap and place the bowl in a large pan to catch any drippings. Set a plate or flat object on top of the pudding and a weight of roughly 3 pounds.

—Refrigerate for at least 18 and up to 24 hours. Once the pudding has set, remove the weight and either unmold by reversing onto a plate, or spoon out the pudding into serving bowls.

—Whip the cream until soft peaks form. Serve the pudding chilled with the whipped cream.

Serves 8 to 10

SECRETS OF SUCCESS:

Pressing the pudding. This allows the bread to become saturated with the juices and allows the flavors to deepen and meld.

The Cassis. This black currant liqueur also adds a vibrant note to the fruit.

The berries. The large amount of berries makes this summer pudding better than any I've tasted.

COCONUT RICE PUDDING WITH STRAWBERRY-RHUBARB SALAD

The Coconut Rice Pudding created by Heather Ho of Boulevard uses only a few ingredients, but the flavor is wonderful: Soft rice surrounded by silken coconut milk with milk, sugar, and vanilla. When ready to serve, whipped cream is folded in to give the pudding an even lighter texture. ✷ It's excellent on its own with sliced fruit or cookies, but Ho adds an unusual element: a salad of strawberries and raw rhubarb. Before you taste it you might be a bit skeptical, but the rhubarb adds a tart crunch to the strawberries, a pleasant contrast to the creamy cool pudding. ✷ Ho, who came to Boulevard from New York, concentrates on simple combinations, but with a twist and a style that melds perfectly with Nancy Oakes's savory courses.

Pudding
½ cup arborio rice
Two 14-ounce cans unsweetened coconut milk
1 cup milk
⅔ cup sugar
½ vanilla bean, split lengthwise

Strawberry-Rhubarb Salad
½ pound fresh rhubarb, trimmed and very thinly
   sliced
½ cup (or more) sugar
1 pint fresh strawberries, hulled and sliced

¾ cup heavy cream, softly whipped

—*To make the pudding:* Blanch the rice in a large pot of boiling water for 5 minutes. Drain, rinse, and drain again. Combine the rice, coconut milk, milk, sugar, and vanilla bean in a heavy-bottomed saucepan. Bring to a boil. Reduce the heat and simmer, partially covered, until the rice is very tender and the liquid is thick enough to leave a path on the back of a spoon when a finger is drawn across, about 1 to 1½ hours. Stir often, as the rice may scorch, especially near the end of cooking. Remove the vanilla bean and cool the pudding completely.

—*To make the strawberry-rhubarb salad:* Toss the rhubarb with ½ cup sugar, or more to taste if desired, in a medium bowl. Cover and refrigerate at least 2 hours or until the sugar has dissolved and pink syrup has formed. Stir in the strawberries.

—To serve, fold the whipped cream into the cooled pudding and serve with the strawberry-rhubarb salad.

Serves 6

SECRETS OF SUCCESS:

Raw rhubarb. The thin slices of rhubarb turn pink when marinated and add a delightful crunch to contrast with the strawberries and creamy pudding.

The whipped cream. The cooled rice pudding is given an airy texture by folding in whipped cream just before serving.

WARM ZABAGLIONE

The hot, frothy *zabaglione*—a simple mix of egg yolks, sherry, and sugar—is one of the best desserts of all times. It has a cloud-like texture and a rich nutty taste. It's great served in a stemmed glass (let it tumble over the sides) with cookies. You can also add fruit at the bottom and spoon the zabaglione on top. ✷ The best example I've found is at Jackson Fillmore in San Francisco and at Cucina Jackson Fillmore in San Anselmo, both owned by Jack Krietzman. ✷ The chef learned to make this dessert at Vanessi's on Broadway, the now closed restaurant that started the trend of installing open kitchens in upscale restaurants. ✷ As Krietzman was getting ready for his cooking tryout at Vanessi's, he practiced making this dessert. It took him about ten tries to get it right. ✷ You won't have quite as much trouble, however, because Krietzman has supplied the recipe. "Given the proper amount of yolks and a strong forearm, the dessert can be very forgiving," he says. ✷ It took us only two tries. The yolk and sherry mixture is whipped constantly over a hot flame. It soon doubles in size and then it turns glossy and frothy. However, if you let it go a few seconds too long, it begins to deflate and pull away from the sides of the pan. ✷ It's a quick dessert to produce—it's done in less than five minutes—but it needs constant attention and must be served immediately. ✷ Use an inexpensive sherry such as Christian Brothers, which is sweeter than the expensive brands. Any white wine can be used, even a generic Chablis.

9 extra-large egg yolks
9 teaspoons (or more) sugar
½ cup plus 1 tablespoon sherry (such as Christian Brothers)
¼ cup white wine
Fresh lemon juice (optional)
Vanilla extract (optional)

—Combine the egg yolks, 9 teaspoons sugar, sherry, and wine in a large copper or stainless steel mixing bowl. Season with lemon juice, vanilla, and more sugar, if desired. Whisk the ingredients to blend.

—Set the bowl on a burner set to high. Whip the zabaglione vigorously with a whisk, creating a tapping motion. From time to time move the whisk around the edge of the bowl to evenly distribute the mixture. The mixture will quickly double in size. Keep whisking and adjust the temperature by moving the mixing bowl on and off the heat. Continue to whisk until the mixture becomes glossy and thickens, about 3 to 7 minutes. Never stop whisking until you serve the zabaglione. Divide among bowls or wineglasses. Serve immediately.

Serves 4

Note: *This recipe can easily be cut in half to serve 2.*

SECRETS OF SUCCESS:

Using sherry and wine. The classic recipe calls for Marsala, but the sherry has lower alcohol so it's easier to achieve a thick, rich consistency.

Knowing when to stop. The yolks will quickly double in size, and you may have the urge to quit, but you need to keep going. The batter will become glossy when it's ready. If you let it go too long it begins to pull away from the sides and soon deflates and turns eggy.

MEXICAN WEDDING COOKIES

I love the interaction between sweet and salty that's inherent in Mexican wedding cookies, regardless of the recipe. But Elizabeth Falkner, owner of Citizen Cake, produces the best. ❋ It's amazing that with only seven ingredients she can create a recipe that's superior to the rest. But then again, Falkner has a way of one-upping other pastry chefs. ❋ An artist by nature, Falkner gained fame for her creations at Rubicon before going out on her own at Citizen Cake, a charming cafe/bakery. ❋ She uses chocolate shards and geometric shapes to make her desserts distinctive, and just about all of them have a twist. The Mexican wedding cookies are no exception.

—Preheat the oven to 350 degrees.

—In the bowl of an electric mixer, beat together the butter and 2 cups of powdered sugar. Add the vanilla and the water and continue to mix on low speed until well combined.

—In a separate bowl, combine the flour, pecans, and salt. Add to the butter-sugar mixture and continue mixing on low speed until dry and crumbly.

—Shape the dough into walnut-sized balls. Roll the balls first in granulated sugar, then in the extra powdered sugar. Arrange on large baking sheets.

—Bake 10 minutes. Cookies should not brown. Transfer the cookies to a wire rack and cool. Roll again in powdered sugar.

Makes 5 dozen cookies

1 cup unsalted butter at room temperature

2 cups powdered sugar, sifted, plus extra for rolling

2 teaspoons vanilla extract

1 ½ teaspoons water

3 cups all-purpose flour

1 cup pecans, toasted and finely chopped

¾ teaspoon salt

½ cup granulated sugar

SECRETS OF SUCCESS:

Two kinds of sugar. The walnut-sized balls are rolled in granulated and powdered sugar before being baked; then they're coated in powdered sugar again after they cool. This helps prevent the outside from becoming gooey.

Short baking time. The cookies only bake for about 10 minutes, producing a moist, although still dense interior.

PROSECCO GRANITA

Few desserts are as easy and refreshing as granitas, or Italian ices. The Prosecco Granita from pastry chef Remi Hayashi of Splendido is particularly easy and delicious. ❄ Prosecco, an Italian sparkling wine, has just a hint of sweetness. The dessert is great with thin lemon or buttery shortbread cookies. ❄ For this ice you don't even need to make a simple syrup as you would in many granita recipes. Just whisk together the wine, lemon juice, water, salt, and sugar, and pour it into a shallow pan or dish. That's it. The only other effort required is to whisk every hour or so until it's set. ❄ Most cooks would recommend that you serve it the same day, but I've found it can hold several days in the freezer.

—Whisk together the Prosecco, water, sugar, lemon juice, and salt until the sugar dissolves. Pour the mixture into a shallow container (such as a 1-quart Pyrex baking dish) and place in the freezer.

—Whisk the mixture every hour to break up the ice crystals and form a slush. In a home freezer this can take up to 6 hours, depending on the depth of liquid in the container. Repeat this process until the mixture is frozen and flaky. Whisk again just before serving.

—Serve the granita in wineglasses or bowls, topped with kiwi.

Serves 4

1½ cups dry Prosecco (Italian sparkling wine)
1 cup water
6 tablespoons sugar
3 teaspoons fresh lemon juice
Pinch of salt
2 kiwi fruit, peeled and diced

SECRETS OF SUCCESS:

Whisking. To achieve the flaky texture, stir the mixture every hour until it's set.

The sugar. Unlike many granitas, this one doesn't need a simple syrup. The sugar just gets whisked in along with everything else.

TECHNIQUES AND TIPS FOR THE HOME COOK

TECHNIQUES:

CHIFFONADE. This is a simple way to cut larger leafed herbs such as basil or mint. Stack the leaves on top of each other, about 10 at a time. Gently roll into a tube shape with the middle vein in the center. Using a very sharp knife, slice in ⅛-inch intervals or thinner. You'll end up with thin ribbons of herbs.

⁜

CLARIFIED BUTTER. Clarified butter can be heated to a higher temperature because the milk solids have been removed. Melt a stick (or sticks) of butter on low heat, then skim the milk solids that rise to the surface. Refrigerate. Remove any remaining milk solids at the top and the milky substance at the bottom. The golden portion in the middle is the clarified butter.

⁜

CLEANING MUSSELS. Mussels are easy to cook, but they must first be debearded. Scrub the shells of the mussels in cold water. Using needle-nose pliers, remove the brown fibers that stick out from between the shells.

⁜

DICING ONIONS. To dice an onion, first cut off the stem end and peel, leaving the root intact. This will prevent the onion from falling apart while dicing. Slice the onion in half through both the stem and root. Place one half, flat side down, on the cutting board and make several vertical cuts to the root but never cutting through it. Then slice horizontally several times, depending on how large you want the dice to be. Begin to slice the onion working toward the root end to produce even cubes. (Shallots are diced the same way.)

⁜

DRESSING A SALAD. Dress all the items individually, tasting for the correct balance. Then toss the ingredients together. This may sound like an unnecessary step, but it makes a huge difference in the finished product.

⁜

GRINDING SPICES. Peppercorns and other spices can be kept whole and freshly ground in a coffee grinder, pulverized with the side of a chef's knife, or crushed with a mortar and pestle. Freshly ground spices impart a pure and intense flavor, while ground spices lose their potency quickly.

⁜

MINCING GARLIC. First smash the clove lightly with a heavy object so the peel can easily be removed. Roughly chop the garlic. Then with the side of your chef's knife, mash the pieces into the cutting board in an outward motion. Do this until you have a garlic paste. This can be used anytime a recipe calls for finely chopped or minced garlic.

⁜

MISE EN PLACE. This French term means "everything in its place," and it works just as well for the home cook as for the professional chef. Look through your recipe and chop, mince, sift, or slice everything before you begin to cook. This organizational step saves time and stress. (To save time during the week, you can also chop often-used items such as onion and garlic on the weekend so they can be used as needed during the week for last-minute dinners.)

⁜

PEELING GINGER. Peel ginger with the edge of the rounded part of a spoon. Grasp the handle of the spoon while supporting the ginger in the other hand. Stroke down to scrape away the brown peel. When slicing ginger, always try to cut across the grain or it will be hard to chew.

⁜

PEELING TOMATOES. Remove the cores and cut a small X into the bottoms. Drop into rapidly boiling water for 10 seconds or until you see that the skins are beginning to peel away from the sides. Drain and plunge the tomatoes into ice water. The tomatoes will then slip right out of the skins.

⁜

SEGMENTING CITRUS FRUIT. Cut off both ends of the fruit and place one end on the cutting board. Slice in a downward motion following the contour of the fruit, making sure to completely remove the peel and pith and expose the flesh of the fruit. Then insert your knife on either side of the membrane that divides each segment. Gently slide the segments out individually.

⁜

SHUCKING OYSTERS. Oysters are not all that difficult to shuck, but the process is dangerous if not done properly. Place the oyster on the cutting board, flat side down. Using a towel that has been folded several times, cover the top of the oyster leaving only the pointed end exposed. Place your hand on top if the shell for support, but make sure the oyster stays on the flat surface. With the tip of the shucker find the soft spot between the two shells right where the oyster comes to a point. Using a horizontal motion, work the tip of the shucker into the oyster. When inserted fully into the shell, twist the shucker and pop the shells apart. Run the knife around the shell to detach the oyster from the top shell. Remove and discard the top shell. Run the shucker underneath the oyster and detach it from the bottom shell while carefully retaining its precious liquor. Look carefully, and remove any shell particles or sand.

⁜

TESTING MEAT. Here's how to tell the doneness of meat. Make a loose fist and press the muscle between your thumb and forefinger with your other hand. Rare meat has that amount of resistance. Follow the same procedure making a regular fist, which feels like meat cooked to medium. For well done, use a clenched fist.

⁜

TOASTING BREAD CRUMBS. A slice of bread will make about ⅓ cup of crumbs. Tear bread into pieces and place in a blender or food processor. Pulse several times to make crumbs. To toast, spread crumbs on a baking sheet and place in a preheated 250-degree oven for about 10 minutes until golden.

⁜

TOASTING NUTS. While nuts can be toasted on top of the stove, the easiest way is to spread them out on a sheet pan and place in a preheated 350-degree oven for 10 to 15 minutes until they start to color.

⁜

USING KNIVES. Grasp a chef's knife by placing your index finger and thumb on either side of the grip where the blade meets the handle. Wrap your last three fingers around the handle. Holding your knife this way will help you to achieve maximum balance and safety. Hold the knife straight, using your arm and not your wrist to cut. Do not put your index finger on top of the blade, even with a small paring knife. *To chop:* leave the tip of the knife on the cutting board and lift the back end up and down.

⁜

WHIPPING EGG WHITES. First bring eggs to room temperature before using. Egg whites whip to their fullest capacity at 75 degrees. Also, be careful that you don't mix any egg yolk in with the whites. This fat will inhibit the white from whipping to its fullest capacity.

⁜

WHISKING. Hold a whisk as you would a pencil. Using only your wrist, move the whisk in a circular motion. Your forearm is not meant to move.

⁜

ZESTING CITRUS. If you don't have a zester, use a potato peeler to remove the zest starting from the stem end and pulling the peeler toward the tip. Use just enough pressure to remove the skin but not the bitter white pith. The zest is then ready to be chopped or slivered. Stack the pieces on top of each other and cut into thin strips, then chop into the desired consistency.

INGREDIENTS:

CANE SUGAR. Cane sugar is preferred in baking, especially in caramelizing the top of a crème brûlée. Beet sugar simply won't do the job. Most brands aren't labeled, but if you pick up C & H you're assured of getting 100 percent cane sugar.

CHICKEN STOCK. Cover chicken bones with cold water and bring to a boil. Skim off the foam and impurities as they rise to the top. To prevent cloudiness, do not stir. Reduce to a simmer, then add roughly chopped vegetables including one part celery, $1/2$ part carrot, and two parts onions. Use a pound of vegetables for every 5 pounds of bones. Season with parsley, thyme, peppercorns, and bay leaf, if desired. Simmer gently for 4 to 5 hours. Strain, cool, and refrigerate. Once the stock is cold, remove the remaining fat floating on the surface.
Note: *In many cases you can use packaged chicken broth for these recipes. The boxed Swanson's product (usually sold beside the canned) is much better than the canned version.*

KOSHER SALT. Most professional cooks prefer this salt rather than the fine grind typically found in grocery stores. The flat, thin crystals of kosher salt are ideal for cooking because they dissolve immediately. Table salt doesn't dissolve as quickly, making it prone to over salting. Kosher salt can be found in the kosher section of most grocery stores.

TAMARIND. Tamarind can be found in pods or in a block of seeds and pulp in most Asian and Latino markets. Soak the seeds and pulp in a little bit of warm water until softened, then strain. This nectar is what is often required in recipes calling for tamarind.

VEAL STOCK. Veal stock is made the same way as chicken stock except the bones and vegetables are roasted. Roasting browns the bones and vegetables and creates a richer stock. Roast at 375 degrees, turning frequently, until browned. Remove from the oven and place them in a stockpot. Turn the heat to high on the burner and add a cup or so of water. Stir the bones and vegetables, then add cold water to cover and bring to a boil. Reduce to a simmer and skim the impurities off of the top. Add herbs and simmer 5 to 6 hours. Strain, cool, refrigerate, and remove the remaining solidified fat.
Note: *Many specialty stores such as Whole Foods and Draeger's carry veal stock in the refrigerator or frozen foods case.*

VINAIGRETTE. To make a classic vinaigrette, start with ½ cup of vinegar. Season with herbs and spices of your choice, including salt and pepper. Measure out 1½ cups of oil. Begin whisking the vinegar and add a drop of oil, continuing to whisk. Add another drop and continue the process of suspending the fat particles in vinegar. Once the emulsion begins to form you can add the oil at a faster rate. When finished the mixture should thicken enough to coat the back of a spoon. Taste and adjust seasonings. A teaspoon or so of mustard in the beginning adds flavor and is a natural emulsifier, allowing the oil and vinegar to blend more rapidly.

EQUIPMENT FOR THE HOME:

BLENDER. This appliance not only produces the wonderful blended drinks increasingly popular today, but it makes quick work at pureeing or liquefying ingredients for soups and sauces. The short blades in a blender allow for the food to become smoother than in a food processor.

CHINOIS. This fine, cone-shaped strainer is used for pureeing and straining foods that you want to be finely textured. You'll need to use the back of a spoon or a pestle to press cooked food through the holes.

FOOD MILL. It looks kind of like a stainless steel bowl with a strainer attached. It's better than a blender for doing such chores as making a skinless tomato or apple sauce, or for getting smooth textures for meats and vegetables that go into soups and compound butters. One of the best is Cuisipro, which costs about $85 at kitchenware stores.

GRILL PAN. These ridged-bottom cast-iron pans (available at cookware shops and many hardware stores) are ideal for in-house grilling of meats and vegetables. They impart a smoky, charred flavor to food with very little fat.

MANDOLINE. A mandoline can be used for thin slicing and making consistent julienne cuts. The secret to using a mandoline is to set it on a sturdy, non-slip surface such as a damp dishtowel. Make sure to always use the guard, as mandolines can be dangerous. You can spend hundreds of dollars on one, but the *Chronicle* Food department found that the Benriner, an inexpensive Japanese model, is the best. Various models sell for $30 to $60 and can be found at Japanese markets and specialty stores such as Williams-Sonoma.

ZESTER. This tool saves time if you need to finely chop lots of citrus zest. Pressing firmly on the zester, start from the top of the fruit and peel down; the zest comes off in fine strings. It can be used as is or finely chopped with a knife.

STORING:

GREENS. Lettuce and other greens will last for a week or more in the refrigerator if wrapped in a damp towel.

NUTS. Because of their high fat content, nuts have the tendency to go rancid. They should be stored in airtight containers in a cool place; they will last for about a year in the freezer.

OLIVE OIL. Most times olive oil is sold in a transparent glass or plastic container, but it is sensitive to light and is best kept in a cool, dark place.

42 DEGREES
235 16th St. (off Third St.), San Francisco
(415) 777-5558
Lunch weekdays and dinner Wednesday–Saturday.

A. SABELLA'S
2766 Taylor St. (at Jefferson), San Francisco
(415) 771-6775
Lunch and dinner daily.

ABSINTHE
398 Hayes St. (at Gough), San Francisco
(415) 551-1590
Dinner Tuesday–Sunday.

ACQUERELLO
1722 Sacramento (near Polk), San Francisco
(415) 567-5432
Dinner Tuesday–Saturday.

ALBONA
545 Francisco St. (near Taylor), San Francisco
(415) 441-1040
Dinner Tuesday–Saturday.

ANGKOR WAT
4217 Geary Blvd. (near 6th Ave.), San Francisco
(415) 221-7887
Lunch Monday–Saturday. Dinner nightly.

ANJOU
44 Campton Place (near Sutter), San Francisco
(415) 392-5373
Lunch and dinner Tuesday–Saturday.

ANTICA TRATTORIA
2400 Polk St. (at Union), San Francisco
(415) 928-5797
Dinner Tuesday–Sunday.

APERTO
1434 18th St. (at Connecticut), San Francisco
(415) 252-1625
Lunch and dinner daily.

AQUA
252 California St. (at Battery), San Francisco
(415) 956-9662
Lunch weekdays; dinner Monday–Saturday.

ARAM'S
3665 Sacramento St. (near Spruce), San Francisco
(415) 474-8061
Dinner Tuesday–Saturday; brunch
Saturday–Sunday.

ASIASF
201 Ninth St. (at Howard), San Francisco
(415) 255-2742
Dinner Wednesday–Sunday.

AUTUMN MOON CAFE
1909 Grand Ave., Oakland
(510) 595-3200
Brunch and/or lunch Tuesday–Sunday; dinner
Tuesday–Saturday.

BACCO
737 Diamond (near 24th St.), San Francisco
(415) 282-4969
Dinner nightly.

BAKER STREET BISTRO
2953 Baker St. (near Lombard), San Francisco
(415) 931-1475
Dinner Tuesday–Sunday.

BARAONDA
2162 Larkin St. (at Green), San Francisco
(415) 447-0441
Dinner nightly.

BAY WOLF
3853 Piedmont Ave., Oakland
(510) 655-6004
Lunch weekdays and dinner nightly.

BELLA
3854 Geary Blvd. (at Third Ave.), San Francisco
(415) 221-0305
Dinner nightly.

BETELNUT
2030 Union St. (near Buchanan), San Francisco
(415) 929-8855
Lunch and dinner daily.

BISTRO DON GIOVANNI
4110 St. Helena Highway, Napa
(707) 224-3300
Lunch and dinner daily.

BISTRO JEANTY
6510 Washington St. (at Mulberry), Yountville
(707) 944-0103
Open continuously lunch through dinner daily.

BISTRO RALPH
109 Plaza St., Healdsburg
(707) 433-1380
Lunch weekdays, dinner nightly.

BISTRO ZARE
1507 Polk St. (near California), San Francisco
(415) 775-4304
Dinner nightly.

BIZOU
598 Fourth St. (at Brannan), San Francisco
(415) 543-2222
Lunch weekdays, dinner Monday–Saturday.

BLACK CAT
501 Broadway (at Kearny), San Francisco
(415) 981-2233
Lunch and dinner daily.

BOUCHON
6534 Washington St., Yountville
(707) 944-8037
Lunch and dinner daily.

BOULEVARD
1 Mission St. (at Market), San Francisco
(415) 543-6084
Lunch weekdays; dinner nightly.

BRANNAN'S GRILL
1374 Lincoln Ave., Calistoga
(707) 942-2233
Open daily for lunch and dinner.

BRASSERIE SAVOY
580 Geary (at Jones), San Francisco
(415) 441-2700
Dinner nightly.

BRIX
7377 St. Helena Highway, St. Helena
(707) 944-2749
Lunch and dinner daily.

BUCKEYE ROADHOUSE
15 Shoreline Highway, Mill Valley
(415) 331-2600
Lunch Monday–Saturday; dinner nightly.

CAFE AKIMBO
116 Maiden Lane (near Grant), San Francisco
(415) 433-2288
Lunch and dinner Monday–Saturday.

CAFE AT CHEZ PANISSE
1517 Shattuck, Berkeley
(510) 548-5049
Lunch and dinner Monday–Saturday.

CAFE FOR ALL SEASONS
150 W. Portal Ave. (near Vicente), San Francisco
(415) 665-0900
Lunch and dinner daily.

CAFE JACQUELINE
1454 Grant Ave. (at Union), San Francisco
(415) 981-5565
Dinner Wednesday–Sunday.

CAFE LA HAYE
140 E. Napa St., Sonoma
(707) 935-5994
Dinner Tuesday–Sunday, brunch Saturday–Sunday.

CAFE MARIMBA
2317 Chestnut St. (near Scott), San Francisco
(415) 776-1506
Lunch Tuesday–Sunday; dinner nightly.

CASA ORINDA
20 Bryant Way (just off Moraga Way), Orinda
(925) 254-2981
Dinner nightly.

CHA CHA CHA
1801 Haight St. (at Shrader), San Francisco
(415) 386-7670
Lunch and dinner daily.

CHAPEAU
1408 Clement St. (at 15th Ave.), San Francisco
(415) 750-9787
Dinner Tuesday–Sunday.

CHARANGA
2351 Mission (at 19th St.), San Francisco
(415) 282-1813
Dinner Tuesday–Saturday.

CHARLES NOB HILL
1250 Jones St. (at Clay), San Francisco
(415) 771-5400
Dinner Tuesday–Sunday.

CHEZ PANISSE
1517 Shattuck, Berkeley
(510) 548-5525
Dinner Monday–Saturday.

CHOW
215 Church St. (at Market), San Francisco
(415) 552-2469
Lunch and dinner daily.

COLUMBUS RESTAURANT
3347 Fillmore St. (near Chestnut), San Francisco
(415) 474-4180
Dinner Wednesday–Sunday.

CUCINA JACKSON FILLMORE
337 San Anselmo Ave., San Anselmo
(415) 454-2942
Dinner Tuesday–Sunday.

DELANCEY ST. RESTAURANT
600 Embarcadero (at Brannan), San Francisco
(415) 512-5179
Lunch Tuesday–Friday; dinner Tuesday–Sunday.

DELFINA
3621 18th St. (between Dolores and Guerrero),
San Francisco
(415) 552-4055
Dinner nightly.

ELIZA'S
1457 18th St. (near Connecticut), San Francisco;
Also at 205 Oak St. (near Gough), San Francisco
(415) 648-9999; (415) 621-4819
Lunch and dinner. Open for lunch and dinner
Monday–Saturday.

ELLA'S
500 Presidio Ave. (at California), San Francisco
(415) 441-5669
Breakfast, lunch and dinner Monday–Friday.
Brunch Saturday–Sunday.

ENRICO'S
504 Broadway (at Kearny); San Francisco
(415) 982-6223
Lunch and dinner daily.

EVVIA
420 Emerson St., Palo Alto
(650) 326-0983
Lunch weekdays; dinner nightly.

FLEUR DE LYS
777 Sutter St. (near Taylor), San Francisco
(415) 673-7779
Dinner Monday–Saturday.

FOG CITY DINER
1300 Battery (at Lombard), San Francisco
(415) 982-2000
Lunch and dinner daily.

FOOTHILL CAFE
2766 Old Sonoma Road, Napa
(707) 252-6178
Dinner Wednesday–Sunday.

FRENCH LAUNDRY, THE
6640 Washington St., Yountville
(707) 944-2380
Lunch Friday–Sunday; dinner nightly.

FRINGALE
570 Fourth St. (near Brannan St.), San Francisco
(415) 543-0573
Lunch weekdays; dinner Monday–Saturday.

GARIBALDI'S
356 College Ave. (near Hudson St.), Oakland
(510) 595-4000
Lunch weekdays, dinner daily.

GINGER ISLAND
1820 Fourth St., Berkeley
(510) 644-0444
Lunch and dinner daily.

GLOBE
290 Pacific (near Battery), San Francisco
(415) 391-4132
Lunch weekdays; dinner Monday–Saturday.

GOLDEN TURTLE
2211 Van Ness (near Broadway), San Francisco
(415) 441-4419
Dinner Tuesday–Sunday.

GORDON'S
6770 Washington St. (at Madison St.), Yountville
(707) 944-8246
Breakfast and lunch Tuesday–Sunday; dinner Friday.

GRAND CAFE
501 Geary Blvd. (at Taylor), San Francisco
(415) 292-0101
Breakfast, lunch and dinner daily.

GREENS
Building A, Fort Mason, San Francisco
(415) 771-6222
Lunch Tuesday–Saturday; dinner Monday–Saturday.

HARRIS
2100 Van Ness (at Pacific), San Francisco
(415) 673-1888
Dinner nightly.

HAWTHORNE LANE
22 Hawthorne St. (off Howard St., between Second
and Third St.), San Francisco
(415) 777-9779
Lunch weekdays, dinner nightly.

HEIRLOOM
110 West Spain, Sonoma
(707) 939-6955
Lunch and dinner daily.

HYDE ST. BISTRO
1521 Hyde St. (near Pacific), San Francisco
(415) 292-4415
Dinner Tuesday–Sunday.

IDEALE
1309 Grant Ave. (near Vallejo), San Francisco
(415) 391-4129
Dinner Tuesday–Saturday.

INFUSION
555 Second St. (near Bryant St.), San Francisco
(415) 543-2282
Lunch weekdays; dinner nightly.

INSALATA'S
120 Sir Francis Drake, San Anselmo
(415) 457-7700
Lunch Monday–Saturday; dinner nightly.

JACKSON FILLMORE
2506 Fillmore St. (at Jackson), San Francisco
(415) 346-5288
Dinner nightly.

JARDINIERE
300 Grove St. (at Franklin), San Francisco
(415) 861-5555
Dinner nightly.

KASBAH
200 Merrydale St., San Rafael
(415) 472-6666
Dinner Tuesday–Sunday.

KATIA
600 Fifth Ave. (at Balboa), San Francisco
(415) 668-9292
Lunch Tuesday–Saturday; dinner Tuesday–Sunday.

KELLY'S MISSION ROCK
817 China Basin (at Illinois), San Francisco
(415) 626-5355
Open daily for lunch and dinner.

KOKKARI
200 Jackson (at Front), San Francisco
(415) 981-0983
Lunch weekdays; dinner Monday–Saturday.

L'AMIE DONIA
530 Bryant (near University), Palo Alto
(650) 323-7614
Lunch Tuesday–Friday. Dinner Tuesday–Saturday.

LA FOLIE
2316 Polk (near Union), San Francisco
(415) 776-5577
Dinner Monday–Saturday.

LA VILLA POPPI
3234 22nd St. (near Mission), San Francisco
(415) 642-5044
Dinner Tuesday–Saturday.

LARK CREEK CAFÉ
1360 Locust St. (at Mount Diablo), Walnut Creek
(925) 256-1234
Lunch and dinner nightly.

LARK CREEK INN
234 Magnolia Ave., Larkspur
(415) 924-7766.
Lunch and dinner daily.

LAS CAMELIAS
912 Lincoln Ave. (between 3rd and 4th St.),
San Rafael
(415) 453-5850
Lunch Monday–Saturday; dinner nightly.

LE CHARM
315 5th St. (at Folsom); San Francisco
(415) 546-6128
Lunch weekdays. Dinner Tuesday–Saturday.

LE COLONIAL
20 Cosmos Place (off Taylor), San Francisco
(415) 931-3600
Lunch weekdays; dinner nightly.

LEFT BANK
507 Magnolia Ave., Larkspur
(415) 927-3331
Lunch and dinner daily.

LEFT BANK
Santa Cruz Ave. (at Doyle), Menlo Park
(650) 473-6543
Lunch and dinner daily.

LHASA MOON
2420 Lombard St. (near Scott), San Francisco
(415) 674-9898
Lunch Thursday–Friday; dinner Tuesday–Sunday.

LIBERTY CAFÉ
410 Cortland Ave. (near Wool), San Francisco
(415) 695-8777
Lunch Tuesday–Friday; brunch Saturday–Sunday;
Dinner Tuesday–Saturday.

LITTLE THAI
2065 Polk St. (at Broadway), San Francisco
(415) 771-5544
Lunch Wednesday–Monday. Dinner nightly.

L'OSTERIA DEL FORNO
519 Columbus Ave. (near), San Francisco
(415) 982-1124
Lunch and dinner Wednesday–Monday.

LULU
816 Folsom St. (between Fourth and Fifth),
San Francisco
(415) 495-5775
Lunch and dinner daily.

MARNEE THAI
2225 Irving St. (near 24th Ave.), San Francisco
(415) 665-9500
Lunch and dinner Wednesday–Monday.

MASA'S
648 Bush St. (at Powell), San Francisco
(415) 989-7154
Dinner Tuesday–Saturday.

MATTERHORN
2323 Van Ness Ave. (between Green and Vallejo),
San Francisco
(415) 885-6116
Dinner Tuesday–Sunday.

MAZZINI
2826 Telegraph, Berkeley
(510) 848-5599
Lunch and dinner daily.

MECCA
2029 Market St. (near 14th St.), San Francisco
(415) 621-7000
Dinner nightly.

MESCOLANZA
2221 Clement St. (at 23rd Ave.), San Francisco
(415) 668-2221
Dinner nightly.

MONTAGE
101 Fourth St., 2nd Level, San Francisco
(415) 369-6111
Dinner 5–11 p.m. daily.

MUSTARDS GRILL
7399 St. Helena Highway, Napa
(707) 944-2424
Lunch and dinner daily.

NAN YANG
6048 College, Oakland
(510) 655-3298
Lunch and dinner Tuesday–Sunday.

NORTH BEACH RESTAURANT
1512 Stockton (at Columbus), San Francisco
(415) 392-1700
Lunch and dinner daily.

OBERON
450 Lombard St. (near Van Ness), San Francisco
(415) 885-6555
Dinner nightly.

O CHAME
1830 Fourth St. (near Hearst), Berkeley
(510) 841-8783
Lunch and dinner Monday–Saturday.

OLIVETO
5655 College (at Shafter), Oakland
(510) 547-5356
Lunch and dinner daily.

ONE MARKET
1 Market St. (between Spear and Steuart),
San Francisco
(415) 777-5577
Lunch weekdays, dinner Monday–Saturday.

ORITALIA
1915 Fillmore St. (near Bush), San Francisco
(415) 346-1333
Dinner nightly.

OSAKA GRILL
1217 Sutter (near Van Ness), San Francisco
(415) 440-8838
Lunch weekdays; dinner nightly.

P.J.'s OYSTERBED
737 Irving St. (at 9th Ave.), San Francisco
(415) 566-7775
Lunch or Brunch Wednesday–Sunday;
dinner nightly.

PANE E VINO
3011 Steiner St. (at Union), San Francisco
(415) 346-2111
Lunch Monday–Saturday. Dinner nightly.

PARK CHOW
1240 9th Ave. (near Lincoln), San Francisco;
(415) 665-9912
Lunch and dinner daily.

PINTXOS
557 Valencia St. (between 16th and 17th),
San Francisco
(415) 565-0207
Dinner Tuesday–Sunday.

PLOUF
40 Belden Way (near Bush St.), San Francisco
(415) 986-6491
Lunch weekdays, dinner Monday–Saturday.

PLUMPJACK CAFÉ
3217 Fillmore (near Filbert), San Francisco
(415) 563-4755
Lunch weekdays; dinner Monday–Saturday.

POSTINO
3565 Mount Diablo Blvd., Lafayette
(925) 253-1975
Dinner nightly.

POSTRIO
545 Post St. (at Mason), San Francisco
(415) 776-7825
Breakfast, lunch and dinner daily.

RICOCHET
215 West Portal Ave. (near 14th Ave.), San Francisco
(415) 566-5700
Lunch and dinner Tuesday–Sunday.

ROSE PISTOLA
532 Columbus (near Union), San Francisco
(415) 399-0499
Lunch and dinner daily.

ROSE'S CAFE
2298 Union St. (at Steiner), San Francisco
(415) 775-2220
Breakfast, lunch and dinner daily.

RUBICON
558 Sacramento (near Montgomery), San Francisco
(415) 434-4100
Lunch weekdays; dinner Monday–Saturday.

SANTA FE BAR AND GRILL
1310 University Ave., Berkeley
(510) 841-4740
Lunch weekdays, dinner nightly.

SCALA'S
432 Powell St. (near Post), San Francisco
(415) 395-8555
Breakfast, lunch and dinner daily.

SENT SOVI
14583 Big Basin Way, Saratoga
(408) 867-3110
Dinner Tuesday–Sunday.

SLANTED DOOR
584 Valencia (near 17th St.), San Francisco
(415) 861-8032
Lunch and dinner Tuesday–Sunday.

SPAGO PALO ALTO
265 Lytton Ave., Palo Alto
(650) 833-1000
Lunch weekdays; dinner Monday–Saturday.

SPLENDIDO
4 Embarcadero Center, Promenade level,
San Francisco
(415) 986-3222
Lunch Monday–Friday, dinner nightly.

ST. FRANCIS FOUNTAIN
2801 24th St. (at York), San Francisco
(415) 826-4200
Lunch and dinner daily.

STARS
555 Golden Gate (near Van Ness), San Francisco
(415) 861-1813
Lunch weekdays, dinner nightly.

STRAITS
3295 El Camino Real, Palo Alto
(650) 494-7168
Lunch weekdays; dinner nightly.

STRAITS CAFE
3300 Geary Blvd. (at Parker), San Francisco
(415) 668-1783
Lunch and dinner daily.

TAVOLINO
401 Columbus Ave. (at Vallejo), San Francisco
(415) 392-1472
Lunch and dinner daily.

TERRA
1345 Railroad, St. Helena
(707) 963-8931
Dinner Wednesday–Monday.

THANH LONG
4101 Judah St. (at 46th Ave.), San Francisco
(415) 665-1146
Dinner Tuesday–Sunday.

THE HOUSE
1230 Grant Ave. (near Vallejo), San Francisco
(415) 986-8612
Lunch weekdays. Dinner Monday–Saturday.

THE MATTERHORN
2323 Van Ness Ave. (between Green and Vallejo),
San Francisco
(415) 885-6116
Dinner Tuesday–Sunday.

THE ROOSTER
1101 Valencia St. (at 22nd St.), San Francisco
(415) 824-1222
Dinner nightly.

THEP PHANOM
400 Waller (at Fillmore), San Francisco
(415) 431-2526
Dinner nightly.

TIMO'S
842 Valencia St. (near 19th St.), San Francisco
(415) 647-0558
Lunch and dinner nightly.

TRA VIGNE
1050 Charter Oaks St., St. Helena
(707) 963-4444
Lunch and dinner daily.

U.S. RESTAURANT (BANDOL)
431 Columbus Ave. (at Stockton), San Francisco
(415) 362-6251
Open daily for breakfast, lunch and dinner.

UNIVERSAL CAFE
2814 19th St., San Francisco
(415) 821-4608
Breakfast Tuesday–Friday; lunch and dinner
Tuesday–Sunday.

UR
663 Clay St. (near Montgomery St.), San Francisco
(415) 434-3567
Lunch weekdays.

VINERIA
3228 16th St. (near Guerrero), San Francisco
(415) 552-3889
Dinner Wednesday–Saturday.

VIOGNIER
222 East 4th Ave., San Mateo
(650) 685-3727
Lunch weekdays; brunch weekends; dinner nightly.

VIVANDE RISTORANTE
670 Golden Gate (near Franklin), San Francisco
(415) 673-9245
Lunch and dinner daily.

WATERFRONT CAFE
Pier 7 (Broadway and the Embarcadero),
San Francisco
(415) 391-2696
Lunch and dinner daily.

WATERFRONT RESTAURANT
Pier 7 (Broadway and the Embarcadero),
San Francisco
(415) 391-2696
Lunch weekdays; dinner nightly.

WINE SPECTATOR GREYSTONE RESTAURANT
2555 Main St. (Highway 29), St. Helena
(707) 967-1010
Lunch and dinner Wednesday–Monday.

YAYA CUISINE
663 Clay St. (between Montgomery and Kearny St.s),
San Francisco
(415) 434-3567
Lunch Monday–Friday; dinner Monday–Saturday.

YUKOL PLACE THAI CUISINE
2380 Lombard St. (near Scott), San Francisco
(415) 922-1599
Dinner nightly.

ZARE ON SACRAMENTO
568 Sacramento St. (near Montgomery),
San Francisco
(415) 291-9145
Lunch weekdays; dinner nightly.

ZARZUELA
2000 Hyde St. (at Union), San Francisco
(415) 346-0800
Lunch and dinner Monday–Saturday.

ZAX
2330 Taylor St. (near Columbus, San Francisco
(415) 563-6266
Dinner Tuesday–Saturday.

ZAZIE
941 Cole St. (near Carl), San Francisco
(415) 564-5332
Breakfast, lunch and dinner Monday–Saturday.

ZINZINO
2355 Chestnut St. (near Scott), San Francisco
(415) 346-6623
Dinner nightly.

ZUNI CAFE
1658 Market St. (near Gough), San Francisco
(415) 552-2522
Lunch and dinner Tuesday–Sunday.

INDEX

TABLE OF EQUIVALENTS

The exact equivalents in the following tables have been rounded for convenience.

LIQUID/DRY MEASURES

U.S.	Metric
¼ teaspoon	1.25 milliliters
½ teaspoon	2.5 milliliters
1 teaspoon	5 milliliters
1 tablespoon (3 teaspoons)	15 milliliters
1 fluid ounce (2 tablespoons)	30 milliliters
¼ cup	60 milliliters
⅓ cup	80 milliliters
½ cup	120 milliliters
1 cup	240 milliliters
1 pint (2 cups)	480 milliliters
1 quart (4 cups, 32 ounces)	960 milliliters
1 gallon (4 quarts)	3.84 liters
1 ounce (by weight)	28 grams
1 pound	454 grams
2.2 pounds	1 kilogram

LENGTHS

U.S.	Metric
⅛ inch	3 millimeters
¼ inch	6 millimeters
½ inch	12 millimeters
1 inch	2.5 centimeters

OVEN TEMPERATURE

Fahrenheit	Celsius	Gas
250	120	½
275	140	1
300	150	2
325	160	3
350	180	4
375	190	5
400	200	6
425	220	7
450	230	8
475	240	9
500	260	10